Wilkes-Barre: Return to Glory IV

THE CITY's RETURN TO GLORY BEGINS WITH DREAMS
AND IDEAS

**Dreams and ideas; plans and actions equal
LEADERSHIP**

by

‖‖ ‖ ‖‖ ‖‖‖‖‖‖‖‖‖‖ ‖‖‖ ‖‖‖ ‖
I0161549

Brian W. Kelly
Lifelong Resident of Wilkes-Barre, PA

Let's Go Publish, Publishers! Wilkes-Barre PA, 2015, 2022

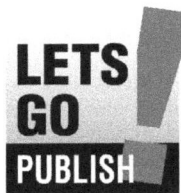

**LETS
GO
PUBLISH**

Published by:LETS GO PUBLISH! PO Box 621 Wilkes-Barre, PA 18701
Editor / Publisher Brian P. Kelly
Email: info@letsgopublish.com
Web site www.letsgopublish.com

Library of Congress Copyright Information Pending
Book Cover Design by Michele Thomas,
Associate Editor—Brian P. Kelly

ISBN Information: The International Standard Book Number (ISBN) is a unique machine-readable identification number, which marks any book unmistakably. The ISBN is the clear standard in the book industry. 159 countries and territories are officially ISBN members. The Official ISBN For this book
978-0-9899957-9-5

The price for this work is: **$16.00 USD**

10   9   8   7   6   5   4   3   2   1

Release Date: February 2015, July 2016, July 2022

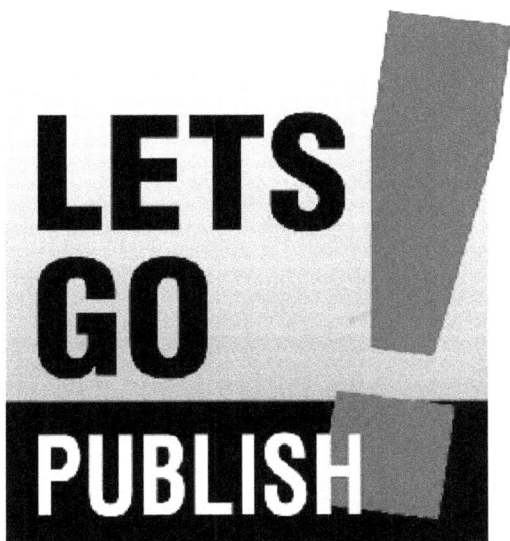

Dedication

To all the people that I have ever mentioned in the Acknowledgments of any book. Please check out <u>www.letsgopublish.com</u> *to read the latest version.*

*Special Dedication to **My wife Pat & children --Brian P, Mike P, and Katie P Kelly***

Additionally,
Dennis Grimes and Gerry Rodski.
Thank you for all of your support in my Writing and publishing efforts.

You all are the best.

*Special Thanks to **Joe Kelly, Ann Flannery, Jim Flannery (RIP), Patrick Kelly (RIP), Paul Radzavicz, + John & Carol Anstett, John Rose & Bernie Hummer***
For your excellent research for this book.

*Thank you to **Irene Jachimiak**, RIP and **George Elias**, my buddies From High Street for the inspiration*

Preface

I have two styles when I write a book. The original book was my fifty-ninth. In its 2ⁿᵈ revision, some might call it my 71ˢᵗ but I am rereleasing this book now in 2022 with some new facts and corrections. This is book # 304

When I write tech books, I figure out what I am going to say and then I outline the book and then I write the book from the outline. The outline is often mental, When I write a patriotic book or a book about trains, such as *Take the Train to Myrtle Beach*, which I wrote several years ago, I start out like I am writing a piece for a newspaper or for one of the online papers for which I write frequently.

When I get past a page or two, I know that what I am saying is too big for a newspaper and I know that my online papers to which I submit material, do not want more than five pages. So, I go where my thoughts take me and I don't stop until I think I have exhausted my material.

In writing this book, I wanted to talk about my home city and its neighborhoods along with a few dreams that I have for Wilkes-Barre City as well as the notion of dreams and ideas, followed by plans and actions being in many ways the definition of leadership. I first wrote this book when I was running for Mayor.

Unlike other writing ventures of mine, I stopped before I was done because as I wrote I had more and more ideas, and I knew this was going to be a book about the glory days of Wilkes-Barre and how dreams, ideas, plans, and actions can help bring back those days of glory to my fair city.

But, at the same time, I felt that I already had something that should interest the two Newspapers that we have in our town. So, I took the beginning in which I talk about dreams, and the end at the time in which I talked about a dream about making Wilkes-Barre a safe city for bicycling, and I put the two pieces together

On January 13, 2015, I submitted the piece to both papers suggesting they might want to run it as a commentary, rather than a letter to the editor. They print much less than half of what I submit to them, and the long ones are the ones that they often don't even bother taking to the cutting room. They just do not call me and ask for permission to print it to assure I sent it. So far, from January 13, 2015, I have received no call. A year and a half later, I expect that I will get no call from either paper. That's OK I got the book out.

In the last week from when I submitted the "article," I transferred all of what I had written in unformatted prose to book format at twelve point type and I was surprised that I had already written ninety pages. When I was still checking book size back in 2015, I looked at the page count on the bottom of the screen I was at 182 and most of what I had written was about Wilkes-Barre's wonderful past, not about its future.

So, my guess at the time when all was said and done would be 250 or more pages. When I completed the book, I was surprised at all I had written, the first cut was actually 384 pages in total. The book dimensions then were 5.25" X 8.25." I made this book bigger at 6" X 9" so it has less pages but many more words.

I loved writing this book so much that I could not stop. Even when I was in final edit, trying to clean the book up of typos and oversights, I added more material about Gerry's Pizza, a mainstay in South Wilkes-Barre, which operates out of the old Luna Rosa site, with a bit of Sable's Music Center being acquired recently for parking and possible expansion. My kids played on Gerry's sponsored baseball team in the little league. Gerry was always a standup guy with the kids, sponsoring a team every year.

I still like writing this book. It is fun. Here I am seven years later fiddling with it. I don't like not having my trusty keyboard with me at all times as I get all kinds of ideas for things that I need in this book. I use a desktop with a great keyboard with tactile and audio feedback so I am spoiled.

In addition to the focus of a return to glory, using dreams, ideas, plans, and actions, I decided to take a tour around my original neighborhood, the Rolling Mill Hill, and I started the verbal tour at the South Wilkes-Barre Colliery. Because of places like the South Wilkes-Barre Colliery and others in the City, there are lots of family stores of all kinds and there are a lot of places where the miners would stop to whet their whistles in the morning and the evening.

After doing a verbal walk of my neighborhood in the Rolling Mill Hill, I decided to enlist the help of some friends who lived in other neighborhoods so I could verbally walk in their shoes through their old neighborhoods. And, so I toured every section of the city. Those sections where I had more material are longer than those in which the material was light. Some, such as Brookside, are actually subsections and not really full sections. But, I got them all.

I also took a walk from the CYC and/or the YMCA Canteen (they were only several blocks apart) downtown to the spots as teenagers, we would visit at halftime of the dances. I took a trip to the center of the Public Square to visit the site of the magical mystical fountain and investigate the disappearance of the stature of Kankakee, the Indian maiden that was once centered there on top of the fountain.

I also walked the business routes of Central City, including the Public Square. I explored many of the important businesses and landmarks in the "business district. My last look at the Square in this book is when I attended the last movie showing at the Paramount Theatre, and just several days after that I was driving an Army jeep in flood mud helping officially with the Agnes cleanup in 1972.

To lighten up some of the stories, I use humor. I hope you find it as much fun as I did writing it. I also tell a story that always gets to my heart. It's about what it was like as a kid in the nineteen-fifties with a twenty-six inch bike, being able to go anywhere in the city. I show how delightful it was to visit the downtown area around Christmas time, and I discuss one of the most extraordinarily wonderful things that happened to me as a nine or ten year old. My friends were asking me for years for me to write a children's book about the incident. Now, it exists as a chapter in this book. Right now, the chapter title is Four Dollars and Sixty-Two Cents.

So, after I got finished with the book's first take, (I was about 95% complete when I touched this preface last) I created a list of the articles that I had written over the last year or so about my plans for a safe city, affordable city, and a clean city. These are included in the last Chapter of the book, right before the Index.

This book is not political, though I had announced my intentions the prior November to run for Mayor of Wilkes-Barre. The things in this book are true to the best of my knowledge, and the things that I think are good for Wilkes-Barre may very well be things that you think are good. I have a sneaking suspicion that I may have made some mistakes on some things. Bernie Hummer, a good friend for years, sent me a note which is included below to help smarten me up a bit. I hope there are not many mistakes. If I am wrong, I would be pleased to correct this book in future editions as Wilkes-Barre moves from stagnation to glory.

I have a standard set of acknowledgments that I have posted on the Internet for the people who have helped me do anything regarding my book projects over the years. All their help keeps me writing. The help of all these people was instrumental in my being able to write 59 books. And, by the way, I had already created a PowerPoint Presentation about a topic that is very important today. I presented to Congressman Lou Barletta earlier this year and he gave the OK to produce the book.

H & D EVANS CORP. t/a
BUILDERS' SUPPLY CO.
MAILING ADDRESS: P.O. BOX 192
504 SOUTH MAIN STREET · WILKES-BARRE, PA 18703
Phone: 717-822-5166 · Fax: 717-825-8020

EMMETT TOOLE'S BAR
+ GRILL WAS LOCATED
AT 22 N. WASHINGTON ST

ON W. MARKET WAS
LOWE'S AT 35 W. MARKET
TREASURE ISLAND 57 W MARKET

ROONEY'S SEAFOOD
RESTAURANT + GRILL
40-42 W. MARKET ST.

The PowerPoint outline was the basis of my 60th book, which was published in mid-2015. Since then, I have written eleven more books. My 65th book is titled. *Great Moments in Notre Dame Football.* I completed it in April of 2016 and I wrote four more books while I was putting together a 650-page book titled *Great Moments in Penn State Football.* The PSU book is my 70th and I just finished it this past Friday July 1. I have dual citizenship with Notre Dame and Penn State as my favorite teams. My book total with this revision is at 304.

I want to especially thank my brother Joseph Kelly, cousin Patrick Kelly (RIP), William Kustas, Paul Radzavicz, Dennis Grimes, nephew James Flannery Jr (RIP), John Anstett, and Carol Anstett for their help in figuring out our great neighborhoods of Wilkes-Barre,

As I have said a few times in this preface, I sure hope that you enjoy this book as much as I have enjoyed writing it.

Sincerely,

Brian W. Kelly, Author.

Table of Contents

About the Author

Brian W. Kelly retired as an Assistant Professor in the Business Information Technology (BIT) program at Marywood University, where he also served as the IBM i and midrange systems technical advisor to the IT faculty. Kelly has designed, developed, and taught many college and professional courses. He is also a contributing technical editor to a number of IT industry magazines, including "The Four Hundred" and "Four Hundred Guru" published by IT Jungle.

Kelly is a former IBM Senior Systems Engineer and he has been a candidate for US Congress and the US Senate from Pennsylvania. He has an active information technology consultancy. He is the author of 58 books and numerous articles. Kelly has been a frequent speaker at COMMON, IBM conferences, and other technical conferences.

In 2010, Kelly ran for Congress as a Democrat against a 13-term Democrat and, took no campaign contributions, spent enough to buy signs and T-shirts, and as a virtual unknown, he captured 17% of the vote.

Brian Kelly ran for Mayor and lost in the 2016 primary to the prior Mayor of Wilkes-Barre, Anthony George. George Brown beat Anthony George in the last election and now serves as hizzonner in Wilkes-Barre. George is a fine Mayor. Brian Kelly would like you to buy this book for your family.

Chapter 1 Good Things Begin with Dreams and Ideas!

All that's left of the great Europa Lounge

Positive change is important

I have a recurring dream about Wilkes-Barre PA. I dream that our fair City can stop its rapid downward spiral and return to some level of the wonderment and the wonderful things that gave us its glory years. I hope you feel the same way. Those of us, who were here before the 1972 Flood might be able to get in the mood for a brand new Wilkes-Barre just by thinking about the great Chile at the Europa Lounge. Mmmm Mmmm! It was on South Main Street right next door on the left side by Fowler Dick & Walker, The Boston Store, now Boscov's Boston Store.

The Classic Front of the Boston Store in Wilkes-Barre pre Boscov's

Wilkes-Barre was quite a town from its birth even before the Constitution was written, through the nineteenth and most of the 20th century. Most of our good fortune in these times came from the hard work of coal miners, and the long-suffering of their families. Mining brought with it a thriving economy that in the 1940's brought our city to its maximum population level of 88,000. Businesses were springing up everywhere as were marvelous theatres, restaurants, taverns, parks and even zoos. We examine these vestiges in this book in our preparation for a rebirth.

Things were so busy in Wilkes-Barre that officials adopted the honey bee as the main focus of the City seal. Wilkes-Barre was busier than a hive of honeybees, and all of the people were the beneficiaries.

There were a lot of dreamers and just as many doers. They are well documented in early Wilkes-Barry history. The doing often began with the dreaming. The look and feel of Wilkes-Barre is still here but there are a lot of holes such as vacant lots that need to be filled to get things moving again. I would encourage Wilkes-Barre residents to begin dreaming again and for former residents of this great city to dream right along with us as we return to glory. Come visit us often.

This book will remind us of the power of the dream by reliving some of the past so that we can prepare well for our glorious future. Let's begin with a dream.

Big ideas and little ideas begin with dreams

Can the Sans Souci Tumble Bug fit in your yard?

Ideas are the first part of positive change. Ideas begin most often as dreams. When in our most quiet moments some of us may begin to think of what it would be like if, say, the moon were actually made of green cheese. This is a dream that may become an idea. The young and young at heart might envision the rides from the old Sans Souci Park operating in our own back yard. I loved the Tumble Bug! This too is a dream that may become an idea. Can there really be better dreams?

Perhaps there are still others, and please include me in the list, who have at one time in their lives, dreamt about a set of train tracks, about the gauge of the old Hanson's train at Harvey's Lake, or the original choo choo at Sans Souci, by the Spook House, built around our very own homes. Why not find a small locomotive to pull a few cars around the front and back yards?

Can you envision when the tracks hit the front and back porches, the underside of the porches could serve as tunnels, and of course, there would always be light at the end of these tunnels! This is both a dream and an idea.

For some, the idea may be impractical and even "goofy;" but for others, it may be the motivation to bring on something entirely new that has never been done before--ever. If not Hanson's size, how about the train below? All aboard!

I have been dreaming all my life about great things in life. In most of my adult work, I had the privilege of dreaming as to how to make things better for businesses that happen to use IBM's largest computer systems. I hope to have the opportunity to bring to life some of my most practical dreams, and perhaps some dreams that may not at first seem practical to life in Wilkes-Barre City. I not only have some dreams. I've got some ideas and I've got some plans.

How about the train on the prior page for around the house? Literally?

In my career with IBM, my peers would often give me a problem and I would give them a solution. I was a problem-solver. I would then work with them so they got the credit. Management sometimes thought my recommendations went beyond a mere solution and sometimes they were phenomenally pleased. IBM made Systems Engineers such as myself, available to our business clients for no charge and we were worth a lot more than the charge. For me, that was when the real fun began.

All my life from when I made my own bikes out of junk-yard parts, I have been a designer and a problem solver, and I do not quit until I get it right. In my client IT shops, there are no marble edifices or ornate decorations standing as the result of my work. Yet, when a client is first able to write a check to pay a bill or develop a new marketing strategy with the help of software that I designed, I smile inside an awful lot. Along the way to my unique solutions in all I do in life, I have lots of dreams and so I have lots of ideas that just the day before did not even exist. There is always a solution to a problem.

Chapter 2   The Glory Days of Yesteryear

Wilkes-Barre City

Fort Durkee was the City's original name

Originally, Wilkes-Barre was named Fort Durkee after Major John Durkee, a Connecticut militia officer, who was instrumental in its settling. Connecticut believed it owned a good part of Pennsylvania and so the Yankee (Connecticut) v Pennamite (Wilkes-Barre) Wars ensued. Fort Durkee had been built by New England settlers in the spring of 1769, on the site of present-day Wilkes-Barre.

And, so the History of Wilkes-Barre shows its founding as 1769, seven years before the Nation's Declaration of Independence. Please note that these were not quite the glory days of Wilkes-Barre. Things were a bit rough in the really early days. The City was eventually incorporated in 1806 after

Major Durkee's death but the Major had a lot to do with Wilkes-Barre, its structure, and its beautiful river banks.

Wilkes-Barre had everything a city needed, with a bounty of water from the Susquehanna and numerous springs, and great soil for farming. The city grew even more rapidly after the discovery of nearby coal reserves and the arrival of hundreds of thousands looking to find peace and well-being in the New World.

The Susquehanna and River Front Park, Wilkes-Barre. Pa.

The city reached the height of its prosperity in the first half of the 20th century when its population reached just over 88,000. It was never as big as Scranton, its twin city to the North; but it was always a dandy place to live, and until the Agnes flood of 1972, it had many periods of glory.

NEPA tycoons and business barons jealously guarded the labor supply

The focus of this book is primarily post 1900 to 1972 as Wilkes-Barre had its climb to the top and the beginning of its fall. No factor was more the cause of the decline than the cause of its rise to prominence, King Coal. It has been said that the Coal Kings in Northeastern PA purposely kept out any industry that was not needed locally. And so, great national corporations were assured by local leaders that with coal flourishing as it was in NEPA; there would be no labor for their plants if they insisted on building them in this area.

In fact, it is rumored that local officials convinced Thomas Watson Sr., the head of IBM at the time, to build his huge plant in Endicott, so it would not be a drain on the labor supply for the mines in the Valley. It was not the first time that officials and dignitaries feathered their own nests rather than help the people they represented, and it certainly shall not be the last.

Regardless of Wilkes-Barre's storied past and what might have been for the people here, I know that I found the city a marvelous place in which to grow up. I did not even know my family was poor until Grade School. I read about the median income in a Weekly Reader and went home and asked my dad about it. He made little of it. Then, I knew we were poor but I sure never felt it. Heck, in grade school, I was about 15 pounds or more overweight.

Reflecting on Wilkes-Barre, PA, many of us have fond memories of our youth spent in some of the finest public and private schools in the country. We were taught by some of the most dedicated teachers in the world. In grade school, the Nuns at St. Boniface made sure I knew the three R's including Algebra, and I admit I was very impressed with the teaching when I went to Meyers for four years after "graduation" from St. Boniface. I was surely a lucky guy.

Since we are all of different ages, our vision of the greatest Wilkes-Barre there ever is affected most assuredly by our own experiences. It is also affected by the many recollections about our City that were passed down from our parents and grandparents. From all of this, we know that Wilkes-Barre is not at its best right now. Don't we all wish we could begin a process to return our city back to its glory days? Perhaps we could even save taxpayers a few dimes while we do it.

Would it not be nice if together, we could bring Wilkes-Barre back to its proper place in our dreams? The City surely has had some fine years of glory, and they were not all continuous. I am not just talking about the Hotel Sterling, which was a symbol of Wilkes-Barre's glory for many years. (http://citizensvoice.com/news/sterling-s-glory-days-1.1523588). There were many other great things that many of us remember.

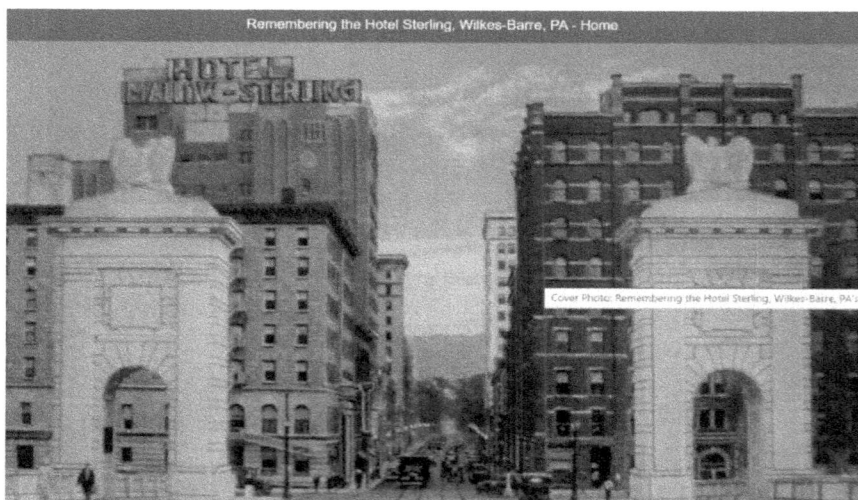

Picture was taken from the traffic lanes of the glorious Market Street Bridge

Two blocks straight ahead from this corner of River Street & West Market Streets was the major attraction of Wilkes-Barre PA for many years—its magnificent Public Square. This picture shows the trolley tracks going from the river to the Public Square.

Another look at the greatest structure in Wilkes-Barre which opened in 1929.

The bridge took pedestrian, horse & buggy, and motor vehicle traffic from Kingston on the left to Wilkes-Barre on the right.

Chapter 3   Tell me about Public Square in Wilkes-Barre, PA

Aerial Photo circa 1940 from the Susquehanna River to the Public Square

Still pristine after many close calls

Let me ask us all to recall our most magnificent Public Square. You may know that over the years, many a business person tried to convince City Officials to commercialize this most valuable piece of Wilkes-Barre real estate. Some wanted to put buildings on the Square and others wanted street traffic to go right through its center.

Thankfully, we still have a Square and none of these destructive notions were permitted by our City Forebears. In 1786, less than twenty years after Wilkes-Barre was founded, Luzerne County was established. Until 1909 or so, you may know that the "Square" was the home of the Luzerne County

Court House. From then on, it was a small diamond-shaped plot of land in the center of town remade for public use. Its use was intended to be a "park."

Luzerne County Courthouse on Public Square circa 1905

Famous Novelist Theodore Dreiser, over ninety-nine years ago offered a great compliment to Wilkes-Barre planners on his visit to the city in 1916. He said that the newly furbished Public Square was "one of the most pleasing small parks I have ever seen." Me too!

Dreiser would later become famous as an author with his timeless work, "An American Tragedy." This now famous man was just one of many people to fall under the spell of the four-acre diamond of grass and trees in the middle of Wilkes-Barre. Some of us now know it as the site of the Farmer's Market, and the rest of us know it simply as that magical spot right there in the center of our town.

I have been asking my friends and cohorts if they can recall a nice fountain in the center of Public Square. I think I can recall this as a child. But, I am not sure. When Dreiser came to Wilkes-Barre, sure enough... there was a fountain right smack dab in the center of Public Square. It was a huge and ornate water fountain shown on the next pages. Wilkes-Barre's return to glory begins with dreams and Ideas. It was lighted at night by a string of colored bulbs. Can you imagine back in the early 1900's?

These were surely the glory days of Wilkes-Barre. However, because of high water bills (The electric fountain used 30,000 gallons of water a day It did not recirculate it.) this magnificent statue of the Indian maiden Kankakee had to be dismantled and supposedly it has been stored in impregnable city vaults for the past eighty years. But I dare you to find it.

My most significant memory of early Public Square besides dreaming that it had a beautiful fountain, was that it also had two underground restroom facilities—one for men and one for women. I can remember using this myself as a kid. I must admit that I was afraid to go into a building that was not above the earth. It was like going into a crypt in a horror movie. But, it was neat once you braved it and got your due relief. It was across the street from one of the identifiable landmarks on the Square—One Hour Porterizing.

Ornate Fountain Indian Maiden Kankakee circa 1911

FOUNTAIN, PUBLIC SQUARE, WILKES-BARRE, PA.

Luzerne County Courthouse circa 1908 River Street, under construction

Less expensive fountain, once in working order on Public Square!

It had steps leading down to a door that appeared to not be part of any building... and of course there was grass growing on top of it. As expected, it offered the great relief that was needed for a young man to continue his adventures on Public Square, completely dry.

It would be nice to find a Wilkes-Barra alum to offer a reward for the return of the Indian maiden Kankakee. It would also be a neat idea to have an archaeological dig across from the Kirby where the underground latrine was. If we find it, maybe we can bring it back. That would be something. Additionally, of course it would be nice to see a working fountain right in the center of Public Square, with its own reservoir of water, so it does not have to flush gallons of costly water into the sewer.

Public Square was originally built to be an attraction because the city leaders at the time understood that attracting citizens into the downtown, or "uptown," as we Wilkes-Barre natives called it, would mean there would always be wonderful places to go uptown. This is still a great notion. Retail businesses like locating where the people are, and the people like to be where neat things are always happening. That was Wilkes-Barre years ago and that can be Wilkes-Barre again as we work together to return the City to our glory days.

I can remember myself in the 1960's and 1970's and beyond, until the flood of '72 that uptown Wilkes-Barre itself was still an attraction. Its historical stores and buildings were mostly intact. When asked "where are you going today?" Many of us would respond, simply "uptown." To repeat, downtown Wilkes-Barre to us was "uptown." Buses were filled with young and old, who held packages and huge shopping bags from trips "uptown." They were great days.

Chapter 4   The Great Places "Uptown" in the Old Glory Days

Neisner Bros. 5c to $10.00 Store With Trolley Tracks in Front

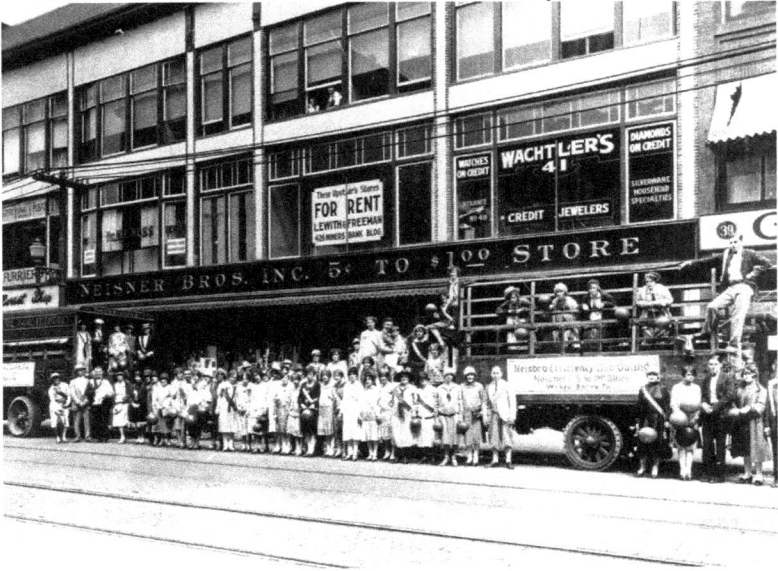

Great places to shop & the Square was there for resting and fun

Some may remember Fowler, Dick, & Walker, the Boston Store (now Boscov's); Pomelos—in its magnificently appointed building (now LCCC "Up-Town"); Kresge's, a unique store in which one could enter on S. Main Street, visit Aunt Clara's Toy Shop, and then exit on Public Square. That's not the end of the story. There is lots more.

How about the Neisner Brothers store at 41-49 South Main Street? It was right down from the Boston Store. My Aunt Ruth worked in the center "Fountain," serving the carbonated fountain drinks of the day. They had great pizza, and a fare that made your mouth water, especially if you were a little kid.

Aunt Ruth always made the "Kelly kids" feel special when we stopped by to say help.

There were tons of furniture stores and of course Bergman's, Bond's, John B. Stetz, The Hub, and the fabulous Lazarus store, which I would love to come back from the dead. Today, Lazarus is covered with asphalt and serves the public as an "Up Town" one level parking lot.

Always an attraction, the Peanut Man was always on the Square by the Peanut Shop, giving out Planters delicious peanuts. Wouldn't it be nice if we could get Nabisco / Kraft Foods to bring him back to the hometown of Planters Peanuts for us all to enjoy again.

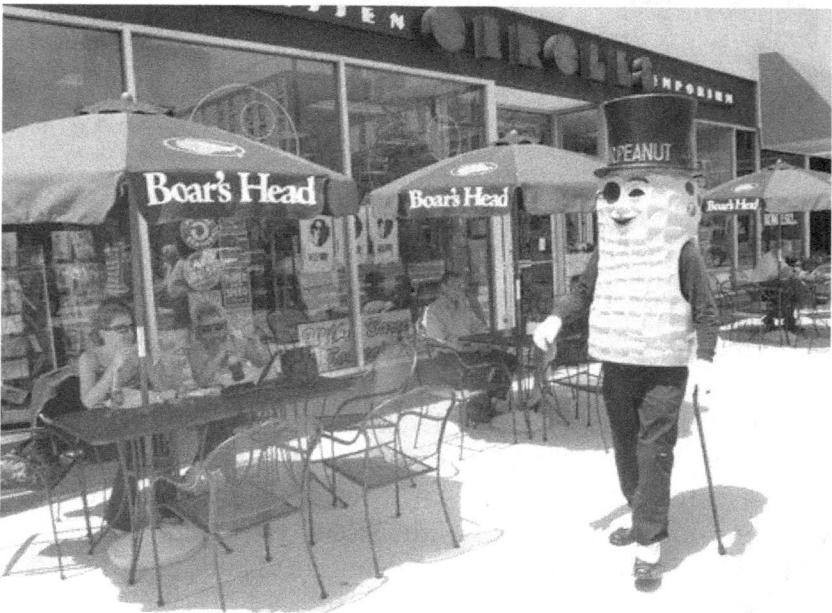

In 2020 Wilkes-Barre brought back the Peanut man who once lived in the Peanut Store on the corner of Public Square and South Main Street. The day's peanut-themed celebration on Wilkes-Barre's Public Square will go on, with a focus on the birth of Baby Nut rather than the demise of Mr. Peanut. Or perhaps it will celebrate the resurrection of the 104-year-old

Mr. Peanut as Baby Nut, as depicted in a Planters Peanuts commercial that ran during Sunday night's Super Bowl.

Barnes & Noble from the Square

Here is how South Main Street looked just one year ago with a view from Public Square. You can see the Barnes & Noble Bookstore which served both the community needs as well as the needs of King's & Wilkes University students for text books. As of July 2021, it became another lost memory. Maybe the Peanut Man can use his influence to bring back this great store.

Barnes & Noble Picture -- Public Square shot--Frank's Photography Site

It also had a very nice coffee house and great coffee. One day I am hoping many from Wilkes-Barre will have the opportunity to enjoy a coffee there while reading a book signed by this hometown author. Wilkes-Barre: Return to Glory (this book) is already in their hands but ironically B & N decided not to stock it. C'est la vie. Now they are gone.

Secret spots for free food

There were other spots on South Main Street across the street from Planters Peanuts main offices, about ten blocks from the Square. Not everybody knew of such "secret" places. But, a guy with a bike finds many wonderful things. I knew what was there and I brought many with me to enjoy.

One of these places off South Main Street was so good that we as kids would sneak to the back of the buildings and eat the sweet popcorn by Hanover Street and Race Street. We never knew where this fine fare, overflowing in huge barrels, put out as waste, had come from. Nonetheless, we stubbornly fought with the bees to get our share. Somehow, we are all still alive. Best of all, we never even knew we were poor. I can remember all the smiles, and none of us ever got stung.

In the back of this Planters Peanuts HQ Bldg. shown below, right next to Mack Bros. Hardware Store ten blocks from the Square was where we found the barrels of junk sweet caramel popcorn. We did not know it was junk. It sure was good!

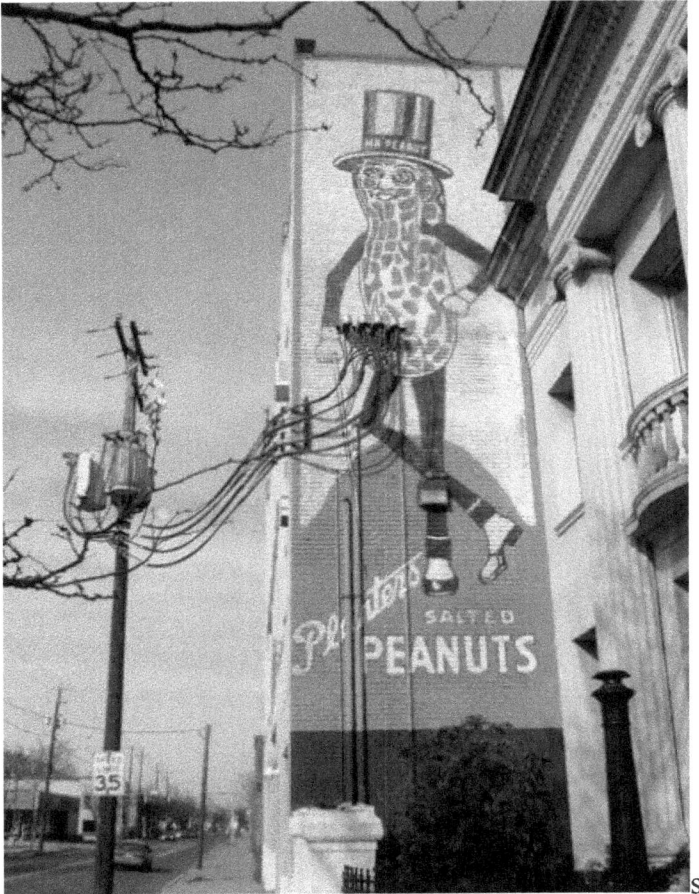

Back to uptown Wilkes-Barre

Looking around the Square in my child's eyes, I can still see the One Hour Porterizing and Martinizing which was placed cattie corner from the Paramount Theatre. Looks like they are still in business someplace.

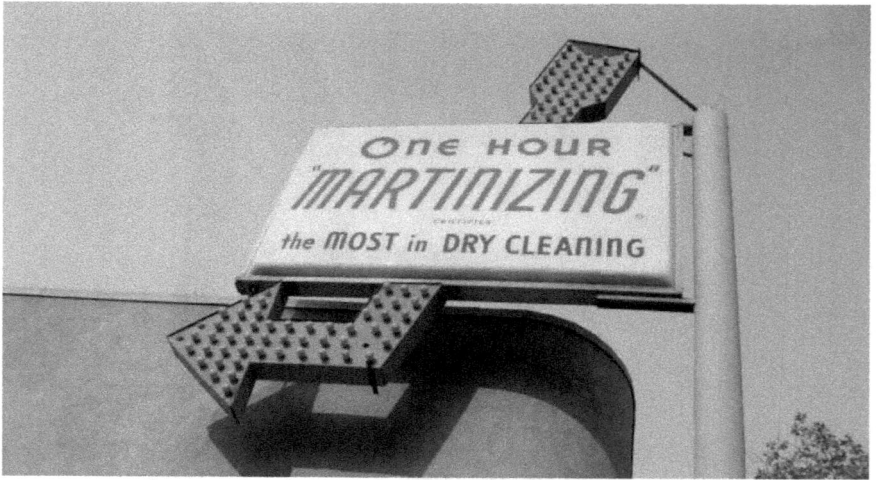

I remember in WB the sign was lit up and flashing

There was not a vacant spot on Public Square. The Comerford Theatre and the Paramount were huge attractions. The Comerford and a lot of other great businesses including the memorable Pizza Casa and Carmen's Pizza disappeared after the 1972 Flood.

After the flood, the Federal funding permitted Wilkes-Barre to build a huge metal canopy system to keep shoppers out of the rain. Lack of painting and rust unfortunately prompted City officials to rip it out recently. It lasted just about thirty years.

If you look at pictures of storefronts before 1972, you will see that the merchants had already solved the shade/rain problem themselves without big government. The merchants simply extended huge attractive awnings over the sidewalks.

Now, without the canopies or the awnings, the malls are the only places that seem to get the shade from the sun and heat of the summer and they get dryness when it is raining or snowing. With more people driving than ever today, it is good that there are so many parking spaces and facilities in the City. This is one of the things that has improved from the glory days. Dreamer that I am, we still have a lot more work to do.

Pictures are rare of the red canopy system that lasted about thirty years in Wilkes-Barre PA.

Chapter 5   The Place to Be in the Glory Days

The trackless trolley (bus) was the way to go

Wilkes-Barre residents of all ages found their way to Public Square for all reasons. It was a great place for out-of-towners with Wilkes-Barre roots also. My Aunt Nina loved coming to town, taking the Grove & Brown Electric Trackless Trolley and getting dropped off on the Square. Coming back on the bus, with my mother, she always had some nice items for my brothers and sisters and me.

By the way, the drivers had to watch how the electric leads tracked the overhead wire to make sure they did not come off. The lines, I can recall seeing the driver coming out and repositioning the leads to make contact with the wires when they did come off. It was another adventure/ You can see the power extensions coming out of the top of the busses on the next two pictures. ffs

Public Square with Pomeroy's; trackless trolley to Parsons; track trolley

Public Square was a great place to be. As a ten year old and younger, I found myself to the Square often riding my 26" bike. I also took the Grove and Brown trackless trolley. I don't recall it being much more than a nickel or dime to ride.

Transfers got you from Rolling Mill Hill to almost anyplace!

I still remember when the King and his Court were playing in Kingston Football Stadium off Pierce Street. Not only did I find my way to Public Square on the Grove and Brown, but I walked to Kingston Stadium from the Square along with a lot of other walkers to see this great event. I could not figure out how to get a transfer.

Electric trackless trolleys were like buses. See the connectors on top!

By the way, Eddie Feigner and company, i.e. the King and his Court, the greatest team that ever stepped onto a softball diamond played its last game in late August 2011. (Like tribute Rock bands, they played without Feigner and most of the originals that I saw.) Eddie died in 2007. This team had been at it its peak for 65 years!

My biggest surprise of this great game was that a young Tommy Yuhas (early twenties) of Wilkes-Barre (the Butcher at Peters Economy Store) got the only hit in the game for the All Star Team picked from the Wilkes-Barre area. This was more than fifty plus years ago. Tommy did well batting against Eddie Feigner, the King, and his four man softball team.

The King pitched from the mound and anywhere else he chose. Sometimes he pitched strikes from deep centerfield underhand of course. He even threw curves from way-out there. The catcher had a tough time reaching Feigner on the return throw. Eddie Feigner, the King, was the pitcher, and the Court consisted of a catcher, and two fielders who played wherever they felt they needed to play to get outs. All of this happened in Kingston's Football Stadium and I could not believe I was there. It was impressive. I got there mostly because of the trackless trolley.

I was there nonetheless. I paid my own way. I could not figure out how to get a bus to the stadium in Kingston from the Square, so I walked the rest of the way from the Square and back to the Square to get the Grove and Brown to go home. I was tired but it was great.

1960 President Kennedy

In the same vein, I either took my bike or I took the Grove and Brown to Public Square on October 28, 1960 to see the next President of the United States, John Fitzgerald Kennedy. Before Kennedy spoke on Public Square after his motorcade had arrived, on the way to the stage, he may have felt the hand of a twelve year old that he was shaking. We did not have words or eye contact, but I sure knew what had happened.

During that October visit to Wilkes-Barre, Kennedy attracted thousands - even more than the large crowd that had greeted Republican candidate Vice President Richard Nixon just a few weeks earlier. My cousin Arline, from NJ, told me just the other day that she had shaken Nixon's hand in Bloomfield, NJ, but she knew in her heart, like I did, that she was for Kennedy. Wilkes-Barre was something back then for sure. Kids like me, who could not vote were still interested in the City and we rooted for the Country big-time.

JFK on the Public Square in October 1960. There was nothing like it!

Chapter 6   Places to Go; Things to Do; People to See

The current YMCA Building on Northampton Street

North Main Street, showing Y. M. C. A. Building, Wilkes Barre, Pa.

<< The original YMCA Building was on 23 North Main Street, built in 1889. This Y was replaced by the new one after World War II. It was replaced by the VA Building, now operated by Blue Cross.

You can't believe how cool it really was!

When I talk to my peers about the late 1950's and 1960's in Wilkes-Barre, we all seem to recall the dances at the YMCA Canteen, and those at the CYC. We had a great childhood in Wilkes-Barre, and as we grew into adolescents and teenagers, we had a great life because of Wilkes-Barre.

You may remember Joe Nardone & the All Stars; Mel Wynn & the Rhythm Aces; and the late Ronnie Stefanko and the Tones playing at the CYC for years when we were kids. Stefanko's rendition of Bobby Vinton's Blue Velvet was better done than the Polish Prince himself.

I can remember Ronnie Stefanko, not much older than I, who married my classmate, the late Bonnie Obelienis, shortly after high school. Last time I saw him perform, he was sharing the stage at the Catholic War Vets picnic just a few years ago with CWV President Ray Walton, a St. Boniface alumnus. Walton, an affable man, was smoking a big cigar, telling us all that we were having a good time. We were! Both of these great guys have passed on to the Lord but I want to tell Ray that he did not have to tell us it was great. Ronnie and The Tones were playing… 'nough said.

Meyers High School Class of 1965 booked the Tones play in 2005 for their fortieth reunion anniversary, shortly after the band made its comeback. Again, they were great!

From the Tones current website, I picked up a little history of the band: The original Tones 1958 through 2003 included Gerald Flora, founder, 1958. First band members included Gerald Flora, Rich Flora—first drummer and youngest in the Valley (13 years old), Andy Macko, Ed Lee, Al Walcheski, Wayne Hughes, Joe Brislin, and Bob Wheeler.

Also performing with the Tones in the early years were Charles "Kip" Weed and Don Bytheway. Other Tones band members through the years not necessarily in order of membership: Tom Evancheck, Bill Strish, Danial Herman, Rocco Marino, Robert (Butch) Malacheski, Don Zlobik, Robert Caleta, John Sopp, William Strish, Edward Arnone,

Tommy Vest, George Drew, Jimmy Calahan, Charles Meyeski, Joe Morris, Jimmy Wynn, Verne Harris, Ron Smallcomb, Ron Stefanko, Vince Saracino & Vince Jr. Just like Joe Nardone's All Starts, the Tones are a Wilkes-Barre band with a lot of history and a lot of glory.

BTW, the Tones still play well and are out there as one of the few bands from "the days," that you can still listen to regularly if you choose. Vince Saracino, longtime member of the Tones & Vince Jr. handles the lead vocalist jobs—el magnifico.

At halftime, the dances at the CYC and the Canteen had what seemed like a half hour or so intermission. Most of "us" high schoolers at the time felt like we were released from the CYC or the Canteen into the uptown, with a return ticket.

The big stores at 9:15 PM or so were mostly closed but the places where a kid could get a soda, a malt, and a hamburg or one or the other always seemed ready and waiting—as long as we behaved and we did not giggle too much.

The Boston Candy Kitchen, Public Square, Wilkes Barre, Pa

Darla Carey 708 followers

There was the Spa Rest-aurant on South Main Street across from Fowler Dick & Walker. The Boston Store, as well as the Twin Grille Europa Lounge right next door to the Boston Store.

Within walking distance from the CYC and the YMCA was the phenomenal Boston Candy Kitchen and the Embassy Restaurant right there on Public Square – situated right by the Bus Stops. The Astor Restaurant was by the Fort Durkee Hotel. If we were adventurous, we could saunter off to the infamous S&W Restaurant on North Main Street. Percy Browns fabulous and famous Delicatessen was right on Northampton between Washington and Main. So it was close to both the CYC and the YMCA.

We were between thirteen and sixteen years old for these dances, and none of these places uptown served alcohol—at least for us, and that too was good. It was such a great experience, we were not looking for diversions. We were there to suck up the greatness of the moment—and there were many… and we were not even grown-ups… yet.

There was of course for teenagers, what I would call Public Square Sticker Shock. I am not sure if McDonalds had even hit the area yet but the prices were nothing like McDonalds or

Handley's Diner, or Elias's Hanover Diner, where Schiel's Family Market now is. But, for just a couple cents more, we were able to partake of the finest places that have ever been part of the Wilkes-Barre landscape.

Because these exquisite food stops were pricey, the boys and girls often traveled at halftime separately each paying their own tab. We always felt that there was something in "uptown" Wilkes-Barre for everybody. They were great days, and Wilkes-Barre itself added to the greatness.

When we were not on or by the Square for the dances, we might go "uptown" at other times for a milkshake or a banana split or just to shop or browse in the many great stores. Wilkes-Barre offered more than uptown and so many of us did not travel so far all the time for we could get all the treats we needed closer to home. There were places like the Stanton Pharmacy Fountain or Leggieri's Pizza or Angelo's Pizza, The D & R in Parsons and elsewhere. In South Wilkes-Barre, there was Luna Rosa, and in other areas of the city there were also great venues for teenagers who knew how to behave.

Chapter 7 A Great City for a Young Adult

Eddie Day & The Starfires
@thestarfires · Musician/band

Eddie Day was not a state representative yet!

Eventually, as we got a bit older, we no longer went to the CYC and the YMCA for dances. Instead we went to the Stardust Ballroom (later renamed the Naked Grape) and the Granada Ballroom and the Starfire Room in Wilkes-Barre. When we had wheels, we might go out of town to Hanson's Park Pavilion and of course the great dance room at Sans Souci Park. And there was a smaller venue but they packed them in at the Spinning Wheel right on the corner of Hanover Twp. & Wilkes-Barre where Joe Nardone & Billy Brown led the weekly bands.

I once thought the Stardust was on the second floor of the Paramount Theatre. However, looking at an old Wilkes-Barre Almanac I discovered that work began in 1929 in tearing down the Joseph S. Coons & Co. store building at the corner of Public Square and East Market. As they said in the Almanac, this was "to give place to a two-story building for stores and a dance hall, with a new theatre in the rear."

The new second floor dance hall was the Stardust Ballroom and it always seemed to be on top of the Paramount to me or the news-stands right nearby. The Stardust later closed and opened up as the Naked Grape. I tried my dancing trade there whenever I could. Kids from the three City High Schools were regulars and got to know each other there.

When I wrote the first edition of the Wilkes-Barre book, I thought that the Granada was right opposite the Stardust on Public Square and S. Main. However, thanks to George Elias, I learned that it was further down South Main Street in the second block. Official address is 162 South Main Street Wilkes-Barre PA, just up from South Street… but it is long gone.

As noted, in my day, these second story haunts were on W. Market and South Main streets. In the 1960's a new place opened up in an old building. We were frequent visitors to the new Starfire Ball Room, the third Ballroom in Wilkes-Barre. This was run by Eddie Day and the Starfires. It was once the old Giant Market on 142 South Main Street right up from the Granada. The Starfires ran their dances upstairs. Those sure were the days. Lots to do for teenagers going on adults,

Those who wanted to stay young found solace in Ricky Jones' and the Sutter Brothers' *Purple Haze*. Roger Neyhard was also one of the founders / owners. It was as if when we needed these places as we grew up; they just showed up. On good sources, the founders enjoyed the income from the Purple Haze and were found at the time with more One Dollar Bills in their pockets than an individual would typically ever have in a lifetime. Hey, great ideas deserve great remunerations. Admission was a buck!

Joseph S. Coons & Sons –one of Wilkes-Barre's Finest Stores

Jos. S. Coons & Co.'s Store,
Wilkes-Barre, Pa.

Our now Representative Eddie Day, one time bandleader, and his group, the Night Timers with Bob Fountain, who is currently with Hollywood and the DUO, as well As Eddie Day and the Starfires; and later Eddie Day & TNT, made Wilkes-Barre a great place for growing kids who were almost adults.

Besides these greats, there was the local King, Joe Nardone and his All Stars. I can recall when Joe Nardone, and the late great Bill Brown teamed up with the All Stars. Wow—especially at the former Spinning Wheel on Carey Av in S. WB—recently razed in anticipation of something greater! That something turned out to be a Taco Bell.

Mel Wynn was there with the Rhythm Aces, Jimmy Wynn was with the Royal Aces, and one of the two Sechleer brothers played with each of the "Aces." They were all great and they took their hand at making records that often hit the top ten on WARM's local chart.

WARM
RADIO 590
5,000 WATTS

JOEY SHAVER
9 P. M. to 1 A. M.

HITS of the WEEK ON THE STATION OF THE STARS

These groups made listening to great bands in Wilkes-Barre a given. What a place to grow up!

Besides the locals, there were also great groups and single acts from outside the area. Just like Joe Nardone hosts DooWop bands and other Oldies Groups at the Kirby periodically, The Granada Ballroom hosted many grand events in its day. This Sunday July 31, 2022 Joe Nardone is sponsoring another great show called the Happy Together Tour.

1959 DION & THE BELMONTS
GRANADA BALLROOM POSTER

When the youth action or young adult action was not on Public Square, the aforementioned Spinning Wheel on Carey Ave, was the home for many a great Friday or Saturday Night dances. By the way, for those nostalgia lovers, on January 20, 2015, the Spinning wheel was whacked by the Axe Man and the wrecking ball. It will soon be a used car lot, so they say! At least it is going to be used for something that can help all of us. I wish the new entrepreneur the best.

As I noted before, it recently became a Taco Bell. I remember being with my cousin Rich Knaus at the Friday Night Dances at the Spinning Wheel and I think before the band started, I tried my feet on Dee Dee Sharp's Mashed Potatoes .

The Spinning Wheel was really close to Meyers High School and so the Meyers people, and those coming to the Spinning Wheel for the music from all parts of the city, often got together at Luna Rosa Pizza (Where Gerry Ricci's Pizza is now) and its seemingly magnetic steps. After or during a dance, or a Friday night football game, nobody seemed to be able to get off those steps. Lennie's Pizza in the Heights was also a similar delight.

King's Dances & Outings

King's College in the late 1960's had great dances every Friday night with groups such as like the Buoys of Timothy fame. The Buoys were an American pop/rock band from the early 1970s. Its membership included Bill Kelly, Fran Brozena, Jerry Hludzik, Carl Siracuse and Chris Hanlon, based in the Wilkes-Barre-Scranton, PA area. They are most famous for the banned song "Timothy", which was written for them by Rupert Holmes. When I was seventeen I was a Freshman at King's and the Holy Cross Fathers really knew how to have fun.

The King's outings were legendary. They had outings in the Fall and Spring at places like Sgarlat Lake and Watahunnee Park. I think the outings went on every Sunday until it snowed in NEPA.

King's Auditorium for me was like having the CYC back in business with its regular dances but we were in our late teens to twenties. There was always something to do other than study from freshman year to senior year at King's. Besides the Sunday outings, there was nothing better than a Friday night King's dance in the 133 N. River Street Auditorium.

Nothing could top the outings or the class parties at the Brother's Four but King's was always doing something special. One time King's had a concert with the Young Rascals and they canceled with one day notice. King's found a group nobody ever heard of. They were great. Their name is the Cowsills. Not one bad song. They got standing ovations,

By the way, Marywood and Misericordia girls literally came by bus-loads to King's events. There was a lot of mixing and when the girls got on the bus to go back to their dormitories, there were a lot of tears on Union Street where they pulled up. At the time, King's was all-male, and the two M-schools were all-female. I can't believe I am 74 years of age now. Boy has time flown by.

As noted previously, The Buoys played regularly at King's. They were great. They sounded like the Bee Gees. I don't remember their hit record, Timothy because it came out in 1970 the year after I graduated from King's. But, we often danced to the music of the Cobra's with Austin people's as lead singer, and Gerry Rodski as lead guitarist. Gerry was one of us at King's and he sure was great with the guitar back then and he is still quite a talent today. Later they changed the name of their group to the East Coast Blues Ensemble. They were great as were all the live bands that played in the King's Auditorium.

By the way, I had a partial scholarship to King's and they gave me a work study job. So, on Saturday mornings at 8:00 I would show up for work and one of my duties was to scrub the Auditorium floor where the dance was held the night before. Sometimes the wads of gum on the floor, and there were many needed a hammer and a chisel to get off.

Chapter 8   Is Wilkes-Barre Doomed to Failure?

Some WB History First
https://www.u-s-history.com/pages/h2131.html

History of Wilkes-Barre, Pennsylvania
Wilkes-Barre is in the center of the Wyoming Valley anthracite coal region. It was founded in 1769 by John Durkee and colonists from Connecticut, and was originally known as Wyoming. Later, it was renamed in honor of two British members of parliament, John Wilkes and Col. Isaac Barre, who had defended the American colonies in parliamentary debates. Fort Wilkes-Barre was built in 1776 as a defense against Indians. On July 4, 1778, one day after the Wyoming Massacre, Wilkes-Barre was burned to the ground by Indian and British forces. It was rebuilt but again destroyed by fire during the second Pennamite-Yankee War. Conflicting claims by Pennsylvania and Connecticut were finally settled in favor of Pennsylvania. Title to lands occupied by Connecticut settlers were resolved by a series of statutes passed by Pennsylvania between 1799 and 1807. In 1818, Wilkes-Barre was incorporated as a borough, with a city charter following in 1871. Coal mining was not the only element of the Wilkes-Barre economy. Charles Stegmaier began brewing beer in 1857 and by 1916 was producing 200,000 barrels per year. Silk manufacturing became important, with companies like Empire Silk Mill importing silk from Japan to be fashioned into women's garments. However, coal was the most important element and its gradual decline impacted the local economy badly. Many of the mines had already closed when the Knox Mine disaster struck in January 1959. Floodwaters from the Susquehanna River swamped the Knox Mine and killed 12 men. In addition, an entire network of underground mines was flooded, ending deep mine operations in Wilkes-Barre and throwing thousands out of work. This was not to be the final

tragedy for Wilkes-Barre. Hurricane Agnes, although reduced by then to a tropical storm, struck in June, 1972, pushing the Susquehanna four feet above the levees built after the 1936 flood. More than 2,000 businesses were damaged, but the city has been completely rebuilt and revitalized since the disaster.

End of Brief History Of Wilkes-Barre, PA

This is the beginning of a book I wrote several years ago when Wilkes-Barre, once endowed with three High Schools was fighting to have at least one High School in the City. Without a single high school in the City, things could be worse but three high schools in Wilkes-Barre made the City's chances for success much better. How could the City Politicians have allowed this to happen. This Description of the book I wrote was the beginning of a book of answers that a group called Save Our Schools put together and there are plenty more.

The Big Toxic School!
Wilkes-Barre Area's Tale of Corruption, Deception, Taxation & Tyranny

A struggle for safe, enduring neighborhood schools.
We can't wait until there are no WB high schools and the tax burden is unsustainable.

In this book, you will learn about the actions taken by a democratically elected board of directors whose job is to manage the affairs of the Wilkes-Barre Area School District.

Unfortunately, in this book and through other sources, you will also learn that though this board was duly elected by the people, they lied about their intentions. In fact, they misrepresented themselves by agreeing, if elected, to represent the people and provide for the needs of the people above all else. We will cite quotations from citizens subject to the board's dictates. You will see that this board has chosen to follow a corrupt course of action rather than follow the known wishes of the people of the area which they serve.

The essence of the issue in dispute is whether perfectly maintainable and well-built and historically relevant school structures in the City of Wilkes-Barre should be abandoned, discarded, and torn down so that the board can build its idea of a Taj Mahal School on top of a toxic mine dump, in a community outside the City expected to give up its high schools for this folly. The three WB City High Schools currently meet the needs of the students and the taxpayers of the city of Wilkes-Barre.

The current board believes it has served the people well. Yet, they have no maintenance plan and have had no plan for the upkeep of school buildings for over fifty years if ever. They have no qualified staff to provide maintenance work in any of the $300,000,000 worth of properties, which are "owned" by the school district. Why is this so important?

If the board had the proper team of in-house builders, and maintainers, and a plan for them to do their jobs regularly, keeping the properties maintained, there would not be an urgent need today to replace the three historically relevant high schools in Wilkes-Barre City with an abomination built outside the city limits on a toxic mine shaft. The board, over the citizens objections, plans to tear down these historical structures because the board itself did not perform its trustee role in maintaining them. The board failed and they are preparing to fail again. The board's dream school shall not be built because the people can do better than the decisions of a myopic school board. Despite grave warnings, this board has chosen to place the health of students at risk. What esteemed body working for the public good would subject those learning or working in Mine Shaft High from breathing in the toxic fumes from the designed school built on top of a hazardous waste dump.

More and more citizens of the Area believe we were duped into believing the words of the Consigliere that putting poor Wilkes-Barre Area citizens in debt up to a half billion or more dollars after the State's contribution, was the only solution to having children well-educated in this area. How long do we think it will be that the foreclosure teams from the county and other taxing bodies would be coming for all the properties of the elderly who won't be able to pay the taxes required for the board's Taj Mahal. Folks, there is no need for this monstrosity and there are a few names you need to know who will change the school board to represent the people instead of the outside interests of board members. These names are Terry Schiowitz, RIP, Robin Shudak, Jody Busch, Beth Anne Owens, and Debra Formola. Folks, reading this book is a must.

Feel free to ask me why I ran for Mayor of Wilkes-Barre in 2015. But, now in 2025, you know a big part of the answer.

In Dickens' *Christmas Carol*, it only might be!

You may all recall that the Ghost of Christmas Future was the spookiest of all the ghosts in Dickens' famous Carol. And so, here we are pondering the future of Wilkes-Bare, and we have no guidance from Dickens' ghosts. Maybe we should be pleased. Maybe our fate is our own.

But, since there is an election for the Office of Mayor in Wilkes-Barre this year, I want you to know that the things that are written right here in this chapter are not things that must be; they are things that simply might be.

Would it not be nice if somebody who loves Wilkes-Barre and has the resources, stood up some day, and said: "I like that and I can make some dreams come true?" Wilkes-Barre's overtaxed payers are not the ones to make such dreams of mine or anybody else happen. But, I dream nonetheless, and I hope you dream too. It is our salvation from the pit our city has dug for itself over the years. Somebody has to dream in order to come up with the ideas needed to get us out of this deep rut.

Having set the stage, let me move to the future just a bit and give you one of my dream ideas that can only be achievable if we think we want it, and of course if somebody else, other than beleaguered taxpayers, chooses to pay for it.

Even if we do not get to do this dream of mine—ever, we should ask ourselves, "Why not?" It sure would help the City if it were to appear all by itself one day; that is for sure.

With good planning many more dreams will come true. We all must demand that our newly elected administration by end of year 2015, grace us with a five year, ten year, twenty-year and even a fifty-year plan for what we would like to make happen in this city's future.

George Patton, my almost favorite US General of all time (Pershing is my favorite), once said, "When everybody is thinking the same thing; somebody is not thinking." Without a plan, many people who want to say all is well, regardless, look for excuses and they somehow divine that what happened must have been planned and therefore must be. That is why mistakes and crises are tolerated.

The fact is the bulk of bad happenings over the years were not in any plan because cities do not like to plan. They like to react to crises, thinking the people sill support them. Those days are gone. It is too costly for any of us in Wilkes-Barre to be dumb any more as our government at all levels is siphoning away our freedoms. It is time to pay attention and elect smart leaders, who will plan for success, and be prepared for any failures.

It's time to demand that the thoughts of our leaders be spelled out early in their candidacies, and then surely during their administrations. Finding out something horrible happened in the eleventh hour like the Hotel Sterling was ripped down, is unacceptable. Was it part of a plan? Was the plan part of something the citizens had approved? Does anybody know those answers? Why the secrecy when public servants are put in office to serve the needs of the public?

On to more positive stuff. Few good things ever get done without having a good dream, a good idea, and a good plan.

So, let me get this thought out on the table and then some more. By the time I finish, the table should be full. It is not a goofy plan for sure, but it is unusual.

Choo Choo Woo Woo for Wilkes-Barre????

Without mincing words here, let it be known that I have often thought about a full-rail sized "choo choo" train circling the outer Square from say two blocks out. Within the train track perimeter, there would be minimal automobile traffic. Only vehicles to benefit the severely handicapped at say 5 miles per hour would be permitted. That's faster than most can walk, anyway.

There would be more free parking spaces on the perimeter and if there are not enough in certain areas, we could build them without busting the City's budget.

It would be an even greater accomplishment if we could get the tracks on the river side of River Street and have them go all the way up to North Street on the river side from South Street—

maybe a little farther but not too far to make the cost too prohibitive.

They would be built like a fortress and would strengthen the dike system in those places, rather than weaken it. Further down the river towards South Wilke-Barre would be a spur and a little garage for the train to be kept dry in the off-months (Wilkes-Barre has many cold winters left) and locked up in the off-hours. The spur would take the train behind Barney Farms, Where its garage and repair area would also be located.

At North Street of in the block after North Street, the tracks could then make a right turn and go up the hill and the north street hill and come down someplace around Pennsylvania Avenue. I have not mapped it all out but I believe when there is a will, there is a way. I think it can work. We might need a little bridge over the tracks here and there or dig out a section and have the train go underground for a bit. Hopefully, it could be done without such major expenses but we should do it right.

Then, after several more blocks in the direction of North Street towards Pennsylvania Avenue, the tracks could turn right again to come down Pennsylvania Avenue, maybe on the opposite side of the Street from Genettis. There are rail-beds there already, so we would have to see if they could be used. We surely would not want to take too many of Gus's great parking spots.

Another option would be to go down to the boulevard and come up. This leg would take us down to South Street again. At this point, we would probably go under the bridge and head towards the river. Of course, we would figure it all out in time as these "dreams" are not yet "ideas." At the river, of course we would get to the other side of the dike and begin a new run.

What a neat idea? Thank You! But, right now it is in the "dream stage." It is not crazy but it is way out of the box, if not a bit off the wall. Perhaps some national figure like a rich ex-president or another philanthropist might even underwrite the whole thing. Wilkes-Barre would be an oasis of beauty and innovation in Northeastern PA, for all to see and for all to visit. And I am convinced that "if we built it, they would come."

I do not care who helps but with the right people, Wilkes-Barre can show how it can be done. I am thinking that perhaps climate change advocate billionaire, Tom Steyer or billionaire Libertarians, such as the Koch Brothers, or perhaps Berkshire Hathaway's Warren Buffet, or Microsoft founder Bill Gates might want to pitch in to help Wilkes-Barre in its trail back to glory. How often do you think anybody asks these gents for a small handout? Maybe Microsoft's Paul Allen, Seattle Seahawks owner, would like to help. God knows we could use the help. My personal pick would be the builder, Donald Trump as he would know how to get it done. Perhaps he could have teamed up with a guy like Paul Allen. This is a third edition so I did learn that Paul Allen passed away on October 15, 1018. Too bad, nice guy!

Hey, maybe Mr. Allen, a sports lover like many of us, would have helped bring a "Wilkes-Barre Barons" minor league team back to Artillery Park to play every now and then if not permanently when Wilkes is not at home. Can you imagine when the new Barons would play the SWB Yankees? The Allen family might want to help in our mission as Jody Allen, trustee, sister and, with her family, sole heir to the estate might think like her brother. I kept the reference to Paul Allen because it was what I was thinking when I first wrote this book in 2015.

Good talk sometimes creates good dreams, which sometimes create good ideas. Let's keep them coming. If I had my way, I would have Wilkes-Barre's greatest development person of all time, my great friend Frank Pasquini, working on all these solicitations. He would have brought them in for sure for Wilkes-Barre.

But God did not have that in his plan. He took Frank to heaven in March 2017 before he had a chance to work on this plan. He was the right guy though as a tribute in the local paper referred to him as "Frank Pasquini, champion of downtown Wilkes-Barre, dies at 67" RIP Frank, you were a great one and the memory of you helps us all.

In my rough plan for the Wilkes-Barre Choo, I am not suggesting that all of these areas would need to be traffic free, especially in the beginning as we perfected the notion. However, the speed limit within the two-block radius would need to be reduced to perhaps no more than 10 miles per hour, while we tried our best to make this work—if of course, most of us think it is a good dream worth putting into a better idea.

I know this is an out of the box notion to say the least. We would have to think really big. A notion is something between a dream and an idea. Being out of the box is sometimes a very lonely notion. I hope somebody is out here with me but, rest assured, I am a quick study and I would be pleased to tell this story as it evolves to anybody who will listen.

I was ready to advise Mayor Tony George at the time, and I am ready to advise the next Mayor, George Brown, who is leading the City for the next four years and even after that, not to take action unless there is a consensus and a probability of success. That's why we need a guy like Frank Pasquini, and his friends with the Benjamins in the bank.

Even some of my good friends, who seem to favor status quo, and would be happy with leadership remaining exactly as it is, would characterize my thinking as "off the wall," and perhaps even nutsy, rather than "way out of the box." They would prefer to continue the long term plan for the City, which as we know has not existed in over fifty years. Have you seen the plan? Neither have I!

When it is built, I would advise a five year version; a ten year version; a twenty year version; and a fifty year version.

Planning can be responsible for the City staying on the mark in the future.

Think about this—Are they the ramblings of a mad man?

Think of this covered, warm and heated passenger train on these tracks in winter, with its windows wide open to the world in the summer. It would need a number of stops, say four—one at each corner at least, to make it effective.

In my ideal dream, the train would be electric, which might convince Tom Streyer to invest in the dream. Additionally, if I had my way, there would be no charge to ride this train. However, if a ticket were issued and verified at some stores, a small percentage (less than one percent perhaps) of the purchase price could be passed back to the City in this electronic age to pay any expenses. These are just raw thoughts. It would be better if it were free.

I would not want any novel idea such as this to cost taxpayers as for sure the people in Wilkes-Barre, the County, and the School District are well overtaxed.

If this notion of a train circling Wilkes-Barre idea were made possible, it would surely be a remarkable accomplishment for Wilkes-Barre—don't you think? People would come far and wide to experience our experience as we returned to our glory days as a city that stepped up to meet its challenges.

Our city would become a magnet and our shopkeeper's and other industries and the job opportunities would benefit big time; as would all of us living in the city. After all, the success of our local businesses have a lot to do with our own success as a City.

Stop the Tram Car, please!

Between the four major perimeter train stops and Public
Square, I can envision battery powered electric tram cars
carrying people from the stops on the perimeter to the
Square… just like at Disney World. Maybe Disney will give us
a few of their Tram Cars to help us out! We'll have to ask the
Lord and our friend Frank Pasquini about those possibilities.

There would be no need for a switching station at the Square
for Tram Car transfers as each car would go the full route and
hit all the streets and stop at every block within the perimeter.
It would be a nice ride unto itself. In my vision, this also would
be no charge but perhaps we would ask for a donation, please.
How many tram cars would we need? Thank you for the
question. Answer: As many as we need!

At the train stops at major Tram Car drop off points, there
could also be entrepreneurs with push carts, like on the
Atlantic City Boardwalk or the Far East. Perhaps you've seen
these clever vehicles on the Boardwalk recently. They seat
about two if large people such as myself are in the cart; three to
four otherwise. They have weather protection for short-
distance travel on bad rainy days. With a strong push-man
working to please passengers; expecting and getting his or her
recompense for a job well done, the trip could be swift, full of
great Wilkes-Barre sights, and a lot of fun.

These entrepreneurs would take their carts full of passengers
over a smooth trail (provided by Wilkes-Barre engineers and
craftsmen) to any destination within the perimeter, including
another train stop. There would also be drop off rental bikes
available as are now prevalent in major cities.

Wilkes-Barre has had bikes available at Gus Genetti's.
https://wbdcp.org/maps-directions/alternatives-to-driving/
See Chapter 34 for more information on this.

WILKES-BARRE BIKE SHARE:

If you would like to explore "Uptown" and the riverfront trails by bicycle here's how. The community bike-sharing program offers free bikes for use from dawn to dusk at Genetti's Best Western Hotel at 77 West Market Street. Cyclists must be 18 years or older (16-17 permitted with parent or guardian). A current, valid driver's license must be left with attendant while bike is in use. Learn more at www.wilkesbarrebikeshare.com

There should also be defined bike lanes for safety and bike parking spots within this area. In my plan with the choo choo, there would be very few if any cars, and those that were permitted on the streets would be going very slow.

Of course a challenge for City officials would be to use the parking spaces in the city without creating a danger. Challenges are welcome and all problems are solvable with the right attitude. Always elect the right officials and voice your opinion to the leaders of the City to represent your line of thinking for a great start on returning Wilkes-Barre to its glory days.

There are naysayers in every project. You may know that it took about fifteen to twenty years for the beautiful Luzerne County Courthouse to be finally finished in 1909. But, the forebears of ours at least had a dream, then an idea, then a plan to make it happen eventually, and they took the action to make sure this beautiful structure now graces the River Common.

Naysayers are good as long as they do not simply declare that Wilkes-Bare is not worth saving, and they move themselves and their belongings out of town. I would advise naysayers to stick around and see what we can do when we have a mind to.

I know it is easy to declare anybody with such dreams as a nut for putting such "out-of-box" solutions out there to be seen by the public. Since it is I, who is doing this, you can see why I am super sensitive about this.

I would bet that since I know what I am doing in making these notions known, most psychologists would say that since I am coherent in that understanding, I am not nuts. Your opinion may differ but that is what life is about—honest debate before action. But, then again, the final determination is yours and my wife's. So far she is on my side...I think!

I do encourage all of those who still use their brains to think independently of government. Use those God-given minds of yours to come up with your own dreams for Wilkes-Barre—big and small dreams alike. I suspect there are few in our City would like us to permit "deterioration" to be a candidate for our city "word," while we wait for another federal grant to pave a few streets or tear down a few more monuments.

I think we can do a lot more than that, even if in the end, we cannot convince anybody to fund our Choo Choo train off and around Public Square. I sure am no Walt Disney, for sure, but can you imagine if the greatest imaginer in America, was shut down simply because he chose to imagine?

Other ideas not requiring a train

What about all those vacant lots on major streets in Wilkes-Barre. Well, we certainly are not going to build a major industrial park in Wilkes-Barre, but we need to do a lot more work on planning and zoning so that we could invite light manufacturing and distribution industries into our city. We have some major streets and then we have neighborhood streets, and we can identify and encourage business uses on certain of our major streets.

We need jobs for sure. They sneak away from our town at a blistering pace. We must stop this. Having good workers and a positive community would encourage companies to relocate here and entrepreneurs would be incented to bring their trade skills right here and set up shop in Wilkes-Barre. Maybe a company would show up that built mini trains in people's yards. OK, I may be stretching it but without dreams, no dreams are ever realized.

A City of Mini-Malls!

There are some pretty large vacant areas in our City, many of which are big enough to support a mini-mall. I am not talking about strip malls with big stores that often become rundown and unsightly. I am talking about places with a nice restaurant and/or a great specialty grocery store and/or a gourmet fish market as the anchor. How about four to ten small stores linking up in the same area with parking or Tram Cars or Coo-Lee service close by.

I bet you have your own ideas for this. In other chapters of this book, we look at our uptown banks that are deteriorating – PNC Bank and Citizens Bank in particular. These all have parking available such as the Boscov's lot, Park 'n Lock etc. Why not make a few floors of the Citizens bank or the First Eastern Bank into mini malls.

Next thing you know, the banks will want to come back down to Wilkes-Barre. I know a nice spot at the corner of West Market and North River Street, where the next successful Wilkes-Barre bank can build its next building. Maybe for nostalgia purposes, it should be called The Miners National Bank!

One of my favorite neighborhood haunts has always been the Barney Inn in the South Wilkes-Barre Section. Its tradition of great food and great refreshments is well known even as the ownership has changed.

The current place, CrisNics is as good as it gets. With regular fare such as Lobster and great steaks, and as my friends Barbara and Dennis had just a short-time ago, Liver and Onions, and a Haddock platter. Dennis said "the Liver &

Onions was as good as he had in his life," and Barbara felt that her fish dinner was almost as good as Lobster Tail. I love their Reuben's, Irish fare, and their pizza with light cheese, extra sauce and extra onions. Can't beat it! And their drinks are good too.

So, in my dreams, I see this little section of Barney Street cut off from the world and made itself into a mini mall with wooden sidewalks, hitching rails, bannisters, bike racks, and a few wooden canopies. CrisNics already has a huge parking lot, and its own great canopy which covers its "outdoor pavilion."

The family is supportive of Wilkes-Barre and I bet they would love to see their immense parking lot become a multi-story parkade, paid for by the efforts of great thinkers such as Frank Pasquini. The lot would have access only from Waller Street. It would take just a few steps to arrive at CrisNics or any other fineries in the new Barney Street Mini-Mall.

I also thinking about a back alley in between Regent Street and Barney to take the traffic over the new bridges. It would be a shame not to use those new bridges. Perhaps some novel store can emerge by the creek and make use of the creek when it has enough water. I am not sure what right now but the noggin is always cooking something.

Abe's and the Barney Street Lunch are already in place as two of the best Hot Dog luncheonettes in the State, and they would fit in perfectly in this new Barney Mini-Mall. Both have a ton of parking that the possible alley from Horton Street might reach effectively.

For big time parking availability, there is a huge vacant lot right now on the corner of Horton and Barney Streets. It is amazing what you can accomplish if you actually think it is possible. If you are not sure of what is possible, and what is not possible, that's where dreaming comes in. If you think Wilkes-Barre can afford none of this; that's where the spirit of Frank Pasquini comes in. All things are possible

Site of Potential Barney Street Mini Mall

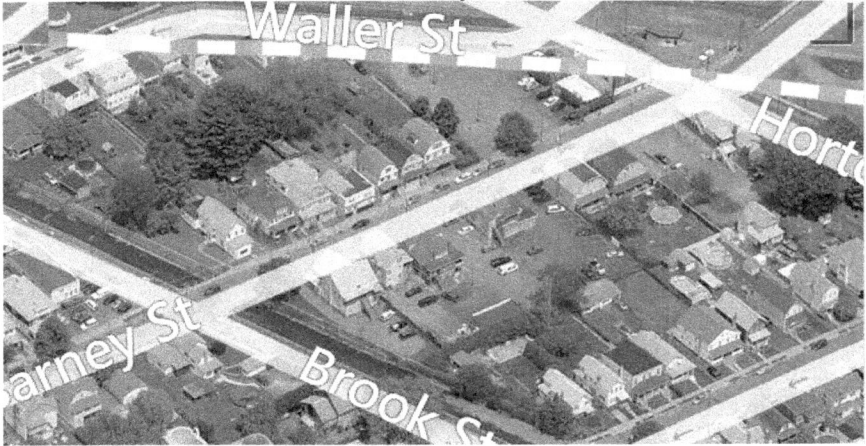

There are also train tracks across from CrisNics, which might be a way to connect to the Public Square Choo Choo if that dream ever materializes. How about a quick way uptown and back down to Barney Street to CrisNics or Abe's, or the Barney Street Lunch or the Barney Street Mini-Mall.

What about a mini-hotel?

Ah, c'mon Brian are you nuts? While we are building the Barney Mini-Mall, we would need to dress up the existing houses a bit with a common old-west theme as a façade or a real front-face. That's how I see it. CrisNics is already in-theme as is the Barney Street Lunch, but Abe's might need a façade to make it look like the Abe's retro of yore.

Once we have the houses looking nice on the front, there may be those willing to sell to the site developer. I can envision craft stores in some of the houses or perhaps a Wawa or a multi-building hotel. There are two or more large former bar and store buildings across from CrisNics. They look like apartments now. If you live in one of those, or any home on this block on either side of Barney Street, fear not!

Nothing happens overnight in Wilkes-Barre or Scranton so there would be plenty of time for your voices to be heard.

Owners of these facilities would have as we would say in the olden days would have "first dibs."

If the owners were amenable, those buildings could be the anchor for the hotel that might include other homes that remain on the block. You would check in across the street from CrisNics and be assigned a room in one of the homes that were part of the "First Dibs Hotel Complex." Obviously, this part would take a lot of planning but can you envision how nice this would be? Why not? Again, benefactors and developers would be needed. The people left behind could not be left behind or this dream, almost reaching an idea could never happen.

There may be other areas of the city in vacant spots of town or almost vacant spots, where rejuvenation and a return to glory is practical, but the folks have given up. No giving up in Wilkes-Barr will be permitted. Frank Pasquini may not be able to make a house call on anybody, but he can offer a lot of Wilkes-Barre prayers for success. With Frank on the Mini-Mall team, nobody has to give up on anything, and he will bring his personal buddy "ole cheerios" Gus Genetti in to work to close the deal.

My message in this chapter of course has been that it all starts with a dream. Dreams become ideas when they seem practical; ideas are translated into plans, and then action is taken to implement the good things that are planned. We can do whatever we choose. If we dream and ultimately pick our best ideas, we might even be able to get a lot of them done. Wouldn't that be nice?

Chapter 9   A 26" Bike Can Take a Kid Anywhere!

Two great junk yards were little more than a block away

I was born back in Wilkes-Barre's glory days, and it seemed that as soon as I could walk, I could ride a bike—I mean a big 26" bike. I was five or six years old. I am not kidding. My dad bought it for me for a dollar. Carly Blaine a kid about ten years old made it out of stuff he had gotten at Solomon's Junk Yard on Parish Street.

Alexander's Junk Yard—Alexander himself was the dad of a great guy the girls in our neighborhood called "Lar Lar." The dad had a spot almost as close to my house as Solomon's but Solomon's was much bigger. Moreover, Solomon's took in a lot of bikes, bike frames, and bike parts. Alexander's always gave a better price than Solomon's for rags, if they were clean. But, they did not like small amounts of papers that I carried in my little wagon. Yet, Mr. Alexander was a great guy, as was George Sr. and Mike Solomon. I admit I was afraid of all the men who ran the junk yard especially when they caught me on one of their piles of junk. .

The Solomon Junk Yard people did not care what kids like Carly Blaine or I took from the yard, or so it seemed. What they could not tolerate, however, was kids on the top of the dangerous junk piles looking for great stuff. We were unbreakable then but the Solomon people did not know it so they would give us the chase when they saw us on top of the big piles looking for past treasures. They did not need a little kid getting hurt.

If we had a good day finding stuff, and we were leaving with some bounty, such as a rim or a shock absorbing bike fork, a sprocket, or a glistening handlebar, they would seemingly pretend they did not see us. Perhaps they just hoped we would leave quickly. They turned their eyes to enable our escape with our loot; but they did not like us ten feet up on those junk piles—no matter how much they seemed to like kids like us.

Carly Blaine had done the deed and had the parts and he had made the bike. I never saw him up there on the piles when I was there; but I knew he did not get the stuff out of thin air.

Looking back, I cannot believe that my extremely cautious dad paid the buck and got me the bike. I was thrilled. He never saw the bike until I was on it the next day. We sorta trusted things back then. We had nine inch "curbs" back then and I needed every inch in order to mount the bike, and then, before I got a little bigger, it was tough getting more than my toes on the petals once I got the launch off.

Once mounted on my mean fender-less machine, I was a bike monster from then on. I never stole anything from anybody. To be honest, when I took things from the junk yard, I never once thought I was stealing. I do not know why! Now I know it was grand theft larceny but back then I did not know. I am sure Carly Blaine felt the same way. That 26" bike changed my life even though, as noted, when I first got it, my feet could hardly reach the petals. I was always able to find a high curb or a set of front porch steps in order to get on it. I had some crashes and they hurt parts of my body I did not realize were actually there. Of course this helped me ride my bike so this rarely happened.

So, with my own bike transportation, I began to frequent any place in Wilkes-Barre that I chose. None of us kids were worried about predators back then because all the kids seemed a lot tougher than the sleaze-balls that might try to bother us.

All I had to do was mount my personal twenty-six inch fat tired bike, and puff! I was in a different world. As previously noted, my "new" bike had no fenders. So, it was not too pleasant riding in rain or snow. But, I managed.

We lived in a great spot (upper High Street) with lots of stores close by so I did not always have to use my bike. However, most often, I had it with me. Places within walking distance from/to our home on High street by Blackman, included great spots such as Brady's Lunch on Blackman St; Peters' Ice Cream Store-- corner of Brown & Blackman; Feighlinger's Store-- corner of Parish and Brown; Mosie's Confections-- Parish close to High; Goode's Dry Goods store-- Parish close to Brown; Daubert's on Blackman Street; Walker's on Jones's Street; and Peters Economy Store-- across from the mine shaft on Parish and High.

There was even Mike Barrouk's Candy & Cigar store in the middle of my block on High Street but it closed when I was about six years old.

Growing up, my grandmother would religiously take me up to Goode's store for a brand new pair of clodhoppers, when my old pair had holes in the bottom. My mother told me I always used to say. Mr. Doodie is a dood man. Karl Goode was a good man as were most of the fine men in our neighborhood.

As noted, Mike Barrouk, Greg Barrouk's Great Grandfather (Greg is a former Wilkes-Barre City official.), ran a candy store on High Street when I was a young kid. It probably was a much more important store in High Street's early days.

Mr. Barrouk had penny candy galore when I was growing up and there were always a few Syrian gentlemen in the store smoking cigars when I would go in for my candy. Sometimes my family members--typically uncles or aunts from out of town—would ask me to go to Mike Barrouk's to get them some change. I still do not know why they did that. The store was less than a half block from my house. Though I was pretty young, the store was three houses down. When I was first permitted to go there. Mike Barrouk always seemed to like it when I came in. I liked him too!

One day, I figured I needed some change myself. In fact what I needed was more change than I had because I knew the more change you had, the more things you could buy.

I did not fully comprehend the value of a coin but I knew that, other than that pesky dime, the big coins were always worth more than the small coins. So I figured on this day, I would put into work my plan of action to get more change into play at Mike Barrouk's store.

I went to the counter and Mike Barrouk was there expecting me to ask for candy or change. He was very patient. I asked for change. He said "What would you like change for?" I had a nickel. I said "I would like this changed into a quarter." I knew that if I got the quarter, I could get two dimes and a nickel for the quarter in a subsequent round of change.

Just then, you could hear a pin drop in the store. Others had heard my request. Mike knew I was too young to be kidding or trying to cheat him, so he asked his friends if they heard what I said and they all got a good laugh about it.

I was perplexed and did not know why they were laughing. When the laughter died down, Mr. Barrouk took the time to explain the value of coins to me. He did not get mad. He was a good guy. High Street was a great place to grow up. I left with my nickel still trying to figure it all out.

When we were looking for neat things to buy, reasonably close by, there was Huntzinger's 5 & 10, on Hazle Street; and the Barney Street 5 & 10, where the parking lot for CrisNics is today. For these stores, bicycle transportation was necessary. All of these venues kept an under ten-year old busy for hours checking out toys, gizmos, sports items, and bicycle accessories and parts.

The City could not have planned it any better.

Chapter 10   Four Dollars and Sixty-Two Cents

Sometimes dreams do come true

I wrote this chapter before I wrote a book with the same title. Every Christmas season from when I was about seven or eight years old, every night, cold as it might be, I went uptown on my trusty bike. It was magical. I always stopped at the American Auto Store (now Marquis Art & Frame), to see the Lionel Trains on display. Quite often they were operating them and the whole place was filled with enchantment.

They had several outstanding platforms upon which to gaze and dream. One was on the right side of the store and the other was way in the back. I made sure I experienced both before I ever left. OK…until I was chased, I stayed and watched in amazement. There was an auto place right next store where they changed oil, batteries, tires, or any part that you bought in the store. It was a great store. When I was sixteen, my dad bought the family a car, and I went there, of course, for anything I needed.

In my younger days, I have already alluded that I had a little junk route on Saturdays that brought me anywhere from 15c to 50c. I took whatever papers and rags I collected to Solomon's Junk Yard, which was no more than a block away from my home on High Street. If I had a lot of rags, which was a real bonanza, I took them to Alexander's, which always seemed to give a better price. It did not take long for this U-10 junk man to know where to go.

I saved a few of those dollars, but I could never afford a Lionel Train. It was the Cadillac of trains. At that time in the American Auto, the least expensive Lionel Train was $14.95 complete. One day, I got my train—the story of a dream fulfilled. It was a Marx Train, and it was a dandy. Here is that story. I'll come back to the glory days of Wilkes-Barre after this story. It is one of my favorite stories about the goodness of Wilkes-Barre and it is 100% true. For me, these were the glory days...

I love trains

I guess by now, you have figured out that I have always had a strong affinity towards trains of all sorts. I still love trains. For example, around my Sunroom today, which has a high, cathedral like ceiling, on a ten inch continuous shelf about eight feet up, I have a Lehman Gross Bahn (LGB) train circling the whole room. It is a step above Lionel and the tracks look like they are overgrown HO scale.

One day I may put a little automatic door in my outside wall, and a train switch, and take the train around the outside deck and back. Right now it is not a plan or an idea but it is a dream and sometimes, when I get serious and discuss it with my wonderful wife. It is an idea...a rejected idea but an idea nonetheless.

When I went to Europe with two friends in the 1970's, we purchased a Eurail Pass (They are still available and are still a deal.) for $125.00. This gave us all unlimited rail travel throughout Europe for three weeks. We traveled through eight different countries often sleeping on the train at night to save on expenses. We were as far north as Copenhagen, Denmark and as far south as Rome Italy. The trains were erste classe (first class).

I recently took a train to Myrtle Beach from Philadelphia with a stop off 100 miles out of town to rent a car the rest of the way. And, I took the Auto Train from Lorton Virginia to

Sanford, Florida, and picked up my wife Pat at the Sanford Airport with my own car, and brought her back to get her return flight. My car and I enjoyed the ride. I do love trains of all sizes.

Christmas is a great time for electric trains

On one of my excursions uptown in December, 1957, it was almost Christmas Eve. I stopped as usual at the American Auto and got my "wow," from the magnificent exhibition of Lionel Trains on the right side and the back. Then, after unrequited satiation, I went to "Bushels" of Bargains or just "Bushels" as we called it, right next door to The American Auto, to check out their train wares. I do not remember what I found that night but I moved on.

In my travels, I would often stop at Rea and Derick Drug store on the next block same side as they had a few trains available. Their ads in the paper were very inviting. I would even stop at Lazarus' sometimes just in case, but their toy store was not built to attract folks like me as they always had little in the line of toys to attract kids.

This particular night, however, I hoped that I might find what I had been dreaming about at a store other than American Auto, where I knew I needed big bucks.

So, I eventually made it to Neisner Brothers, right down from the Boston Store. We called it Neisner's.

On my many trips uptown, I had checked out the less expansive trains at Neisner's. So, I knew their Marx trains were substantially less costly than Lionel. Yet, I had never checked to see exactly how much they cost.

Optimistically, I was hoping I could afford one, but even if not, at a minimum that night, so close to Christmas, I figured I would get to check them out, and I would continue the dream.

I had accumulated $4.62 cents. I had been selling ice cream cakes for Peters' Ice Cream Store. I had been shoveling sidewalks with Peters' as my prime location. I was working my Saturday junk route. And on top of all that, knowing in addition to keeping the life going, I needed some real profits at Christmas time to make an impact on gift buying etc..

So, I had bought some "stuff" at Huntzinger's 5c & 10c and to get some extra pocket money, I actually made Christmas corsages from Holly and Pine cones. I sold only one corsage to Abe Solomon's pretty daughter on Parrish Street for 50c. It paid for every other corsage I had made but had not sold as Huntzinger's was a reasonable store.

I always hoped that somehow I would accumulate enough cash to be able to buy a Lionel Train. My $4.62 was there in a bid wad in my pocket; but I knew for sure it could not get me a Lionel Train by almost a mile. My trip to the American Auto this night sealed the deal in my thinking.

Thinking about home

In reflecting on how old I was at this time, I can recall that my grandmother Mary McKeown, died when I was just 11 years old. Grandmom was definitely alive this night. So, I think that I must have been about nine years old at the time.

I remember that this particular night, I felt a little different about everything. I cannot explain it. I had some hope because I knew that that $4.62 was not just a buck plus a few quarters. It was real money and it took a lot to earn it.

Perhaps that night something good would happen, and with $4.62, I was ready just in case it did. But even I, with my glowing anticipatory eyes, would never have expected what happened that night. All the while, my trusty 26" bike was waiting for me just outside of Neisner's store.

When I went into the Neisner Brothers' store, I did not even stop at the Fountain for a coke. I wanted to have all of my funds available. I went right down the steps to where the toys and trains were sold. There seemed to be no customers and no sales personnel in the Neisner's basement that night. It was "dead."

I went around to the train displays and I looked longingly as I always did at the boxed Marx trains. There was enough train showing through the cellophane to make them look almost as glorious as the Lionel's that I had just seen at the American Auto Store.

I was disappointed to see that the least expensive Marx boxed model was priced at about $8.99. I had never priced them, more than likely because my big plan was to buy a Lionel one day. I did have $4.62 so I thought I had a shot at a Marx train but even this did not seem like it could happen. It had happened many times for me in the past and though I always dreamed about a train, it had never happened and it sure looked like I would have to wait another year or so.

Ready to accept disappointment

Though lots less expensive than the Lionel's, I realized that I still could not afford any train—even at Neisner's lower prices, but I kept browsing, nonetheless. I had been disappointed before. So, maybe next year I would save up enough! I had made myself OK with how I figured it was going to end. That's the way it had always been.

Out of nowhere a man who looked like he was a store manager came up to me and asked if he could help me. Most stores did not really seem to like a kid to be hanging around a lot of loose toys. I suspect it had to do with being concerned that something might be stolen. This gentleman looked like he wanted to help me find what I wanted. He looked like a regular store guy but he did not act that way.

I told the man that I was looking for a train but there were none there that I could afford. He did not react to my answer but instead, he simply and gently asked me how much money I had. I knew I had just $4.62 and that is what I told the man. I expected him to walk way but he did not.

Instead, he looked me in the eye and he reached down and pulled a huge Marx Train box out from under one of the counters. It already had a load of track in it and a transformer; but nothing else. It was not a set.

Was the man really an angel?

He asked me to come along with him. I was not sure why. He got some more track and said that ought to be enough track. He then went about finding Marx Electric Train cars and putting them into slots in the box he held. Finally, he found a painted diesel shaped engine (not a locomotive) and he put that into the box. Everything seemed to fit except the why?

Each time he did something like this, he would ask if this was OK or that was OK. I would say it was OK. I was not 100% sure what he was doing but the dreamer in me thought he just might be building a train set for me. I knew deep down that I would not be able to afford this fine train as it grew in size inside the biggest train box that I had ever seen. And, in case you may not recall, I was sort of an American Auto expert.

He then looked puzzled and he started walking quickly from one area to another. Then, he came back to me with a red Pullman (Passenger) car. He said, "I cannot find a caboose but this looks an awful lot like a caboose. Will this car be OK to use as a caboose?" I said sure.

He then closed the box and took it to the register. He was also the guy at the register. He had built a whole train set from pieces while walking around the counters. He sealed it so it did not come apart, and then he asked me what I thought of the train. I told him how much I liked it and he said "that is great."

I could not contain myself so I then asked him the question of which I dreaded the answer. I asked "How much is it, sir?"

Thank you sir!

He looked at me like he knew what he had done and he said: "Why; it is four dollars and sixty-two cents…that's how much you told me you had, right?" I was crying with joy inside but I showed no tears because my dad always taught me that men do not cry. I said "Thank You Sir."

I took out the $4.62 from my pocket. It was in the form of a lot of change and a few bills. He stood there smiling and waiting patiently for me to finish counting and then I handed it to him. It was an exact count. He took the wad of money, thanked me for the business, and he rung up the sale.

I thanked him again and he said Merry Christmas, and it sure was a Merry Christmas for me and my family. I could not believe what had just happened. I wanted to hug him. I wish I had.

The ride home was exciting

My 26" bike was waiting patiently for me outside. It was cold but I did not feel any cold. I put the huge box on the handlebars of my twenty-six inch bike and drove it down South Main Street. I walked it up the big part of Parish Hill, by George Elias's house on Parrish, and I rode it over High Street to our home.

I could not wait to show everybody. All the while that I was riding my bike, or pushing it, I was dreaming about setting the train up and running it for mom and dad, grandmom, and my brothers and sisters.

We had never had a train. When I got home, nobody could believe that I had gotten a train for $4.62 so I had to tell them the whole story that I just told you. Our Christmas tree was already set up in the corner of the parlor, and there was a white sheet surrounding it at the bottom and it extended for quite an area. The train would look great running on track on that beautiful white sheet.

For the dry run, I set the train up on the living room rug. It was huge with straight track galore. It was almost as big as the living room (parlor as we called it) or so it seemed.

Tommy Mehm Helped Me

I had learned enough about trains from my best St. Boniface School buddy, Tommy Mehm, RIP, from Blackman Street, who had a Marx Train with similar track. Yet, at first, I could not figure out how to connect the transformer to the track.

My dad found us some small gauge coated copper wire for the transformer and it was easy to screw that on. But, I did not understand that I could tape the other end of each of the wires to a track so that it made contact and then the two wires would power the tracks for the train. I knew I needed something. What was it and what was it called?

I figured out from recalling Tommy Mehm's train setup that what I was looking for was called a lock-on. I had seen these at the American Auto displays also. All their trains had one.

I hoped that a Lionel lock-on for its standard O27 gauge would work if I only I had one or could get one. But, I had no money at all. I confessed to my generous grandmother that I needed a part. She gave me a quarter and without hesitation, I got on my bike again. and went into the winter cold and back to the American Auto.

I knew that Neisner's did not have parts like that and I knew American Auto would have the part. They did. It was fifteen cents. I bought it and came home, all again on this dark, cold, December night.

We had already placed the train on the track before I went uptown for the lock-on. So, I connected the lock-on to the track and then connected the wires to the lock-on and then I plugged the power cord of the transformer into the wall. Everything fit and the train worked for the first time like a charm. Everybody in the house was there watching with glistening eyes.

We then disconnected all the track after running the train for a long time. We then took just the circular pieces and put them around the tree on the pristine white sheet.

It all worked and it was like magic when the train went behind the tree and came back out the other side. It was surely a blessed Christmas for a kid with a dirty face from High Street in Wilkes-Barre, and a family that was in awe of having a train make its trips around the tree.

These were Wilkes-Barre's glory days for sure. As I think back, I sure wish I had taken notice to the name of the man who helped me get the train for $4.62. I often wished I had written him a letter because of how good he made me feel as well as my whole family.

I guess to do what is right, I will have to begin hanging around Wilkes-Barre stores looking for some dirty faced kids so I can help get them their first train set along with all the smiles it might give. Thanks for letting me tell this story. Isn't it nice to know such great people exist in this world? And, at this time in my life, my whole world was in Wilkes-Barre, PA.

Chapter 11   The Young Had Many Choices in WB Glory Days

Sports, Swimming Pools, Games & Theatres

Besides the great restaurants and other eateries which catered to teenagers who had a buck or two to spend, there were many great opportunities to do neat things in Wilkes-Barre. Many of the places I mention are gone or are smaller in size; and their absence and/or right sizing has taken away some of the glory of our town.

<<<
**Miner Park
Wilkes-
Barre with
Memorial
Placard**

A boy or a
girl could
play
hardball,
softball,
wiffle ball,
basketball, or football at Eyerman Park off Gilligan and
Andover Streets; the Company Yard on High Street by Parish,
Espy park by Espy St. parsons, the bottom of Scott Street,
Huber Park in the Mayflower, Miner Park on Old River Road
and Hanover Street, Pine Ridge in Parsons, and Coal Street
Park off Coal Street.

There were a host of places across the city to play organized
sports such as Little League, Teeners' League, and Senior
Teeners' leagues. Most importantly, there were vacant lots
upon which homes had never been built, such as the one by the
Homestead on Brown Street and the one by Mamary's Funeral
home on Parish before Mamary's was even there. Every
Neighborhood had its places.

And because there was not always a field or a vacant lot
available, there was always the street where tag football, wiffle
ball, and basketball were played from morning to night. And,
of course there were the night time games—Hide and Seek,
Relievio, Statue of Liberty and others that made life in Wilkes-
Barre's glory days, worth waiting for the sun to come up.

It was as nice as it could be. Nobody was poor because we all
had Wilkes-Barre to make things great. Maybe neighborhoods
would be closer and friendlier and safer if we could bring some
of these notions back today.

My wife met me at the Parish Street Swimming Pool. The pool was very new, built in the late 1950's. When she met me, I did not know it. Parrish was a great pool and I was there almost every day in the summer. It was a lot of years after she met me that I finally met her.

Thank the Lord, she did not remember me. When saw me from a distance the first time, I had a huge bathing suit and a larger waist than most of my childhood / teenager peers. The bow on the string that tied my bathing suit was about a foot long. That's how oversized my bathing suit was. But, it never fell down.

My wife told me years later that she had remarked to her best friend, Mary, who at the time looked like my wife's twin, that I was pretty icky looking. Hey, even I thought I was. Hah! She was not impressed by my fine duds and my great crew cut. She also commented on my crew cut, which never really worked for me with my curly hair. Until I met this same fair maiden and many years had passed, I was unaware these words about me were ever spoken.

Others more than likely in their youth had similar experiences I am sure as Wilkes-Barre was the proud sponsor of three additional pools including Hollenback, the Griffith Swimming Pool, which, before Coal Street, the Heights folks enjoyed, and of course the fabulous e Miner Park Swimming Pool with its magnificent, but scary for a kid, fountain right in the middle. Those of us from the Rolling Mill Hill frequented Miner Park and ate picnic lunches under the trees on Hanover Street until the Parish Street Pool was built.

Kids and adults in Wilkes-Barre did not have to go to the Mall or the huge Cineplex eight miles away in the 1960's to see a movie. The theatres were in our neighborhoods. We saw our share of these movies because the price was right, and the Goobers Peanuts were enough to get a hungry soul through a double feature. I'd sure love to see community theatres come back. Maybe in some of the vacant lots in the City or in the new Mini Malls?

There were so many theatres in Wilkes-Barre that there is a long list of those that I had never seen nor heard about until I researched this book. These include the Gaiety Theatre (formerly the Nesbitt Theatre), S. Main St.; Capitol Theatre, Public Square; Grand Opera House, S. Franklin St. near W. Market St.; Irving Theatre, S. Main St. opposite old post office.

We had a number of great theatres right in Wilkes-Barre in the neighborhoods and downtown, no more than a fifteen minute walk away from where anybody lived. The Hart Theatre was off the main path but it was very classy, situated on Hazle Street. Back then, Hazle Street was a fine Wilkes-Barre street. Movies at the Hart Theatre were typically twenty cents except on Sundays or if they had a Disney Movie. Then, the price was 25 cents.

The St. Boniface school kids, about thirty or forty in a class, often went as a group to the Hart Theatre for some spooky shows on Friday nights. I suspect other grade schools like Dodson or Palmer did the same as there were lots of kids in the theatres at the time.

When we got to High School, the places to go were the Comerford and the Paramount. I also went to the Penn before I was a teenager. Downtown theatres were the big date venues in the 1960's. And if there were a few sheckles left, there were all those great spots on the Square to extend the date with a soda and something else.

The "Bucket" aka the Barney Street Theatre, which is now part of the parking lot for CrisNics Pub (Barney Inn) was always a nickel cheaper than the Hart Theatre. Then again, the movies at the "Bucket of Blood," had been out for a few months longer by the time they reached "The Bucket."

The Penn Theatre on South Main Street disappeared perhaps even before the 1960's. It had been Poli's Vaudeville Theatre before it was the Penn. I remember my brother Ed, RIP, who took me there just one time as I recall. The double feature that day was *The Creature with the Atom Brain* and *The Beginning of the End.* It scared the crap out of me.

The walk from High Street to South Main Street seemed to go on forever. The shows were exciting for sure and that is how Ed intrigued me to go with him. To show I remember the titles the one trip I made, it was a double feature with "Creature with the Atom Brain" and "The Beginning of the End" as the two movies. Maybe you were there? Scary!!!

It was the scariest adventure I had ever seen. For years it haunted me, especially since a good guy I had known as "Frank Smith," who was Joe Friday's first partner in Dragnet, became one of the bad guys and he got an atom brain. I could not believe he would go bad. Wow, for me it was so real.

But, I loved the fact that the Penn Theatre was there in the same area as the roller rink (South Main Street Armory, and the fantastic GAR Building). To put things in full perspective. Back then, there were five theatres in Wilkes-Barre that I knew about and today there are zero.

We have to ask ourselves, "How is that better for kids or for the rest of us?" Taking our high schools out of our neighborhoods appeals to me just about as much. TV and Video games are no replacement for the social and friend network one created just by going to the movies and going to a local high school...

And the popcorn, huge pickles, and Goobers Peanuts were unbelievable! Maybe we should serve that stuff in the high schools also to encourage friendship.

Chapter 12   The "Miners" & the Importance of Coal for Wilkes-Barre

Small Coal Mining Operation from 1898

Miners made it better for the whole city

Wilkes-Barre, as many towns in NEPA in the early days, was a mining town. Miners had tough lives. They would work 12-hour or longer shifts and there were many times in the winter, in which folks like my Uncle Gene McKeown, who lived on Brown Street and worked for Glen Alden, would go into the mine in the morning when it was still dark. When he would come out after his shift, it was dark again.

Only the light on his helmet and the few lights in the mines kept his eyes from being all pupil. No wonder the miners enjoyed their respite at the huge bounty of taverns built just for them by Wilkes-Barre tavern proprietors across the city.

The whole day had passed by the time the miners were ready to call it quits. The good news was that there was plenty of work for the miners, who often started their careers just after they turned ten years old. John L. Lewis's United Mine Workers' Union kept wages to the point where miners made a decent living. But, with the coal dust, and the long hours, the miners, both young and old had really tough lives, and their lives were shortened by the conditions under which they toiled.

In August 1830, Charles Miner put pen to paper to describe the burgeoning coal industry in Pennsylvania's Wyoming Valley for Hazard's Pennsylvania Register. Miner knew the anthracite industry well – he had been intimately involved with the first mining venture at Mauch Chunk that sent coal down the Lehigh River to Philadelphia on an ark during the War of 1812.

Charles Miner – University of California

The mines were a scary place to work as many over the years had lost their lives because of one type of accident or another. Wherever there was a mine, there were always a lot of taverns close by, ready to serve the needs of the miners. The taverns did wonders for the dry throats which often plagued the miners after and sometimes well before a day in the deep mines.

Many a miner chose not to call it quits for the day when the shift was over. Instead, he would find his favorite tavern (for some right across the street from the colliery), and they would enjoy a few local brews such as Stegmaier's or Gibbons' as well as a few schnorkies. In the morning, before the shift began, the taverns would open early to give those heading down the long shafts a few schnorkies to help give them the courage to face yet another day.

My father thankfully was never a mine worker. He would have done anything to make a buck to feed his family five kids and my mom and her parents living in three bedrooms. However, he did not get the job. He was hired by fortune at Stegmaier Brewery in the 1940's when he happened to apply for a job just advertised. Ed Kelly Sr. worked there until the Stegmaier Brewery shut down.

Many in Wilkes-Barre on the day of the shutdown said the Brewery had shut down. By habit, many of us in Wilkes-Barre chose to drop that early "r." And so the Brewery or Burey it was, and not the Brewery for many. Regardless in October, 1974, Stegmaier Brewing Company shut down for good.

My father as a teenager picked coal off the train tracks to heat his parents' home but he never had to work in the mines as my uncles on the McKeown side did. But, when my dad married my mom, eventually he lived in the same house with my grandmother and grandfather. Our home was less than a full block away from the big shaft in the South Wilkes-Barre Colliery.

When my father was a kid, he picked coal off the tracks in the Parsons area and sometimes, the picking would not do so well and some of the "boys" would pick from the loaded railroad coal cars. That was verboten and against the law. My dad spent one night in jail for picking coal. We heard that story a lot. From the time of the late nineteenth century, the Pinkerton Detective agency would be hired to prevent pilfering of coal that was ready to ship out.

They hired as guards in critical areas in a lot of states including Pennsylvania and the Wilkes-Barre area especially. During the twentieth century, Pinkerton rebranded itself into a personal security and risk management firm. The Pinkertons were dreaded by those families wanting to keep their homes heated for the winter without paying for it.

As dad got older though it was the depression, he looked for work wherever he could find it. As a Stegmaier employee, as you might suspect, it was a sin in our home not to like Stegmaier Beer. Worse than that sin, a bigger sin was to bring Gibbons or Bartels into a Stegmaier Brewery Worker's home.

It was loyalty and people could be fired for less. So, the empty foreign bottles would need special disposal by either de-labeling or smashing before they could be put out to the trash for Wednesday pickup by the G-men. Otherwise the neighbors would see that the faithful brewery worker was "drinking" another brewery's brew.

My uncles who worked in the mines came to our home all the time because my grandmother, Mary McKeown, their mother, lived right there with us with Grandpa. One day I can recall the uncles coming in with some Gibbons. They were not thinking. Back then, you never entered a home in which you intended to drink beer without bringing the beer with you for you and for the host to drink

And, so, caught with Gibbons in their arms, and knowing my dad's conviction to drink only Stegmaier, they presented their offerings nonetheless without regret. My dad first tried to be a gentleman but after a few of those nasty Gibbons under his belt, he asked why they would bring Gibbons into his home, knowing his predicament with competing breweries. The uncles scurried for a response and finally answered a different question. They said: "Ed, All beers are the same!" I am sure they felt that way.

My dad told this story so many times over the years because it infuriated him—and I heard most of them. He was getting laid off periodically when business slowed down and he was always a cheerleader for Stegmaier, as he had five children to support, plus two of my grandparents, and he and my mom—all living in a six room home in half a double on High Street. He hoped the uncles would buy Stegmaier, because their mom and dad and our family needed my dad to work.

Not being able to make Stegmaier sense to my uncles, he decided that if all beer is the same; then all coal is the same. Prior to the uncles coming in with the competitor's brew, my father was loyal to the mine company where they worked—Glen Alden. That is why he could not understand their lack of loyalty to Stegmaier.

In our home on High Street, we had a Heatrola coal stove in between the parlor and the dining rooms to heat the whole house. We had no furnace, ever. We had either a Pittston Coal Stove or a Wilkes-Barre Coal stove with an oven and a hot water back in the kitchen to heat the hot water for bathing.

Like most in Wilkes-Barre, coal from the sweat of the miners' brow was very important to us as it provided heat for our homes, hot water, and we cooked for it. The miners and the mines also added big time to the economy of the city. Unlike most in Wilkes-Barre when we were growing up, we had no coal furnace, just the stove in the dining room and the cooking stove in the kitchen. It was tough in retrospect but while we were living that way, we just thought it was how it was.

As a side note, after many years, on High Street, we got ourselves a Magic Chef Gas stove and the Gas Company put gas piping in our home from the curb. No longer in the summer did my father have to keep the fire dampened on the kitchen stove for cooking and baking, and of course hot water for bathing. The gas stove provided all our cooking needs. I can recall when we tried the first kettle test and it was from our perspective *instantaneous* that the kettle of water got hot on the gas stove. I remember the smiles on my parents faces.

We still had the kitchen coal stove because the hot water plumbing was connected to it, and in the cold months, the Heatrola was not enough to heat the whole house. Quite frankly, we all slept under a few blankets and a quilt each night to stay warm and sometimes in the morning, since there was no furnace sending the good warm air upstairs, and we had a closed stairway, and a dampened fire in the Heatrola, so it did not burn out overnight, a glass of water on the dresser was often partially frozen with a rim of real ice on the top. .

Back to the uncles' story wrap-up

The Kellys on High Street clearly burned more coal from Glen Alden than the McKeowns from Brown and South Grant Streets drank Stegmaier. Our biggest flirtation with disloyalty to that point was that we had a gas stove for cooking and would not burn coal in the summer for cooking.

But, until the time of the uncle's indiscretion, we always bought Glen Alden coal because the uncles worked for Glen Alden. Once all beer was the same and family loyalty did not matter, all coal was the same as far as my dad was concerned. Lehigh Valley coal was not more expensive than Glen Alden and so my dad operated in kind and he began to buy from coalmen who would deliver Lehigh Valley rather than Glen Alden to our home.

I never heard more about this but I do believe that if I knew about this as a sub ten-year old, my grandmother knew about it and my mother knew about it. Since the uncles never stopped coming because their sister and mother lived with us, I suspect they learned that they were being warmed by Lehigh Valley coal. I must admit that I do not know that for sure. I do remember never seeing another bottle of Bartels or Gibbons again in our family dwelling on High Street. Amen to that story!

Chapter 13   Rolling Mill Hill-- Lots of Choices in the Glory days

The Wyoming Valley including the Wilkes-Barre Area were littered with mine remnants

Something everywhere for everybody

Let me now walk you from around the South Wilkes-Barre Colliery, a block from my boyhood home, to the many places where the miners and the rest of the adults in our neighborhood would find both comfort and fun. The Colliery was, what we might say, was in the foothills of the Rolling Mill Hill Section of Wilkes-Barre. It was the first thing you saw.

The miners and the neighborhood folks and many from outside the neighborhood frequented the taverns close by in the coal years, which before I was born were also the war years. Folks from the neighborhood and from all around Wilkes-Barre, frequented many of these spots long after the baby boomers were making demands. There was and still is lots to do in the Rolling Mill Hill; just not as much as in the glory days.

Tommy Rowan Sr. had a fine tavern on Parrish & High Streets. It was directly across Parrish Street from the mile high mine shaft where the coal cars would go down empty and come back filled. Tommy passed away at a young age and his wife Arline took over. Her son Tommy Jr. married my first cousin Mary Brady and so I got to see a lot of Arline's Tavern from the inside. I got pretty good at Shuffleboard. Later establishments included a second Arline's, a Perugino's for a while and today the place is Margherita Azoul's a nice restaurant.

Before I get into telling stories of the great Rolling Mill Hill, my neighborhood, and there are many stories, please indulge me since I lived on High Street until I was 23 years old.

A wonderful lady, a neighbor, the daughter of Mary Nick Solomon, as she was known, and Nick Solomon, had bugged me all my life about being something she thought I should be. She loved it that I ran for public office in 2010 as a congressional candidate, and she kept telling me that I should run for Mayor of Wilkes-Barre. Well Irene, I heard you. I agree. It was my time. Thank you for the urging.

Irene who passed away just a few years ago, R.I.P. was a mainstay to the neighborhood. Everybody knew here. She and her husband Ralph and children lived on Holland Street just two doors up from High Street. It was one happy place. I was proud to know her.

Irene knew that I wrote books and when I wrote this book in 2015, this was my fifty-ninth book. Now this major revision is my 304th. How time flies. A few years ago, she asked me to work with her to write a book about growing up on High Street. I always planned to do it but not until those in the queue were completed. Right when I was writing this book as # 59, I had just one more on the way. Instead of a singular book about High Street, I puffed up Revision 2 and this one has more stuff in it about High Street. I did not want to let Irene down. I loved her like a relative and never thought she would die.

It was a wonderful experience growing up on High Street, as everybody—Syrian, Irish, Polish, German, and others—always knew we were all Americans first. Irene helped make us all know that we were Americans.

I always expected to be off to Irene's High Street book. I knew this wonderful lady was going to dictate the contents. I am so sorry she is no longer with us. In my humble opinion, Irene Jachimiak ought to get a Hall of Fame nomination for Wilkes-Barre as she was always such a wonderful Wilkes-Barre Patriot.

My good buddy George Elias from High Street, reminded me a book or so ago, that I had missed a few folks from High Street in my first book when I wrote my acknowledgments. He is right! So, let me correct the record. First of all, Mrs. Irene (Nick) Solomon Jachimiak is my favorite resident of all time from High Street and I have a lot of folks there that I love like brothers and sisters. I have great regard for all my old neighbors. So I am going to make a trip around High Street and close surrounds right now. Please come with me.

Let's begin at Peters' Ice Cream Store on the corner of Blackman Street and Brown Street. Moving down Blackman Street to High to Parish, in that sequence, you would find my buddy "Thunsie" Peters, who invented Peters' Ice Cream. I shoveled his sidewalks and I sold and delivered his delicious homemade ice cream cakes before I was ten years old.

Angel Albert Peters Sr., Angel Emily Peters, and entrepreneur Butchy Peters, the current Godfather of the Peters' Ice Cream dynasty and Pete's convenience stores were all associated with the store. Butchy now runs the dynasty. All lived and worked in the High Street area. The ice cream of course was Thunsies's recipe. The Peters' lived on Blackman Street midway between Brown and High. Thunsie is still with us thank God but he no longer makes homemade ice cream but the brand they got to replace it is very good. Butchy wanted

me to tell you that try it you'll like it. None is as good as his
fathers but they sell a good ice cream at Peters Ice Cream store
which was where it still is from before I was ten years old.

The Peters' household was a great brick home in the middle of
the block between Brows & High sts. Up just a little bit up
from The Peters' homestead was Henry Vivian's Barber Shop.
He was a great barber and one of my paper customers. After
Vivian's, Stanley's Bike Shop took over in the same building.
Now it is a house / apartment complex.

Across the street from Stanley's was the Galardi family, paper
customers of mine. They ran RoKay Flower on South Main
Street. Going down the block from the Galardi's a few homes,
were the Namey's. Leo's family was on the left moving down.
They were right next door to the Alexander family. Down the
street just a bit was Daubert's Grocery store where Betty and
Russel Daubert minded the business for years. Across the
street from Leo Namey was the Mike Namey family. All were
my paper customers. The ones I skipped were not customers
and I did not know them well. Mike Namey Sr. just recently
passed away. His son was the Meyers Football Coach for
years.

My best buddy after William, who I will discuss in the next
few paragraphs, moved to back mountain early in life. He had
lived in the second house up from High right next to Mike
Namey's. I called Bobby Broody--Bibska. He was a really nice
person. Next comes angel Cathy, Ben and Lois Witos on the
corner of High and Blackman. Then on High Street. , there
were the Blaine family, followed in the same home by the
Donnelly's. Dad and Mom were Dan & Berti, and the kids
were Jimmy, Larry, Debbie, and Brian. Right next to them
were the George and Lizzie Volpetti family and son George
who is a retired Wilkes-Barre surgeon. .

They were the best. Their son is a great guy also. He is a
legend as a great surgeon. I know from friends that one time
after his dog was hit by a car and was almost dead, George
operated on his own dog to save him. The vet knew the

anatomy and George had the micro-surgery skills to save the family pet. Except for one day when out of nowhere, George hit me between the eyes from across the street with an excellent pea shooter shot, George has a great record with me. We're both Kings College graduates.

Across the street from the Volpettis' at 363 High was my family. There were nine of us in three bedrooms, and we were fine. Next door to us on High Street was the Sallitt family. I do not remember Mom and Dad, when I was really young but kids a bit older than me were George and Mary Ellen Sallitt. Over time the Kitchens moved into this building with Red and Loretta, Joan and Chester. We loved them and their cats and Rinny the Dog for sure.

Then came a driveway and early on before I turned six I played with my best buddy William, who was exactly my age. His siblings were Edna, Rudolph, and Johina. They all moved south when I was five and it really ripped my heart out losing my best friend at six years old. I never saw him again. Hazel and Frank Nockley, Sr. moved in after them. Franky Jr. always had a great car such as his classic Ford Galaxy convertible. My buddy George Elias who passed away earlier this year, said it was a 1963.

Across the street from us again we have Angels Ruth and Joe Solomon—Ricky, Danny, & Marilyn, who are wonderful people, always ready to help. Danny is a Doctor and Rick runs the family business. Then next to the Solomon's were the Pahler's—mom & dad (John), Helen, Chazzy, Rita, Shirley, Jim, and Joe. Joe Pahler and Carly Blaine were always working on bikes. My father paid Carly a buck for my first bike ever. I

Across from them were Ham, Zacqua, and Sadie Abraham. I shoveled their sidewalks and cut their grass with Ham's electric mower when I was a kid. Ham was most concerned that I did not cut my toes off and that I did not cut the extension cord... I think it was in that order.

On Holland Street today is my good buddy Irene and her husband Ralph Jachimiak and son Ralph. Also on Holland were Bobby Stanton, George Yuhas, Steamboat Joe Radzavicz along with Annie, Murph, and Barbara Feldman.

Back to High Street and Holland. The Elias family lived there all my life while on High Street. Mr. & Mrs. Elias, and Jenny, Helen, George, Eleanor, and Joseph "Skippy" Elias made a very nice family. I hope I did not miss anybody.

Across High from the Elias,' who are not the same Elias's as those on the corner of Parish and High, were Mike and Sam Barrouk. Mike was the grandpop of the family (Jiddou) who ran the great candy store right across the street from the end of Holland Street.

They lived on the left side of the house. On the other side of the duplex was Steve Sr., Carmella, Steve, Jr. and Beverley Barrouk. We have always been friends. Then, came the Eget family when I was an adolescent. Before them were the Davis's – Ernie, Esther, and Emily. I had not seen George Eget in a while but we just made contact again about a year ago. Nice guy as always.

Dave (Dy) Amos and the Amos family including Jackie Dare sometimes lived right next to the Eget's. Mr. Amos was a blacksmith and he rented the garage behind Arlene's Saloon to apply his trade. George Elias's grandparents lived across the street on the corner. We played hard-ball catch across High Street with the Elias garage and Dave Amos's Blacksmith shop as backstops. We were there almost every morning every summer. Mr. Amos was OK with that. At one point, the Zekus' family lived next to the garage after it had been vacant for many years.

Then there was Mrs. Louise Dailaida / Hogan and Ann Lee Hogan and Michael Daelida, RIP. Michael died way too young. They lived right after the Amos's house and before the Zekus'. Ann Lee was my sister Nancy's really good friend after the Davis's moved out. Emily, Ester, and Ernie Davis, his wife, and another daughter whose name also began with an E, lived there before the Egets. The Davis' eventually moved further up on High Street / Virgin Lane right by the Roper family.

And, of course across from all of these folks was Nick, and Mary Nick, Zeke, and Joey Solomon. Zyrah, Stan Fidrych's mom (Stan was one of us who played ball all the time on High Street) and Irene Jachimiak lived there early on before these two daughters of Nick and Mary Nick were married.

On the corner of Parish Street and High my good friend George Elias's Jiddou and Sittou lived there and George spent lots of time with them. It made him more accessible to all the ball games and activities on High Street.

Across Parrish, from High and up a little bit, and that is as far as we are taking this sub-trip into the Rolling Mill Hill, lived Mr. Clem Eydler, and Mrs. Eydler, and my buddy Billy, who was an honorary member of High Street. Peters Economy Store was at that corner for years. The colliery was across High from them.

At the last corner of High and Parish was Arlene Rowan, who ran Tommy's Place and then Arlene's. This tavern made the street a lot nicer for the miners across the way at the South Wilkes-Barre Colliery. We will return here when we finish discussing the Rolling Mill Hill in lots less detail.

Wilkes-Barre Section: Rolling Mill Hill

Let's begin again now that our "George Elias High Street tour," is behind us. We will get a different tour of the Rolling Mill

Hill. We will start at the South Wilkes-Barre colliery at the corner of High and Parrish streets, and at the end we will come back to this same block. Essentially, our tour begins where the High Street tour left off if you cancel out the short run up a few homes to Billy Eydler's place.

Working down High Street towards the uptown area on the Eydler side of Parrish Street, we would pass Peters' Economy Store's original site. When I was a teenager, they moved up a block to Brown on the opposite side of Parrish. Continuing along on the left side of High Street after Parish were mine buildings and at one time a lot of mine track where the coal was shipped from one area of the mine yard to another.

Back on the right side, before we hit Glen Street, was an area that was always open and still is. It was called the company yard, where we played ball when we wanted to be off High Street and be sure we did not knock out anybody's windows. We batted towards the mines. In the fall, we played football between the company field and the mine buildings right on the paved street.

So, starting again, from the South Wilkes-Barre Colliery on Parrish & High on the opposite side of High Street, we eventually reach Glen Street. As we move up Glen Street on the right side towards Brown, we would find a fine spot named Rocky's about half-way up the Glen block. Rocky's was known for its pizza. Rocky's Pizza was great! I can remember as a kid going over there, waiting, and getting some of their fine creations to take home.

Moving up Glen Street just before the corner, we would find my good friend, and Tony Weiss's good friend Joe Pienkowski's house right before the corner. Joe passed on just a few years ago and it is still hard to believe. The Pienkowski's were also Wilkes-Barre Record morning paper customers of mine so I saw them all the time.

At the time in history as a kid, my snapshot of the Rolling Mill Hill is taking me, the Glen Tavern was run by Tony Yudisky. I am not sure if he owned it. He too, was one of my paper customers. Over the years, other famous people, such as boxer Billy Strauss ran the Glen but Tony was the guy in my youth that I remember.

The Glen had a "kitchen" and my father would take the family there every now and then for "lunches." My mom liked to call dinner at a bar, a lunch. It was wonderful. Recently the facility has been renamed Ike's Glen Tavern. I am not sure if it is open any more. We have pictures of us at a booth at "Tony's" having a nice family "lunch."

Up Brown Street to the left from the Glen Tavern was Tony Suchadelski's Tavern, which was the cleanest tavern in the area. I know, because I went in every two weeks to collect for the paper. It now operates as Billy's Sports Bar. I see Billy all the time and last time was about a month ago. Mike Danowski Cheryl's former husband just had his 75th birthday party at Billy's. I gotta get back up there.

I know the place was always pristine because at ten years old I was the paper boy. I delivered the papers to all the taverns. It is still clean with nephew Billy in charge. Mike Danowski, who worked for Billy for years recently retired as one of the main bartenders ever at Billy's. Billy and I enjoyed our 40th Meyers Reunion in 2005. The next day was Memorial Day. My family and I did the grave ceremonies and then went to Billie's for some free food, and he did not disappoint us. Both he and I needed Visine from the reunion the night before.

Delivering papers at 5:30 AM was tough!

My brother Ed gained a paper route from Wilkes-Barre Publishing Co. for the Wilkes-Barre Record (wilkesbarrerecord.com) when he was sixteen and I was ten years old. Our "guy" was Mr. Walters. He made sure we were OK so he could be OK!

We had 84 paper customers. I delivered my half at 5:30 in the morning every day except for Sunday. So did Ed. Our dad was working for the Stegmaier Brewery at the time. He had to be at work early and he walked to Stegmaier from High Street every day so he had to get up early himself. He did the honors of waking us up each morning.

I took over the full paper route when I was thirteen after Ed graduated from Meyers High School at age 18. It was too much. After delivering in the AM I no longer had a chance to go back to bed for an hour. All the time was gone.

My brother Joe was enlisted to help. He was only nine years old when he began peddling the Record with me every morning. He was thirteen when he took over the whole route after I graduated from Meyers at 17. It was a tough job for sure. I only did the whole route a few times. Joe really had to work hard. Now, let's go back to the Rolling Mill Hill Tour.

The route on Brown Street took us all the way to Stanton St. but we stopped our tour at Billy's. Right across the street from Billy's is Jones Street. If you go up Jones Street past Dodson School and take a left onto Airy Street, you will find the Airy Tavern. I don't think I was ever inside it but I suspect my dad was but not too often. He never spoke about it. So, let's go right back to Billy's and then back to the Glen.

We're going back to the Glen Tavern for positioning the tour properly. Moving to the right down Brown Street from the Glen, you would encounter Julie's Homestead, which at the time had a nice sized vacant lot next to it. That was where my friends and I played tackle football with no helmets.

Moving to the corner, on the right was the Ferris family with a huge grassy lot in front of their home towards Brown Street. It is now a paved parking lot. Often there were big balls of shinklish—pronounced *shawn kleesh* (a Syrian cheese concoction which is dried in the sun for a week.) The Ferris' also were on my paper route.

Across from them one time was Feighlingers Ice Cream Store, which later became the new Peters Economy Store, which eventually became Parrish & Brown Printers.

Right across Brown Street from this in our day was the only pharmacy we had ever heard about. It was like O'Donnell's in Parsons, but at the time, I had never been to O'Donnell's. Its name was Colley's Pharmacy. Unlike today's pharmacies, there were few goodies there but I recall they did sell paper and pens.

The place smelled like a pharmacy, and all of our prescriptions and many of those from the Rolling Mill Hill were filled there. When you got up to Stanton Pharmacy territory approaching the Mayflower, they got the business. Today, Colley's still looks like a three story fortress and it is a nice apartment building. It is still attractive. I am glad it has lasted these years.

Going back to Julie's Homestead. If we move right around the corner from the Homestead to Parish Street, past all the shinklish, we would find Eddie Williams' Tavern. Over the years this changed hands. It was once Par Four; then Schnapsies, and others. Driving by the other day, I noticed it is again reopened under a new name, Frosty Mugs. Best wishes!

Across from Eddie Williams' was The El Hussain Syrian American Club, which went out of business when I was a kid. It no longer exists. Bob Amory's Barber Shop garage replaced it. Now, Bob is enjoying life with his son in warmer weather. He was a good barber.

My dad never had to buy a car. Everything was in walking distance. The neighborhood was so packed with places to go and things to do that my dad never had to drive. His toughest trek was walking to Stegmaier Brewery for work each day, which he did judiciously ever day while I lived at home. He had five kids to support plus my mother, grandmother, and grandfather. He was a real hero in my book.

Back up to Brown Street again to Colley's side of the street. .
Let's now keep heading southwest on brown. Right across
Holland Street, on Brown, you would be greeted by Bohn's
Tavern. We knew it for its food, served upstairs while there
was a regular neighborhood bar downstairs. My dad never let
us go into the bar when we went out to dinner. We entered
Bohn's from the outside via a steep set of stone stairs.

Once a year in the summer, our dad would take the whole
family there and they served a fine lobster tail dinner with
three tails, French Fries, and Cole Slaw for $1.25. It reminded
me of Joe Zalewski's in the Mayflower as the food was just as
great. My father did not make much more than $60.00 a week
then but every now and then, he would give the whole family a
great treat at Bohn's. It was typically during my sister Nancy's
birthday in July.

One of my brothers (Joe) and one of my sisters (Mary) are
twins, and they love cole slaw. At the time we got to go to
Bohns; I hated mayonnaise and by extension, cole slaw. The
Twins would trade me one of their lobster tails for my slaw.
Amazingly, they took turns as to which of them would get the
slaw.

I knew I had the better deal. Dad would order a few dozen
clams and I have no idea how inexpensive they were but he
would ask for bullion and make himself his own version of
clam chowder with the crackers. They were great times.

Moving to Blackman Street on Brown from Bohns' if you
made a left up Blackman, and went a few blocks to Loomis
Street, there were two more taverns. They were far enough
away that I never got there as a kid so I have nothing to report
about their original names.

One of them became successful as Gallagher's in our recent
past. Dad and I and my brothers were there a few times. I
include these two as it took just a few minutes more from the
typical neighborhood route to get there. They were definitely
in the "Hill." There really were tons of places to go.

Back down to Blackman and Brown from Loomis, and down one block more on Brown. You would pass Bradford Street, which was really an alley and run into McLean Street. After making a right, moving to the bottom of McLean Street, you would find on the right side, another tiny neighborhood tavern that was not a regular stop on my dad's route nor mine. But it was no more than four blocks from our homestead. We were there one time as I recall but for the life of me, I forget its name.

Back again to the corner of Blackman and Brown from McLean. This time, we'll cross Blackman Street and move down the street just two and a half blocks passing Essex Lane on the right. The next small building after a few double blocks was the site of Brady's Lunch. "Brady" offered the best food in the walkable section of the lower Rolling Mill Hill.

Leo "Brady" Moses ran the place and he was also one of my loyal Wilkes-Barre Record www.wilkes-barrerecord.com customers. I loved the guy and without asking, I know my brothers did too. Mr. Moses returned to the Lord on November 26, 2006. "Brady" had the best dogs in the Rolling Mill Hill and perhaps the country. His burgers with "everything" were super also. What a wonderful and unique chile hot dog sauce. I loved the steamer they had right on the counter. The buns were always fresh.

Bowling and fun at the 2nd Wilkes-Barre Republic Club.

Right across the street from Brady's lunch was the site of the second location of the Wilkes-Barre Republic Club. "The Club," this building, burned down some time in the 1990's. It had originally been formed by the folks in our mostly Syrian neighborhood and the founders made it so that ethnicity did not matter.

Many people from Wilkes-Barre frequented the place because it had six bowling alleys and they showed Sunday night movies for free, when there was no VHS or DVD technology. Additionally, a main attraction was that Carl Prohaska's food was so darn good. Sometimes for major events, a guy I know well, Joseph A. Kelly would cook for crowds over 150 in the back room. They could really pack 'em in; and did.

Oh, did I mention that folks also liked to go to "The Club," because they often had bands play on the weekends such as Danny and the Excels. The bands played for the patrons' enjoyment in the extensive back room. It was like a YMCA for adults.

Before "The Club," had burned down, my dad had become a lifetime member and my two brothers, a secret Indian Chief named Joe LaSarge, and a great glass thrower named Joe Ferro, were members and officers at various times.

Edward J. Kelly, my dad was an expert shuffleboard player. He was as good as it gets at "The Club," for sure. He as pretty good at darts also. Besides the original, Wilkes-Barre Republic Club, WBRC, he mostly played shuffleboard at the Glen Tavern, the old Club, Arlene's, and the New WBRC.

He played just about anywhere else in the City including SuCaLis in the Mayflower section and Stan's in the Heights. He was so good that players from across the City would come in and challenge him for a game. Sometimes the game stakes were as high as $20.00 for one of those challenges.

There were also a lot of side bets. Dad's friends from the neighborhood told me that he never disappointed them, and they always knew their side bets were safe when Ed Kelly was on the board, and they were always on the Kelly side of the bet.

My father could put a double chipper up on the right side of the board by throwing with his left hand. He would then watch his opponent try to knock it off in the game of 21. Rarely was there a knock-off.

Dad would then throw a double chipper on the left side of the board with his right hand. FYI, A double chipper means that the thrown shuffleboard weight or quoit, as some call it, is leaning not just over the edge at the end of the board but on the edge of the side also. Depending from which side it was thrown to, it would be leaning over the opposite edge of the board, making it next to impossible to knock off. But, good players can knock them off, but, very rarely.

I never wanted to beat my dad but I always tried. I was always glad to simply score points when I played against him. He got no pleasure beating his kids either but he did like to see that the three of us could beat just about anybody else in shuffleboard but him. He had taught us well!

As noted previously, besides Darts and Shuffleboard, cards, and poker machines, the Club on Blackman Street had six bowling alleys further back from the "back room." When I was 12 years old, in addition to my junk route, and sharing my brother Ed's morning paper route, I told one of my earliest lies in life. I promised that I was fourteen years old and on the strength of that lie, I was hired on my word, by the Republic Club's Bowling Managers, Boots, and John Mellus, as a pinboy.

I worked as a pinboy for a year or so before I got a better job delivering soda on the Eagle Bottling Works (Zep-Up) truck with Murph Solomon and my dear departed cousin Richard Knaus.

Yet, I left the pinning game under my own terms. It was not just because it was the worst job I could have ever had. I got out of the pinning racket as soon as I could, as the soda truck job was perfect, and Murph made it fun. Eventually when I graduated High School, my brother Joe, who worked sometimes on the truck with me, took over the whole Job. With the soda truck job and the paper route, eventually Joe had to give up the paper route. I know I could not do that whole route by myself.

The job of a pinboy

The Club had semi-automatic pinspotters. That means nobody spotted the pins on spikes in the floor; instead, we picked them up off the pit and inserted them into a machine that spotted them perfectly each time. The holes were still in the bottom of the pins from days past and the spikes in the floor still could be raised if we chose. We did not since the semi-automatic machines worked so well, and we were afraid the spikes might not go down if we raised them.

The Club Bowling Alley needed kids like me and others, known then as pinboys, to pick up the pins and put them in the pin spotting machine. We would take one or two alleys for nine cents a game, and would first send the ball back and then set the pins inside the machine. The objective was to have a fresh set of ten pins down before the bowler got his / her ball. We pulled the cord on the machine which set the pins, often saving the last two pins until the machine was actually on its way down.

As pinboys, the pay was not so great but it was pretty good for a twelve year old. At the time the bowlers were paying 35cents a game, and on league nights, the bowlers threw in an extra nickel a game. Besides that, we pinboys could bowl for nothing on Saturdays when and if nobody came in to use the lanes for open bowling. "Loser pins" is a good way to be motivated to learn how to bowl quickly. After a short while, young as I was, I rarely had to pin for the others.

After a major fire wiped out this great building, many years after I was a pinboy, the Club eventually reopened further up on Blackman Street past Hazle Street, still in the Rolling Mill Hill. This place recently morphed into Beer Solutions, itself a fine place for glassware and beer supplies. More recently, "The Club" moved to its current location on Dana Street in the old Sucali's building in the Mayflower Section of the City.

Our route among the taverns and places in my neighborhood is now almost complete. Leaving the second incarnation of the WBRC and moving back up Blackman Street a block and a half to High Street--just a block before Brown Street, if you were to make a left and go to the next block, you would be back at the beginning of our tavern tour, right at the South Wilkes-Barre Colliery.

There is one tavern location I did not speak much about yet. It was directly across Parish Street from the Big mine shaft / elevator. From this venue, you could see the coal cars full of all kinds of sizes of coal surfacing from the deep mine shaft. We all knew that miners, as much as a mile down, had placed the coal inside the cars. The train tracks were small it seemed, almost like the gauge of a Sans Souci or Hanson's, or Rocky Glen Park train.

The Original Wilkes-Barre Republic Club

The Tavern across the street from the mine on Parish Street began as The Wilkes-Barre Republic Club. It was the first WBRC. We just talked about this club when it was on Blackman Street. But, it started out on Parish and High. They had music and dancing at this club just as the other.

It was so popular in the City that my father, originally from Parsons would either hitch a ride or take two buses to be there. He and his friends came from the Parsons section to High & Parish so this club had to be a special place. The Club as noted was originally an ethnic Syrian establishment, but it quickly reshaped itself into an ethnic-neutral spot. Dad told me that there were always these nice neighborhood girls and they were so friendly that they taught him how to dance.

My Aunt Nina and my mother would also go to the Wilkes-Barre Republic Club for socializing. It was less than a block from our double block house on 363 High Street. One day my mother and father met each other for the first time at the "Old Club," and you know a lot about the rest of the story. What you don't know is that my mom and dad loved each other when my dad had no job and my mom worked in the silk mill next door to our house on High and Blackman Streets.

They loved each other so much that they got married with nobody's knowledge. My dad was twenty-However, because my dad could not support my mother during the depression, they kept their marriage a secret. When my father got his job at R.A. Davis Plumbing, before Stegmaier, they announced that they had been married for about six months.

Each night before this, he would go home from High Street to Scott Street in Parsons, and my mother would go to our home on High Street. When dad had enough of a salary to support the whole family, including at the time, grandmom and grandpop, mom and my dad, he moved in and our public life as the Kelly family from High Street began.

Several years later, my brother Ed was born, and our little family began to grow. Dad got a job at Stegmaier Brewery which was steadier than RA Davis. Then three years later my sister Nancy was born, and I showed up another two and a half years after that. It was almost four years more before the twins, Mary and Joseph appeared on the scene. If they were triplets, you know what the third name would have been? *Jesus!*

Dad would joke that once they started coming two at time that was enough. We had a very loving family and still do, and it all began at the Wilkes-Barre Republic Club on High and Parish a long time ago.

That is not the end of The Club Story. As we already divulged, the Club itself relocated to Blackman Street, and then a different venue on Blackman Street and finally on to Dana street where it now stands.

The Parish & High building was sold to Tommy Rowan Sr. He opened the establishment as Tommy's. Tommy died early in life and his wife, Arlene took over the business. Eventually, since there was no Tommy Sr. any more and Arlene never remarried, the name was appropriately changed to Arlene's.

You may recall seeing it for years on the corner of Parish and High. Arlene had several children, Betty Jane and Tommy Rowan Jr. Ironically, the next owner was also named Arlene so the name did not change for years. Along the way for a number of years after the second Arlene sold, it was Tony Perugino's, and most recently it is Margarita Azul. The food there is reported to be excellent and most generous, and the place is very clean and the atmosphere is friendly.

You may remember that in the beginning of this Parish and High Street Club adventure, my Aunt Nina accompanied my mother, the baby of the High Street McKeown family to the Club. Not only did my mom meet my dad in this fine historic building, But, Aunt Nina Brady's first child, Mary Brady met Arlene Rowan's 's second child Tommy Rowan Jr. and they fell in love, got married, and moved to New Jersey.

When they came home to Wilkes-Barre, they stayed with the first Arlene in a wonderful apartment on top of the tavern. What a neat building. Don't tell anybody but as a kid, because of our relationship, I learned how to play shuffleboard there when it was not busy.

So, the Kelly family had a relationship with Arlene's for many years until she retired and sold the building and the business. Arlene's as the original Arlene's was a mainstay on Parish and High for many years in the glory days of Wilkes-Barre. Being directly across the street from the major mine shaft, the South Wilkes-Barre Colliery, many a miner enjoyed a quaff of Stegmaier or Gibbons there after a hard shift under the earth.

Generosity in the glory years of High Street.

I have one more story to tell and a few more spots to visit around the top of Parrish Street, before we take a look at the other sections of the City and uptown" as in the glory days.

When I was seventeen years old, I was hired by Peters' Economy Store when the store was on Parish and Brown. My job was to fill their delivery truck and drive the truck to take the orders to those who could not make it to the store. I was very busy, and I got the feeling there was more to some of the orders than that they were *call in, deliver and pay* as I think certain people were assisted in their purchase by the store itself.

The Peters' family was well known in the Rolling Mill Hill as being effective, efficient, and very kind and generous merchants. The Pete's Delis around town now are an offshoot of the Peters' family run by Butchie Peters, the youngest son of Albert Peters from Blackman Street.

My dad always had a book for Daubert's store on Blackman Street, and a book for Peters Economy store which was cattie corner to Arlene's (The original Club) and across High Street from the old South Wilkes-Barre Colliery (now a WB fire station). Many had such charge books. My dad and many others were paid in cash once a week and when they were paid, they paid off the balance on the book for food and merchandise bought at the store during the prior week.

My dad told me that Albert Peters was one of the nicest and kindest men he had ever met. During the depression and whenever people could not come up with enough to pay their bills, Albert Peters was so concerned that he not only permitted them to extend their credit but he also granted permission for them to continue to buy food to keep them going.

Mr. Peters, as I knew him from respect, more than likely never got paid back by everyone when the economy got better after the depression and then the war. But, he was the kind of man who was so kind, that he would smile knowing he had helped. He was a model for many a fine person who grew up in our neighborhood.

After World War II, there was a feeling of jubilation in the streets of Wilkes-Barre and throughout the US and the world. Albert Peters was such a caring man, and he too was so thrilled that the US had ended the war with a victory that he helped all of his neighbors celebrate. It was late summer in 1945, so nobody minded being outside.

My dad told me that Mr. Peters "put a keg out in the middle of High Street" for the celebration. And quite a celebration it was. I had the pleasure of knowing Mr. Albert Peters in a number of different roles, including being his paperboy on Blackman Street. The words "kind and generous" are not strong enough words to describe him. He was the best. May God rest his soul in heaven.

Thunsie Peters reminded me that I had left out from the first edition of the book the fact that he could not be with the folks on High Street for the celebration because he was still in Europe as a soldier mopping up after the war. So, I added this story to book 2 in 2016. thank you very much Thunsie. BTW, Butchie Peters sold the first edition of this book at his store on Blackman St. Nice people!

Parish Street Theatres, Med. Offices, Stores, Swimming Pools, & Churches

The Hart Theatre was located at 459 Hazle Street to the right of the A&P shown below. It was a great place and added to the delight of the kids and the adults in the Rolling Mill Hill, The Mayflower, and the Heights. We have two pictures below as a tribute to the Hart. One is a poster about its grand opening in 1938, and the other pictures shows the A&P and the Hart, right before demolition circa 1989. How time's change when magnificent structures are not maintained.

A&P and the Hart Theatre Opening and Closing

Be among the first to greet this triumph of theatre elegance **!**

Grand Opening
SATURDAY, JANUARY 22nd
INTIMATE
ELEGANT
MODERN

Comerford's New
HART Theatre

HARLE and PARRISH STREETS

Offering the theatregoers of this vicinity the last word in safety, comfort, novelty and first screen entertainment!

Opening
ATTRACTION

The film that is removing various wide portions by pictures and screen stars!

MICKEY   SOPHIE
ROONEY   TUCKER

JUDY   C. AUBREY
GARLAND   SMITH

— in —

"THOROUGHBREDS
DON'T CRY"

PERFECT SOUND
by LATEST MIRRO-
PHONIC SYSTEM

Ultra Comfort
by Air Conditioning

The HART Policy

Matinees Daily at 2 P.M. Evening at 7 P.M.
New Shows Every Sunday, Tuesday, Thursday
and Saturday

PRICES . . . Matinee Children under 12 yrs. 10¢
Adults 25¢
Nights 5 to 6 P.M. Children 15¢
Adults 35¢
Shows Continuous Saturday, 1:00 P.M. to 11:00

Hart medical Center Corner Parrish & Hazle Streets

Hart Medical Center & Dr. Patrick Kerrigan

Dr. Patrick Kerrigan, a great doctor and healer and friend, runs his medical center right up by the Hart Theatre and just down from St. Patrick's Church and the Parrish Street Swimming Pool.

I bet he spent as much time in the Hart Theatre and the Swimming pool as I did, though he is a lot younger than I. As you can see in the picture above, he remodeled the old Hart Building on Hazle Street for his medical practice and he has it looking pretty sharp. Dr. Kerrigan is a great physician and he takes care of people, not just his Medical Center.

Dr. Kerrigan is my family doctor, and he is the best. He is so good that in all the books I have written since he became my doctor, he is a highlighted feature of the acknowledgments section. Every member of my family has needed his help at one point or another, and have received it. Here is an excerpt from this book's acknowledgments at www.letsgopublish.com:

"A special thank you also goes to Dr. Patrick Kerrigan, our family enabler. Several months ago I was in for a tune-up and I have had the stress test, the colonoscopy, and all other things including a facial exam, and all is well." [Thankfully, my two sick adult children have already been to see you and are now fine. Thank you.]

"Every now and then one of us needs an emergency appointment when we get sick. You are right here at the beginning of my acknowledgments list because you make sure we are all OK. We love the medicine provided by Doctor Patrick Kerrigan, our man of the year, every year."

"After making sure that nasty cyst did not come back and helping me find the right surgeon for my knee replacement, I am glad that we can share Notre Dame moments again. May the light of the Holy Spirit always prevail with Dr. Alexander's assistance of course!...."

"Everybody in Wilkes-Barre and beyond loves Dr. Patrick Kerrigan. A testimony to that was the 'Man of the Yea'" award from the Friendly Sons of St. Patrick just in the past several years. I hear testimony from your dedicated staff on each visit. You have assembled a fine team and they love working for you since you are one of the great Doctors in life and you really care for people, and you smile as people get well."

"You are a humble man who loves his God and Country and of course my books. For our family, you are the man of the decade with many more decades to come; Dr. Patrick, thank you for keeping us all well. Thank you for curing the spider bites, internal issues, strep throat, colds, flu, thyroids, and all the other maladies that befall us all."

"Thank you for being the kind of doctor that will do your best even if you are saddled with government regulations... I know you will persevere and do the best you can. Thank you for your vigilance and for fighting to keep the doctor / patient relationship in tact as your work exemplifies the value of that relationship. Thank you for making your patients your life's priority."

"Special thanks for the help from the kind and overall wonderful staff at the Hart Medical Center, where this group of experts helps Dr. Kerrigan complete his daily toils. Mary Beth, Barbara C., Mary, Colleen, Sandy, Jamie, Susan, Barbara S., and Kim Ann all contribute to helping make the experience very professional. Thank you all."

Parrish Street Pool

In 1956 City Council cleared the way for a public swimming pool on Parrish Street. In 1957 it opened and became a reality. Like a lot of good things in Wilkes-Barre it soon fell into disrepair. It was well out of the flood area, yet it was not maintained. It was a dandy place. Nonetheless, in 1980, it was closed down as a swimming pool and sold to the Sheet Metal Workers Local 44, shown in the picture below

It was located on 248 Parish Street. It shared a corner with Lloyd's Lane and across Lloyds was one of many churches on Parish Street.

Bathers would go in the front door of the building and show their City patch on their bathing suits. These permitted swimming in City owned pools. From there, the boys went left and the girls went right. There were rest facilities, benches and showers. It was the same deal at all City pools.

You would get a basket. You would put your clothes in the basket and get a number. Most wore their bathing suit under their clothes to make the process quicker. When you finished swimming, you would take your number, take a shower, dry off, put your dry clothes on, put your wet bathing suit in a towel and roll it up for the trip home.

Going out to swim, you would come to the shallow pool and then a deep pool which had three diving boards. The one in the middle was ten feet high and it was scary; but it made swimming exciting. Red Cross certified lifeguards made sure your swimming was safe. There was a snack bar that had all the goodies that kids would like.

In 2001, a gang from the Rolling Mill Hill planned a get-together of those who frequented the Parish Street Pool and the Hart Theatre. Ironically they scheduled it out of Wilkes-Barre at Firemen's Memorial Park in Ashley.

Sandra Skies Ludwig of the Times Leader reported that Cathy Capristo Scocozzo, then 43. helped organize the reunion. At the time, she still lived in the "old homestead" on Parrish Street where she grew up. Cathy said: "We sat there, talked, played cards, swam, and had those early teen romances...We hung out every day, every night. We were like wall-sitters. That's where we ended up." You can see the front part of the wall in the picture on the prior page.

Cathy continued: "The businesses and people in the neighborhood - Angelo Ricci [Angelo's Pizza], Bill Karlheim of the Stanton Pharmacy, the Hart Theatre manager—these people were genuine godsends...The Brennan yard was another place to hang out. Mrs. Brennan was an angel from heaven. She's a prime example of the neighborhood families who accepted and welcomed the kids. She's since passed on."

The Brennan yard was right across Lloyd's Lane from the pool. It still is as big as a park. There were enough Brennan kids to fill the pool, the "park," and the home, but Mrs. Brennan always loved to have more in the yard. It was like the beach to the pool.

Parrish Street at one time was loaded with functioning parish churches of all denominations. They were all operating in the 1950's in the days of the Parrish Street Pool.

The **Welsh Bethel Baptist Church** is located at 290 Parrish St, Wilkes Barre, PA, 18702. Its Pastor is Don Hartshorne, and its email address is BaptistChurch@frontier.com

According to its web site, the mission of Welsh Bethel Baptist Church is "to be and to make fully devoted followers of Jesus Christ." A follower, or disciple of Jesus Christ is one who prayerfully and intentionally seeks to know and obey Him through daily worship, fellowship, study, and ministry. We offer many ministries to aid the follower to develop and grow."

The **Berean Baptist Church** is located at 260 Parrish St, Wilkes Barre, PA, 18702. Wilkes College lists this church as Independent. Services are Sunday at 11:00 AM and 1:00 PM

The **Wilkes-Barre Parrish Street ME**, a former Methodist / Episcopal church. is located on the corner of Collins and Parrish Street, Wilkes-Barre. It is a castle of a church, built like a fortress. It is no longer occupied. Its historic conference is the Wyoming Conference of the Methodist Episcopal Church. Last references were in 2005 when there was a motion to discontinue; remaining financial resources to Albright UMC. Driving by today, there is a sign outside the church saying "House of Judah Ministries."

There were several other "Protestant Churches" on Parish Street that no longer are operating. One church that was once between the two Baptist churches has been demolished. Most of the other buildings are in use for other purposes.

St. Patrick's Church is an extremely beautiful church, located at 316 Parrish Street. It is the designated church for St. Andrew's Roman Catholic Parish in Wilkes-Barre, PA. It is on the same block as the Bethel Baptist Church and often competes for street parking spaces with the church. The parish message is below:

"We the people of St. Andrew Parish, members of the Diocese of Scranton and the Roman Catholic Church, come together in faith, to worship and serve God. We yearn to grow deeper in our faith, through a meaningful and conscious celebration of the Eucharist and other Sacraments. By living the Gospel message of love and compassion, we desire to be a light to others striving to obtain salvation."

St. Patrick's RC Church – Worship Site for St. Andrew Parish

The Pastor of the parish at the time of the first two books was Rev. James E. McGahagan. The Deacon was Francis J. Bradigan. Parish Secretaries are Dolores Bradigan and Theresa Lisiewski. The Choir Director/Organist is Jeffrey E. Papciak, and the Director of Religious Education is Debra Potsko. They can be reached at 570-823-1948 or 570-822-8330 and stbonstpat@verizon.net

Now the Pastor is Father Kearney and Deacon William F. Behm – Parish Life Coordinator

St. Patrick's Church Inside View Circa 2014

St. Patrick's Church is where worship is conducted Saturdays at 4:00 P.M and Sundays: 8:00 AM & 10:30 AM.
St. Andrew Parish was established in June of 2010 as a consolidation of three former parishes: St. Patrick, St. Boniface, and Holy Rosary

St. Boniface Parish on Blackman Street was founded in 1896 by Bavarian immigrants and a parish school opened in 1913, with the Sisters of Christian Charity. The parish closed June 6, 2010.

Holy Rosary Parish on Park Avenue was founded in 1906 by Italian immigrants and closed June 13, 2010.

St. Patrick Parish at the present address was founded in 1921 as a territorial parish and the upper church dedicated in 1930. It officially ceased to exist as a parish in June 2010, Sacramental records for all three parishes are maintained at St. Andrew Parish.

Holy Rosary Church at 363 Park Avenue, Wilkes-Barre is now the Iglesia Cristiana Pentecostal Nuevo. Picture is below:

Iglesia Cristiana Pentecostal Nuevo / Formerly Holy Rosary Church

St. Boniface Church is now the Wilkes-Barre Mennonite Church. Its Pastor is Mark Weaver, who can be reached at Home Phone- 570-837-6219; Cell Phone- 570-490-4282; Email-wilkesbarreweavers@gmail.com. Church mailing address is 225 Blackman Street, Wilkes-Barre, PA. 18702

Inside View of St. Boniface Church, Circa 1960

Chapter 14   A Town with Many Sections

Both sides of the Susquehanna

Lots of stories in all sections of the city

There were many other neighborhoods in Wilkes-Barre's glory days just like ours in the Rolling Mill Hill, where there are many great stories to be told. It's time to look at a few other 'hoods and tell as many stories as we can. But again this is from my own eyes and so my coverage cannot be as complete as a native of the many sections of Wilkes-Barre. So, in many instances, I got help from the section natives.

It can be argued that some neighborhoods on the fringe and not close to the heart of their particular section, such as the Heights, the Mayflower, and the Iron Triangle are in multiple sections. But each resident "knows" the section in which they live. If you are not from that section, however, it is easy to be wrong. Other than Parsons and Miners Mills, both of which once were mapped out Boroughs and had separate governments, the sections of Wilkes-Barre are somewhat mythical but nonetheless they are all magical.

Many of the taverns left over from the mining days are still in place in all sections of the city but most are not really thriving. The best thing I think we can do regarding neighborhood taverns, stores and activities is to support them to help bring back some of the former glory.

For example, one thing we can do is help these many establishments. I know Tony Suchadelski's secret and now Billy's Sports Bar on Brown Street, how to keep a place neat and pristine. You work hard. Billy's is darker than Tony's but it is definitely a clean place.

Tony's looked like you could eat off the floor. A good City administration would provide the health inspections and perhaps even some down-home training to make sure the inside and outside of these older facilities can be maintained and beautified and kept clean for the whole city to enjoy. I am not talking about harassment. I am talking about help. I see no reason why for simple electrical or plumbing issues, the inspectors, to stay crisp in their trade would not help out in the poorer areas to assure the job is done correctly.

Being from the Rolling Mill Hill my whole life in the glory days, my personal vision of the historical glory days of Wilkes-Barre is somewhat limited to my experience. I would like to consider this Volume I of Return to Glory, version III and I would welcome a walking tour of other neighborhoods by other authors in those Wilkes-Barre sections that we cannot cover as well as we try to do in this one book.

After all, in Wilkes-Barre's early 20th century glory days, the population was almost 90,000. Right now, as I type, this document, I have written just 26,279 words and of course each word adds to that. If we just printed the first and last names of everybody in the City back then, this book would total 180,000 words, and would be mostly unreadable and unenjoyable. So, we'll save some stuff for Volume 2.

Nobody that I know from the Rolling Mill Hill stayed 100% in their own neighborhood. Just like we all got to Public Square a lot, and my bike served me so well in that regard, there were a lot of neighborhoods explored by adults and children in other sections of Town.

I am sure these sections in their glory days were just as exciting as the Rolling Mill Hill. Let's look at them now.

Chapter 15   Wilkes-Barre Sections: The Heights & Iron Triangle

Most of the Iron Triangle buildings now gone!

The Iron Triangle was once a vibrant area southeast of uptown, centered between East End and Mayflower. It still contains small parts of Wilkes-Barre Boulevard (formerly Lincoln Street); South Welles Street; Hickory Street; Metcalf Street Park Avenue; East South Street; Hill Street; mid Dana Street; mid Moyallen Street; lower Hazle Street; and perhaps part of Loomis Street.

The Heights is adjacent to Iron Triangle to the north; principally the area dominated by Lincoln Plaza, Okarma Terrace (boulevard Townhouses), South Welles Street, East Market Street, & Park Avenue. To the right of Northampton Street is technically the Mayflower as the locals tell me.

Iron Triangle Playground

Because the Triangle has been taken out of the "Iron Triangle," and some joke that it is now the Iron Quadrangle, many in Wilkes-Barre, who are not from that Section believe, rightly or wrongly that the Iron Triangle Section is no more. However, as reported by the CV in 2010, the neighborhood known as the Iron Triangle built itself a very nice playground that year at the corner of Hickory and Metcalf streets. it is right smack dab in the "no triangle" Iron Triangle Section of the City.

The big buildings in the area associated with what for years was called the bowery are mostly gone other than Murrays and buildings that once made up the Penn Ave complex. All that once was on Hazle Street before the city was rearranged and most of that area gutted. At the very end of Hazle Street and Ross Street, The Flatiron Building was one of the most distinctive structures in Wilkes-Barre. You can't find It today as Hazle has been rerouted to Academy Street.

Flatiron Hotel – Ross on the left and lower Hazle Street on the right.

Lawson's Flat Iron Hotel, Wilkes-Barre, Pa.

The FLATIRON was the triangle

The FLATIRON was located on a triangular piece of land where Hazle Avenue (now relocated a block south) and Ross Street met South Main Street. The "new" South Main Street Post Office and its parking lot occupy this spot now. See the picture of the FLATIRON on the prior page.

Hospital in the "Triangle"

Wyoming Valley Homeopathic Hospital, established in 1911, was located on 147 Dana Street, Wilkes-Barre. it was originally a general hospital service that was maintained under homeopathic auspices for a number of years. For the last thirty or more years it operated as the First Hospital of Wyoming Valley. Like many things in Wilkes-Barre, the building was demolished in the Fall of 2014.

First Hospital Wyoming Valley

The old First Valley Hospital – New One in Kingston went out of business in 2022

The Heights

If you find yourself on Coal Street, you are most assuredly in the Heights. Technically again, the Heights is the area southeast of Downtown centered between East End and Mayflower. Most people that I know from up that way just say they are from the Heights. I think to disprove any sectional claim, we might have to bring in a person with a PhD in City Sectionography!

When I was growing up, my dad worked for Stegmaier Brewing company located purely in the Heights Section of "Brewery Hill off East Market Street. East Market Street was the original home to Kransons' Clothes, Kornblatt's Bakery, and the Keystate Bakery. Lennie's Pizza was also up there someplace.

Now that we are comfortably situated in the Heights, let's go up either Hillside street or Northampton and back down. Either way, you would run into two nice taverns at the bottom of the hills. Kramer's was the first name that everybody remembers regarding the small tavern on the corner of East Northampton and Empire Streets. it later became Sofa's Bar and Grill and was a great place for $1.50 spaghetti and other bar fare. It is now Elmer Sudds.

Elmers Sudds, according to its patrons, and from my own visits, is a gem of a bar / club. It is unique. They took the bar / back room model from Sofa's and Kramer's and opened it up so that the bar now has two sides and the backroom is in full view. Elmer's It is always a great visit to visit to enjoy great beers and mixology products such as the ever popular Elmer Overwhelmer—all in a relatively quiet, relaxed atmosphere.

In a recent review a writer noted that Sudds is "without recently-turned-21 morons screaming and ripping shots of Jack Daniel's and vomiting in the bathroom." It is a lot more than that. The pub is very charming. It is a great place to sit and have quality beer with many unique brands on draught. The conversation is always nice. You can also hang out with your friends and watch the game. **Elmer Sudds' is good for Wilkes-Barre City and would be part of any rebirth of the glory years.**

Across Northampton Street in a joined corner with Hillside Street still stands Stan's Café, one of the few taverns left in the City with a shuffleboard. Stan's nephew runs the place now and he is open for dinners and refreshments, and of course, shuffleboard. That has been our new spot for Shuffleboard since the Blackman Street Club burned down.

Northampton Street also has many other famous establishments including Bucky Joseph's Ten Pin, and former WB Councilman McCarthy's Saloon. More recent add-ons include the famous Philadelphia Subs, which is close to Georgetown. This is not to be confused with Phillies Phinest on Carey Avenue in South Wilkes-Barre.

Up East Market Street in the Heights was another neighborhood favorite, Kazimir's Tavern. At the corner of Meade and Market was a place known as "The Hill" Additionally on E. Market in the Heights, was a popular joint called The Brass Rail.

East Market Street was what those in the Heights saw as the business part of their section. It was all lined up with stores, apartment buildings and restaurants. It was one of the busiest streets in the city until the Axe Man completely tore it down after the flood. The federal dollars had to be spent It was the era of redevelopment and Wilkes-Barre lost a lot of its character during this period, and the Heights was not spared. If the Heights were to hide in a Time Warp, it might have been spared. But, the Axe Man is relentless.

The Heights Elementary School and its playground occupy most of this spot now, at the old Hancock Street intersection, with a small shopping center and a block of homes taking up the rest. A former bank building at the end of the block to the left still stands. It could have been done a bit more surgically for sure. Always a rush so those federal dollars do not have to be sent back!

There are a number of new spots in the Heights section today, and this is the good part. One of them opened up a few decades back as the Black Rock Brewing Company on 380 Coal Street. It is now the Arena Bar and Grille, still known for its fine brews.

The Arena Bar and Grill is an award winning casual bar and restaurant. For the beer connoisseur, the place packs 50 unique beer spigots on its back bar; and it actually has 50 beers on draft, as well as 450 different bottled beers. Besides, their uniquely crafted martini creations, this fun place offers inexpensive bar appetizers, normal fare appetizers, Angus burgers, hand-cut Steaks and fresh pasta. It will quickly make it to your favorite's list.

FROM THE BAR

PINK WHITNEY ADULT SLUSHIE
FAT HEADS HEAD GROOVY JUICE IPA (OH) 7.1%
BLACKBERRY MARGARITA
HIGH NOON BLACK CHERRY SELTZER
STRAWBERRY SANGRIA

APPETIZERS

FRIED PICKLE CHIPS   7.99
PHILLY CHEESE STEAK EGG ROLLS   9.99
BUFFALO CHICKEN EGG ROLLS   9.99
BATTERED ONION PETALS   7.99

SANDWICHES & SALADS

CANDIED PECAN AND STRAWBERRY CHICKEN SALAD   12.99
COWBOY PULLED PORK SANDWICH   14.99
HONEY & BRIE CHEESE BURGER   14.99
PIEROGIE GRILLED CHEESE   11.99

ENTRÉES

FILET MIGNON   26.99
BLACKENED CHICKEN CARBONARA   19.99
GRILLED PORTABELLA MAC N' CHEESE   20.99
BAKED HONEY BRIE CHICKEN   21.99
SALMON WITH SPINACH & MUSHROOMS   21.99

DESSERT

BROWNIE TOPPED CHEESECAKE   PEANUT BUTTER EXPLOSION
CHOCOLATE MOLTEN CAKE   CHOCOLATE TRILOGY
REESE'S PEANUT BUTTER PIE   CRÈME BRULEE CHEESECAKE

From 1936 to 1964, Wilkes-Barre maintained its own incinerator where refuse could be dropped off and burned. Businesses found it especially useful. I was sixteen when the incinerator days ended. Nobody knew why.

The modern days of tighter environmental regulations put an end to the huge fire pit and the belching smokestack along Coal Street, and it was demolished in 1973. There are a number of new apartment buildings and the biggest city recreation complex is standing there on neatly landscaped ground. But, each time the Axe Man came, Wilkes-Barre lost more than it gained.

Chapter 16 Wilkes-Barre Section: North End

Public Square looking towards North Main St., Wilkes Barre, Pa.

Connects to central city on the north side

This is the area northeast of the Square / Central City. It comprises a number of urban and suburban communities, and is renowned for its interesting and beautiful architecture.

Some notable buildings include Wilkes-Barre Publishing Company, now The Times Leader building, Social Security, III Guys Pizza, King's College, Walkers' Pub which some thought was an actual part of King's in the 1960's before its site was consumed by King's, and of course the HQ of Blue Cross of Northeastern PA.

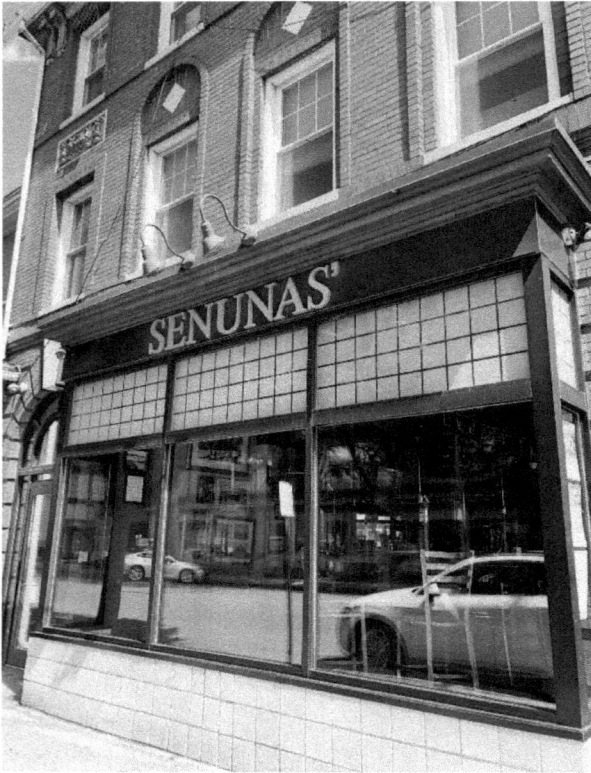

If you keep moving from the Square you'll bump into Helen Senunas' old place, which is now part of King's but across the street is her son John's spot, also called Senunas' which has the look of a fine New York or Philadelphia Pub. Moving up after a few double block buildings, there is the infamous S&W Restaurant. This is the site of many a late night meal.

Continuing where King's North Main Street "Margaritaville" building is now, you will pass the space once occupied by the original Rodano's, and right at the corner in the newest King's building, would be where the Mary MacIntosh Laundry once stood.

©2015 Property of GWBAR

Most of the rest of North Main Streets and North Washington and Penn Ave streets are in North End. As we take a walk around central city a few chapters from now, we will be back in North End.

Margaritaville Dorm built later to the left of the VA Bldg.

Technically, the Coughlin High School building, which consisted of the former Wilkes-Barre High building that was over 105 years old when decommissioned and a newer structure can be considered in central city but they are also in North End. Those from nearby sections, including those from Parsons and Miners Mills most often attended Coughlin until the New High School in Plains PA took over.

Coughlin Circa 1919 as Wilkes-Barre High

JAMES M. COUGHLIN HIGH SCHOOL, WILKES-BARRE, PA.

Coughlin Recent Times – In Danger of the Axe Man

A nice spot way up on North Washington St. is Lombardelli's and there was a place about which I am trying to recall its name—that was the first pizza joint in the City to make Victory Pig Pizza like Victory Pig. Mmmm!!!

A relatively new spot in North End is **Cork's Bar and Restaurant**, 463 Madison Street. Corks is a unique establishment with a very homey look and feel. It brings an innovative concept in dining to the North End of Wilkes-Barre close to downtown. They mix a strong focus on the power of hospitality and they serve delicious food from great appetizers, steaks, seafood as well as mouthwatering pasta dishes. Their bar menu, features an array of juicy burgers, and the liquid bar fare is top shelf.

Pat Patte's Sports Bar above on Hollenback street by General Hospital is by far the highlight place to go for Northenders, and in fact this popular place gets its clientele from all over Northeastern PA. It really is a Sports Bar and has been forever. Patte's as it is called, graduated years ago from a small neighborhood bar to a landmark restaurant and tavern in Wilkes-Barre's *North End.*

The Inside of Patte's—where the good stuff is.

Wilkes-Barre General Hospital Tallest Structure in North End WB

General Hospital was founded in 1872. Until 1874, it was maintained wholly by voluntary subscriptions but since then State appropriations have been made. In 1875 John Welles Hollenback donated a tract of four acres, on River Street near Mill Creek. In the next year, the hospital building was erected. The General Hospital continues to grow.

Wilkes-Barre General Hospital, an affiliate of Commonwealth Health in Northeastern Pennsylvania is a leader in local healthcare with loyal employees and a family work environment. It is a general medical and surgical hospital in Wilkes-Barre, PA, with 412 beds and over 400 allied physicians, It is also accredited by the Commission on Accreditation of Rehabilitation Facilities (CARF). In a recent survey the data available shows that 58,533 patients visited the hospital's emergency room. The hospital had a total of 17,245 admissions. Its physicians performed 4,587 inpatient and 8,289 outpatient surgeries. Of course the numbers are probably higher now.

North End runs into Brookside

The North End area goes all the way down North Washington Street until it hits a small sub section of the City known as Brookside. What a name. This is the section of Wilkes-Barre that gets whacked all the time when there is excessive rain.

<<<

Here is a recent picture of 20 Brookside Street in the Brookside section. Wilkes-Barre is known for its winters.

Chapter 17   Wilkes-Barre Section: Parsons

George Avenue in Parsons Section

A one-time self-sustaining borough

This is a quiet part of town with a suburban atmosphere. It once was its own geographical and political borough. It includes two city parks, a golf course, and a number of factories. Most of the factories, such as Craft Associates and Carter Rubber / Footwear that were fully operational in the glory days have been closed for quite a while after limping for a few years after the flood.

In many ways, this was the end of manufacturing as a source of glory-time income in Wilkes-Barre proper. Muskin Pool company in Miners Mills, lasted a bit longer, but my cartography skills are so bad that I cannot tell if Muskin was really in Miners Mills, Plains, or Parsons. Nonetheless, Lots of jobs left the immediate area when Muskin pulled out.

There were and in many cases still are a number of great establishments to enjoy. Though it moved from its glory days location when it was run by the Vitali family, the Anthracite Café is still a mainstay of Wilkes-Barre's Parson's section.

They cater not to fine dining per se, though their dining is fine; but to that larger segment of the population that views food as fuel and who look upon dining as simply a means to an end. Nonetheless, the Anthracite has one heck of a nice menu even today.

My dad "Ed" and his six Kelly brothers, Mart, Mike, Phil, Pat, Joe, and Johnnie, from 913 Scott Street loved the Anthracite. For years, they called it *Vitali's.* Even after dad moved to the Rolling Mill Hill and most of the brothers, except Uncle Pat who stayed in Parsons, had moved out of town, they still had their reunions until late in the evening at *"Vitali's"* and then over time, they began to call it *The Anthracite.*

The original building is on the 1100 block of Scott Street. it began as The Anthracite Hotel. Like many places of the day, the "Hotel" was more recognized for its bar fare than its food fare. The House proudly served Stegmaier Gold Medal Beer from the brewery where my dad worked for thirty-one years.

In 1920, Guilio Vitali purchased the Anthracite and his family ran the place for four generations. As noted but worth repeating, the Kelly brothers, born in the early 1900's, who, by the way, had their own basketball team (only needed 5 good players) played various teams around the valley in the 1930's. They saw the Anthracite as a friendly and inviting place where great beer, as well as tasty and affordable food was served.

In 2003, the Anthracite Café moved from its historical beginning to its current, more spacious location. In the recent past, this iconic dining establishment is under the ownership and management of Mike Prushinski, a local restaurateur born as a Wyoming Valley native. Even after it left its glory roots, it is still a place to behold and enjoy

George Avenue was always another great place for the Parsonites to frolic. Though Scott Street is the big street in Parsons, George Ave was its main street.

When my dad was an usher at the Parsons' Theatre on George Avenue, his toughest job was to convince his friends not to try to get in for free. Later the theatre became the Parsons Theatre Hall, a catering hall, and then the Golden Palace, and now it is A Touch of Class. It was and surely is a hallmark of Parsons and a great place for wonderment. I bet mostly all of us have been there for a great function like a wedding or graduation. A lot less of us were there for a movie.

The Parsons Theatre Hall in Parsons Section of Wilkes-Barre

Parsons had an American Legion, a VFW (originally across Scott Street from the Host Motel.

The time I recall the most was after the Vietnam War when a lot of returning veterans frequented these two establishments.

To the left is an old miners bar unidentified where the miners would stop before and after their shifts to whet their whistles.

Right next to the Parsons' Theatre on the right was Whitey's Café. Moving up George Ave towards Scott you would find Benedetti's Diner next to the Parsons Bank, International Color Printing was a little further up from the Bank, by the original Vitali's Bar.

On the left side of the Theatre looking on was the American Legion. The Parsons YMCA was also on that side of the street. Across George Avenue from the Theatre Hall was the D&R, Primo's Bakery and later Arnold's Pizza.

Lots of high schoolers in the 1960's, mostly from Coughlin, hung out at the D&R, which was right next door to Schumacher's Bar and across the street from YMCA. The high school kids spent a lot of time at the Parsons Y with pool, ping pong, bowling, basketball, etc. These same high school kids today are in their mid-seventies to early 80's. Time flies.

The Y was in many ways a pool hall and the young at the time played pool in the basement which also had ping pong, and two bowling lanes. Basketball of course was the main course and many of the kids from Parsons learned how to play quite well. On top of all that, the Parsons Y had a wrestling team.

Those who know, tell me that in the 50's and 60's as noted above, the main hangout was the D&R. They say it was like the restaurant on Happy Days, and so they all went there. One source suggests that D&R stood for Donnini & Raggee, but he is not sure of the spelling. Parsons had a lot of life then and it still does

Don's Den took over for the original Schumacher's Bar next to the D&R. This bar was named after the late Donnie Pryor. Eventually Donnie sold to a group who put together a place called Grannies'. It did not look too much different than Don's Den.

In 1974, Grannies got a face lift and reopened as Mr. Bojangles. I was a partner in that enterprise and I helped remodel Granny's along with George Mohanco. I remember the bywords of our first ad: *Mr. Bojangles: Where it is all together!* Hah! I still do not know what that means.

We sold the business after about a year and rented the building to Dave Carey, a Parson's boy who opened up Speak Easy East. As Speak Easy West became more and more popular, Dave chose to close his east side establishment. The place opened briefly for a while and now it is a house. When I ran for Mayor I visited the house right by where my friend Frank Krakenfels lived.

Next door to Mr. Bojangles was O'Donnell's Drugs, and down further was the Parson's Pharmacy. These were needed for local patrons to help alleviate the pain from all the fun that they had at Bojangles and other fine spots on George Avenue in particular.

Occasionally, Tim O'Donnell, son of the Pharmacy owners, who is a great bartender, would do the honors at Mr. Bojangles.

In the same building as O'Donnell's after they retired, one of my best buddies in life, Eugene Aloysius Michael Burke RIP in 2014, a former electrician and a successful iron worker, opened up Soccer '94. My kids bought their stuff (shoes, socks etc.) from Gene. He also did the Soccer pictures for the SWB Skyhawks! He was great and he spoke soccer first at all times! Believe me I have the goods on Gene Burke but I won't spill them here. He was simply a great man.

Gene's Dad was once the honcho, of the powerful electrical union in NEPA before he stepped down.

Next to O'Donnell's was Harry Parri's Bar and then the Parsons Pharmacy and then on the corner was the Imperial Bar, which has been on George Avenue under various names forever, it seems.

Across the street on George Avenue was the Giant Market and Frank Caligairi's Barber Shop, which was one of three Barber Shops on George Ave.

<<Blake Collins Wake House

Haslins was the spot for a nip after a wake at Blake Collins place. It was to the left. After you move down the street further on the Imperial Bar side was Parson's Floral, and Mickey Haslin's, place, now run by his son Michael. Mickey was a relative of the Kelly Family as my dad and my uncles always said. He was a former major leaguer, with the NY Giants a few years, as documented later in this book in a different chapter.

Liparula's was located down on the next corner where Hun's Café' 99 (99 George Ave) is located now. Hun's has wings and other Friday night food and it is good. My Friday night happy hour contingent always loved to go there.

Down the road from Hun's on George Ave were a number of old Parson's standby establishments. One of them is the Blake Collins Funeral Home shown above where most of the people from Parsons choose to be waked and buried. Many of the Scott Street Kelly / O'Boyle family were buried from there.

Almost as if he knew it would be needed after a wake, Mickey Haslin, the great baseball player noted above built his tavern right next to Collins'. My dad and I would enjoy a few there after going to a wake at Collins' for a relative or friend of the family. Dad grew up on Scott Street in Parsons.

There were and are still so many establishments in Parsons that even the long time locals can't recall all the names on George Ave, Scott and all the side streets. Parsons surely is a thriving mini metropolis.

Those that we can count include the S&S (Soldiers &Sailors) on the corner of Mill St and Calvin. St. Dominic's, now St. Benedicts Parish was always there to help. It is on Calvin St along with grade schools.

St Dominic's Catholic Church, now closed, was there to soothe the souls that enjoyed Parsons' just a bit too much. There were also several Protestant churches that helped to assure that their congregations had the proper credentials to get through the Pearly Gates.

Thanks a million to my first cousin Patrick Kelly RIP for his help on the Parsons section.

Chapter 18   Wilkes-Barre Section: Miners Mills

An old postcard depicts the grain mill that once operated on Miller Street in Wilkes-Barre for generations

Check the last photo on the prior page. Interesting buildings in Miners Mills. Moosic Resident Nick Rosati has his eye on

this building to the left in the photo. He has plans to turn the place into a distillery. Good Luck Nick

Miners Mills: Once its own Borough

This huge section of Wilkes-Barre is named after an early prominent local family with a last name depicting the major industry of the area at the time. It is the last neighborhood on the northeastern border of the city.

Miners Mills extends well north and was the borough that brought lots of life to the area. I suspect those in Miners Mills, when it was a borough—an independent governmental entity, felt that they could keep the borough moving right through Plains, and Hudson, and the trail that grows from there. If you live there, know that I am only supposing.

Most of the surrounding areas of NEPA, even though they could not afford their own police, fire and other services were not interested in being a part of a larger community such as Wilkes-Barre. Miners Mills and Parsons Boroughs, recognizing that a shared municipality would be better for them, chose to join Wilkes-Barre City and now they make up two of its largest geographical "sections."

With Wilkes-Barre not in its finest hour today, spots such as Plains and Hudson, and Wilkes-Barre Township would righteously feel they have done what was best for them. But, I, your humble author, am not sure about that. It may be so.

The notion of being a big fish in a small pond keeps bad politicians in operation. In too many cases, these charlatans should be kicked out of office for dealing less than the right amount of honesty in those small ponds.

In small bergs across the nation, such politicians fly under the radar undetected, as if they love the people, while they really love the power. Miners Mills and Parsons now think of themselves as does the Mayflower, North End, and South

Wilkes-Barre, as integral parts of Wilkes-Barre City. All for one and one for all. We will all recover together.

So, it was a good thing for Parsons and Miners Mills to join with Wilkes-Barre proper when they did to make life better for both communities. If all of us were honest to ourselves we would recognize that Plains, Wilkes-Bare Township, and Hudson, would do well along with Wilkes-Barre, being part of an even larger community. Heck if it were so, the newly enlarged Wilkes-Barre or whatever it would be called would then have its own high school.

There is no denying that it would be good for the people but in most cases, it would not be good for the entrenched politicians in the bergs who influence the people—who place the people last. That is why people from all communities need to wake up to the chicaneries of their "friendly" politicians.

Wilkes-Barre for its part, to look like an attractive candidate to be asked to be part of a total community, would have to become a model community. It would have to look to the future with a real plan for glory. And, why not?

Maybe the glory choo choo train needs to go through Hudson and Plains. Maybe the train needs to go up Northampton street to Georgetown. Don't stop dreaming. And of course don't start having nightmares if you are from Plains, Hudson, and/or Wilkes-Barre Township.

These are simply some random thoughts that might spawn even better thoughts if somebody considers them. They are not even close to being dreams but I think they are good thoughts.

Perhaps Hudson, Plains, and Wilkes-Barre Township should merge into their own governmental unit until Wilkes-Barre gets its act together. Then, if Wilkes-Barre does get its act together, maybe they might invite us in. It helps to remember that the bad guys, growing every day, always win when small communities cannot protect themselves. Who wants that?

Miners Mills, a long established neighborhood.

I recall Miners Mills mostly from frequent visits to Penn Lee Footwear, which still is in business there on East Main Street. For years with IBM and later as an independent consultant, I remember Miners Mills from my many visits to the Muskin Pool Company.

I saw the goodness of Miners Mills again on my birthday several years ago. I was searching for St. Clair Street. I got to see Penn Lee again. Penn Lee still has a great selection of some of the finest shoes that money can buy, and they do not ask you to leave your whole wallet at the store. In other words, they have very reasonable prices.

After Karl Goode's store on Parrish Street in the Rolling Mill Hill went out of business in our neighborhood, my dad, through his friends in Parsons and in the Brewery, found Penn Lee Footwear. Penn Lee, like Goode's was economical for the neighborhoods. It still is.

If you type in your web browser the *words miners mills neighborhood scout Wilkes-Barre*, you can learn even more about this section of Wilkes-Barre. There are a lot of *for examples*.

For example: did you know that the Miners Mills neighborhood of Wilkes-Barre, has more Polish and Welsh ancestry people living in it than nearly any neighborhood in America? It is true! In fact, 29.2% of this neighborhood's residents have Polish ancestry and 2.5% have Welsh ancestry.

Miners Mills is also pretty special linguistically. When I did the research for this book, there was a time that 1.5% of its residents five years old and above primarily spoke Polish at home. While this may seem like a small percentage, it is higher than 97.2% of the neighborhoods in America.

A great establishment in Miners Mills

At the corner of East Thomas and St. Clair Streets (59 E Thomas), you will find Teberio's Pub & Pizzeria, a very, very nice place. The Teberio family bought the place about ten years ago. This past year I spent my birthday evening there. John was on duty then. He may not be there any longer but he was a great bartender.

Ron Norakus, operated Norakus' Bar in the 1970's and 80's on the same turn of the century site after taking over from his parents. His parents created the place over 100 years ago. Ron gave Mike Teberio a tour of the building after he bought it and he gave Mike a big history lesson to boot. It is a great lesson. I just found this place today and already, I planned to get there very soon, and in fact I did,

Too late! While editing this paragraph on January 31, 2015, I must admit that I was there last night for my birthday celebration. John the bartender, who is as good as they come. I promised him on the 29th that if he could fit us in, I figured about 14 folks from our Friday Night crowd would be there. Well, there were 17 and every one of us thought the place was wonderful. Now it is going on 2023 and we have been there quite often. Shhh!!!

Mike Teberio has his share of experience for the last ten years so we expect this to be a successful outing for him and significant other. The Norakus's likewise ran a great Pub and restaurant. They insisted the place be built in a first class fashion.

The Norakus family "imported" the bar structure itself from Chicago Illinois at the turn of the 20th century. Try to do that today. Their hard work had just begun after getting the bar on a train in Chicago. When the train got to its stop just down from Norakus's yet to be christened establishment, they wondered how to get it to the bar from the train stop. At the time, the best solution was to use a horse and buggy.

They moved it piece by piece, and laid it in well over 100 years ago, in 1909—in a structure estimated now to be about 113 years old. The finished product is amazing even after Teberio recently had to clean up after a major fire.

Mike Teberio & fiance' Brenda Phillips, at Teberio's Pizza & Pub in WB (TL pic)
Soon after their opening

Soon after opening

When you go there, please check out the intricate carvings on top of the wooden pillars behind the long, mahogany bar, which as noted, and I will say it again. It was constructed more than a century ago. The newly created back bar is also wonderful and it blends in well with the surroundings.

The Norakus family ran their bar for decades until the place changed hands and became Captain's Quarters, a popular restaurant featuring German and Italian cuisine in the 1980s and '90s. For a short time after Captain's Quarters, it was also an Italian restaurant before it was closed apparently for good. But Mike Teberio bought it. At one time it was up for a Sheriff Sale but regardless of how that worked out, Teberio brought it back from death and the rest is some great Miners Mills and Wilkes-Barre history.

In addition to pizza, right now, Teberio's menu includes salads, hoagies and bar foods. Great pizza! After the pub becomes a little more established, Mike Teberio promises that he will be expanding the menu. Looks good to me already. My wife and I sampled the fare right before I wrote the initial edition of this book. The food was excellent. Happy Birthday, Brian!

Chapter 19   Wilkes-Barre Section: South Wilkes-Barre

Logo of Skyhawks Soccer Founded Circa 1985

Makes up a large chunk of Wilkes-Barre

This is the section of Wilkes-Barre directly southwest of uptown central city. In its heyday, it was home to the national headquarters of Planter's Peanuts and the Bell Telephone Company—back in the 20th Century. Both of these companies are gone from Wilkes-Barre and in fact they no longer exist as corporate entities. Planters Peanuts is now owned by Kraft Foods and Bell Telephone became Bell Atlantic, which is now Verizon and they are currently headquartered in NY City.

Wilkes-Barre by many standards is a much better place to live and raise children than NY City but companies love NY as a place to set up their HQ sites.

The tallest church in Luzerne County is in Wilkes-Barre, and it still exists. St. Nicholas Roman Catholic Church, dominates the south end skyline at nearly 200 feet. Today, Monsignor Joseph Rauscher RIP November 2019, shepherded one of the largest parishes in Wilkes-Barre. Today St. Nicks is even bigger than then due to consolidation. Here is the list of the people who are St. Nick's today in 2022.

- Pastor: Rev. Joseph D. Verespy
- Parochial Vicar: Rev. Fidel Ticona
- Parochial Vicar: Rev. Mark J. DeCelles
- Deacon: Deacon Michael Golubiewski
- Pastor Emeritus: Monsignor Joseph G. Rauscher
- Director of Faith Formation: Deacon Joseph Sudano
- Office Manager: Rita Kaminski
- Administrative Assistant: Lynn Humanik

As Scranton Diocese consolidations have continued to occur, occurred, many displaced parishioners, who love the German Night and the St. Nick's Smoker, and the great St. Nick's Bazaar, and of course the welcoming attitude of the pastor's team, have opted to join the parish. The Times, they are a changin!

Nicholas Church circa 1910

Rudy's is another place in the same vicinity. In Wilkes-Barre's heyday, it was located under the South Street bridge on the way to the Heights/Mayflower. A fine establishment it was according to all reports. Many South Wilkes-Barre natives continue to belong to St. Nick's Church along with many more from other sections of the City.

These and many others, including Protestants, had been known to partake of the golden liquid in many of the spots of the city over the years, including Rudy's.

Recognizing that South Wilkes-Barre and the Iron Triangle might be contesting this next spot, I choose to list it under South Wilkes-Barre even though there may be claims of inclusion by as many as four sections of Wilkes-Barre.

In the interest of full disclosure, I cannot bring Rudy's up without saying something about Goldey's, which was also under the bridge. Recent sources for this telling information remain anonymous.

As the story goes there were older guys from King's who found comfort, as in Paul Simon's, definition of comfort, in Goldey's whenever these older students had some breaks from hard studying.

Reportedly, Goldey's was a house of not the finest repute that was well known and yet, very illegal in the city. When it was scheduled to be torn down, as folklore goes, some gentlemen from King's who must have also spent some time at Rudy's and thus were aware of Goldey's, made sure they were able to get a few bricks from the treasure of its demolition to keep as personal treasures.

We definitely will not be asking Goldey's to return to help bring back Wilkes-Barre to its glory days but, it is an interesting story, nonetheless. Many of the bricks are reported to have disappeared.

Moving from under the bridge

One of the reasons why people are so smart in Wilkes-Barre is that we had great schools growing up. In South Wilkes-Barre, the High School before the major consolidation was Meyers but Meyers is unfortunately gone and the building is for sale. Citizens of Wilkes-Barre must pay attention to charlatans posing as representatives of the people.

The Old Ladies Home in South Wilkes-Barre was located right across Carey Ave from Meyers. It is shown below as a magnificent building.

The Old Ladies Home was a charitable institution caring for aged and homeless women in the community. It had room to house up to 40 women either temporarily or permanently as needed. Along with much of Wilkes-Barre's legacy, the "home" was torn down shortly after the flood of 1972.

Meyers High School in its glory years

In late December, before Christmas in 1964, when the bank temperatures displayed 5 degrees, at least twenty Meyers High School male students walked Wilkes-Barre and sang Christmas songs for donations. We began our evening singing a number of songs for the ladies in what we always called it, *The Old Ladies Home*. We did not ask the ladies for donations.

Old Ladies Home Carey Ave Wilkes-Barre

Old Ladies' Home, Wilkes-Barre, Pa

When we left, we showed up anywhere in South Wilkes-Barre that was warm and the place was open and we sang and sang and sang. When it got late, we figured we were done and so we walked uptown to the WBRE radio station as I recall and we sang on the radio and we gave the personalities the loot we had collected to donate to charity. It is amazing how much fun one can have while doing something good.

Mercy Hospital / Geisinger South Wilkes-Barre

Mercy Hospital, 196 Hanover Street, Wilkes-Barre, was the hospital for South Wilkes-Barre and beyond for many years until 2005. It was a general hospital run by the Religious Sisters of Mercy until it was sold to Geisinger. Mercy was founded in 1898 to benefit poor people in need of care.

Over the years it grew substantially with new services and a larger bed capacities than in the early 1900's when it was stable at 177 beds. Eventually Mercy could hold 250 beds before its acquisition by Geisinger.

Geisinger announced that it would be focusing on same-day and short-stay inpatient services at the South Wilkes-Barre campus, thereby eliminating about 400 positions from the former Mercy Hospital campus.

Mercy Hospital Wilkes-Barre Circa 1920

Mercy Hospital, Wilkes Barre, Pa.

Food Places Galore in South Wilkes-Barre

There still are a lot of food places for shopping and for dining in South Wilkes-Barre. There were many more choices in the glorious past but there were also about twice as many people living in Wilkes-Barre itself.

Mercy Hospital Wilkes-Barre Circa 1960

Mercy Hospital, Wilkes-Barre, Pa.

Some remember an Acme in the plaza on South Main Street, and an A&P on Carey Ave. General Radio & Electronic which disappeared a few years back, was once an Acme also. Now, we have Schiel's most welcoming Hanover Street store, which once was a Giant Markets, and before that, a Food Fair. The Target Fruit Market, located at the Crossroads, which technically is in Hanover Township was also a great spot. Jeff Gritz, graduated from Meyers with me. His dad ran all the Target Markets in the area, and he lived in South Wilkes-Barre on Amherst Ave.

Mesko Plaza is new, relatively. It is very nice and is on the Wilkes-Barre side of Division Street, towards uptown from the Target Market. Today it once hosted the Daily Donut, WahMeh Chinese Restaurant, and my personal favorite, Philly's Phinest. The faces and the names have changed in the last few years.

Philly's Phinest, run by Steve Bollinger, RIP, is so good that at a recent wine tasting event in a South Wilkes-Barre neighborhood, the host chose to serve Abe's Hot Dogs from Barney Street, and eight large boxes of Philly's Phinest Pizza in many delicious flavors. It was great. The guests were pleased that Philly's and Abe's, were the palette cleansers for the evening rather than sherbet. . What could be better?

The "Phinest" is known best for its Philadelphia style subs that are the best in the area for sure. They buy their buns fresh from Amorosa Bakery in Philadelphia. This bakery supplies the buns to the great Philadelphia Cheese steak houses places in the big PA City – Pat's Steaks, and Geno's. They ship them to Wilkes-Barre's best place that meets the truck in Allentown to assure fresh Amorosa buns for Wilkes-Barre's Phinest every day.

Philly's Phinest is one of the places that is going to help bring about Wilkes-Barre's return to glory. The place is so good that there ought to be a lot more of them in town.

To give you an idea of something great, which Wilkes-Barre has to offer, consider these two sample reviews of Phillies Phinest randomly picked off the Internet.

Review # 1
"Food was fantastic! Service was exceptional and we couldn't have been happier... Family owed for 25 years.... They are doing something right!."

Review # 2
After feeling iffy about reviews me and my band mates decided to give Philly's Finest (sic) a shot.

I expected a mediocre sandwich and ok service at best based on what I read......wow was I wrong....this was my experience.......

Upon entry the decor will not give you an "eye-gazm" and you may feel like you're at a beer package store rather than a food joint....then you smell the amazing aroma coming from the back.

The staff was prompt to greet and shared some casual jokes while we read the menu. I ordered a traditional cheese steak with whiz, onions and green peppers....my bandmate ordered the chicken cheese steak with American cheese and sweet and hot peppers. Then we saw a two for one deal on a few different choice brews and asked if we could get the same deal with the beer we wanted and the manager quickly replied yes. I was already sold.

Next the food came out.....what a treat for my pallet!!! The first bite of my steak had a perfect blend of whiz, steak, onions, peppers and bread!!! All flavors were... and I was able to separate them in the one bite. Next came the bite with no whiz....still a tasty sandwich! The meat was juicy, the veggies were cooked yet crunchy not soggy, the whiz wasn't overbearing and bread was a perfect blend of chewy yet soft!

Before we could set our sandwiches down from the first couple bites the nice server brought us a fresh order of fries on the house just to be nice.

.....if you are looking for a delicious traditional Philly in the Wilkes-Barre PA area, "Philly's Phinest" should be your destination!!!!!

End of reviews Amen

And as Congressman Daniel J. Flood would say, "That's praise from Caesar." On top of being the greatest mid-speed food place in Wilkes-Barre, it is run by the nicest people, the Bollinger family.

Steve was a great guy but he passed too young. He was my daughter Katie's softball coach when he was remodeling his space years ago in Mesko Plaza. He and Cindy worked hard to build the place and the business. Folks like them and Cindy's irascible sister. Folks like the way they run their business. Already it looks like Wilkes-Barre is reliving its Glory Days. The Bollinger family need to be on any Wilkes-Barre revitalization committee.

Please! Check out their modest store front in Mesko Plaza below. Meanwhile, it helps to know that there were a few other old places in WB's glory days. Gone but not forgotten!

Philly's Phinest – South Wilkes-Barre's Phinest

Other spots in or by Mesko Plaza

To the left of Philly's Phinest a few stores down, you once found a dry cleaning establishment called **The Clothes Hanger**, which really came in handy. They moved to Kingston by the UPS Store. In days of old, when I lived on High Street, the Palace Laundry had a truck and they would pick up your clothes and return them in a week. One hour Porterizing on the Square was also great as was Mike's on Hazle Street.

At the very end of Mesko Plaza is **Mesko Glass**, which also comes in handy for windshields or any other of your glass needs. They are really good and they do not rip you off. My rear view mirror fell off the windshield last year, and it was on in a jiffy. Thanks Mesko

Moving down Carey Ave another block or so on the same side, was **Steve's Tailor Shop**. It is between Willow St and Stark next door to where Dr. Gawain Carlin ran his chiropractic clinic for many years. Steve could fix anything. But no more as Steve packed up and moved in 2016. He has fixed pants, dresses, hats, coats, and even jeans for our family. Thanks Steve for your skilled work.

At the corner of Horton and Carey Avenue in the glory days was Luna Rosa Pizza. Pizza was great and it was a regular Meyers stomping ground. After football games and any excuse, crowds would be on the steps right on Carey Avenue to enjoy the conversation and the excitement of boy meets girl and vice versa.

Today the old building is gone and Angelo Ricci's son runs Gerry's Pizza from the site. He moved his building back from Carey Avenue so he can fit three cars in the lot now, and he has a drive through. Gerry also has a drive through on the side making it really convenient to pick up take-outs. Sometimes he will throw in a big wad of cheese for a dog if he is aware, unless that honor was always reserved for Chance Elinsky (RIP)

Hanover Diner

In the gone but not forgotten category, a great old time lunch room in South Wilkes-Barre was the Hanover Diner. it was located on Hanover and South Main streets. (12 Hanover St.). Its location is part of the present site of Schiel's South Wilkes-Barre Store. It was run in those days by Mr. & Mrs. George Elias with some help from their son, George, Jr.

While writing this book in 2015, George Jr, RIP one of my best lifelong friends from High Street, told me that my late brother Ed, and his best friends, Jim Malacarne, and Bob Stanton lived there from the time school (Meyers) was over until approx. 4:30—Mon. thru Fri. Nice tribute to such a fine diner. I wish I could show a picture. At his annual Fourth of July fest, one time, George recounted the story of how a new customer came in and sat where my brother and the other amigos sat when they came from school. His dad loved these three guys. My brother was his paperboy. Mr. Elias told the new customer he had to move because the three Meyers' guys would be there shortly. Thanks for the story George.

The Elias's lived in the back of the place until the diner was sold to The Food Fair. Over the years, as noted above, it was also the Giant Markets, and now it is the site of the very successful and very well run Schiel's' Market, where my wife and I do just about all our food shopping. Schiel's is another store that is already helping Wilkes-Barre on its comeback to its glory days. Keep it up guys

Foley's & Boris's

Al Boris Elected Chairman of City Council

Boris Sworn as Chairman
Another Boris, WB to Observe

President Becomes Vice Chairman
Judge Podven Does the Honors

The most popular two places in South Wilkes-Barre in its glory days, during a Meyers Football game besides Wilkes-Barre Memorial Stadium were no doubt Foley's Tavern, and Al Boris' Bar, both on Carey Avenue. Al Boris was a WB Councilman.

Boris's, for years run by the late Al Boris, a popular Wilkes-Barre Councilman, is no longer in business; but the beautiful building still is in business. Foley's became Carlos and then Salerno's; and then unfortunately the whole thing burned down and it is now a parking lot.

There are too many spots like this on Carey Avenue waiting for some Wilkes-Barre lovers to set up shop. Don't forget these desolate deserted vacant lots can all become mini-malls with mini boutiques so Wilkes-Barre residents looking to bring forth an idea can take a shot at being an entrepreneur without bankrupting their families.

Welcome Inn & Schmidt's Fiesta Lounge-Quite the Show!

The Welcome Inn on Wood Street had some risqué entertainment in the 1960's that attracted many, as did Joe's Fiesta Lounge on South Main Street. Of course at the time, Wilkes-Barre had many more churches than now, so forgiveness may have simply been a street-corner away.

Whiskey Business now thrives in the old Welcome Inn building. A lot of young folks and those who think they are young, frequent this popular establishment. The Riverside Bar is another great stop for the young and young at heart. it is on Old River Road. Their pizza is uniquely great.

Page III was another great haunt on South Main in the glory years as was McCool's Irish Pub, which succeeded it in the South Main Plaza. Of course even before the plaza existed, there was the Ovolon Night Club and the Club Baghdad. I recall how interesting and inviting the front of the Ovolon was, but I was so young, I did not even know what the term, "Night Club," meant.

This was surely a happening town and a great section in the real glory days. Wilkes-Barre was a fun town. I bet there were people back then that did not feel compelled to take a vacation just to get out of town. Town aka Wilkes-Barre, was a great and exciting place even when guys like me did not understand what it was all about.

Moving uptown from this area was Joe Schmidt's Fiesta Lounge, and The Leader, a great Pizza Parlor. There was even a hotel close by around the turn to the twentieth century. It was called the "Little Delmonico Hotel." It was at the corner of Hazle and South Main streets. It had to be past the FLATIRON building.

The FLATIRON and the Little Delmonico are gone. They were replaced by our newest Plasticville Post Office Building, which is no longer a fully functional regional post office. The great original post office building still functions as a Federal Courthouse up the street on South Main and South Streets

Sam's Steaks was right across South Main Street from the Plaza. Their steak sandwiches were so good everybody in Wilkes-Barre knew about them. Murph Solomon told me Sam would freeze beef and then cut it on a sharp slicer very thin— almost like minute steaks are made but much, much better. Sam's skinny building spot was right across the street from the Ovolon. It existed long before there was a South Main Plaza.

By the way, Sam's delicious mini-cheese steaks are still served at Abe's Famous Hot Dog spot on Barney Street, and elsewhere in the Abe's local chain. You can't go wrong. The Abe's on South Main street run by the Leo family is also a great historical spot with wonderful fare.

<< Abes on South Main

While we are at it, another nice Wilkes-Barre Hot Dog Place is the Barney Street Lunch. Abe's and The Barney Street Lunch grew up together on Barney Street, and they are both still alive, unlike the Bucket of Blood Theatre, and my favorite in my pre-adolescent years, the Barney 5c & 10c shop.

At the corner in the picture below, at the intersection of Barney & Horton is CrisNics, by Waller Street. It is as good as it gets. On its left down Barney Street just a hair is the parking lot which is the former site of the "Bucket" theatre and right down from that is the former site of the Barney St. 5c & 10c. See the big green tree in the picture...you're there.

Former Site—Bucket of Blood Theatre & Barney St. 5c & 10c Store

With my 26" bike in days of yore, I was able to check out the prices between this 5C & 10C in South Wilkes-Barre and Huntzinger's on Hazle Street in the Rolling Mill Hill. A fella had to have good 26" bike transportation to pull off such comparison shopping in the glory days.

Ironically, as previously noted, the other Abe's, whose family were from the Rolling Mill Hill, are located by the other plaza on 419 South Main Street close by where Sam's Steaks was.. They also serve nice dogs and lunch fare. Unlike Sam's however, there is no "Bug Juice." That is the name for a drink that Sam's served up that was made from "Blend."

One of our favorite "home game" places in South Wilkes-Barre is across from the other Abe's on the corner of Barney & Horton Streets. It was once the Barney Inn; then it was McCabes's Barney Inn; then Fish's Barney Inn, back when the late "Fish" Fisher had the place.

CrisNics Irish Pub in South Wilkes-Barre – Lots of Tables on left

Always ready to make you feel welcome at CrisNics

Now, it is **CrisNics**, named after the two Flaherty daughters, Chris and Nicole. In this establishment, the Flaherty's show the neighborhood folks as well as those looking for great adult refreshments and great top of the line food, how to make it look easy. It's our favorite place to go. As a recent side benefit, my talented daughter Katie Kelly, a folk/jazz singer and guitarist plays there on a regular basis.

Chapter 20   Wilkes-Barre Section: East End

East End: where life is just a holiday!

This is the area directly east of uptown Wilkes-Barre. East End, along with the Heights and Mayflower, are fairly new areas compared to the rest of the City, having only been developed in the 20th Century. Old pictures of the Stegmaier Building (which is the oldest "high-rise" in Wilkes-Barre and the last one on uptown's eastern border show that everything east of uptown Wilkes-Barre early on, was just forests and coal mines.

Though relatively new, East End has its own history, and a good percentage of its population are Irish, who just as the miners of yore, still enjoy their schnorkies. So, there are a lot of "establishments" within walking distance of all homes. It was planned that way as some suggest in East End.

Long-time glory day's Brader's Pub on Bowman Street for example is one such place. It eventually changed hands to Mahon's Pub during the 1980's or so. It now operates as Keats' Pub.

Scott Street (the part that is not in Parsons) is full of other fine local establishments. The all-time favorite of East Enders— mine and my father's too was the Silver Queen Hotel, run by the Toole / McKenna family for many years. It was sold and the new owner found it burned to the ground one early morning.

Regina M. (Jeanne) Toole Kopec ran the Silver Queen Hotel as a great Pub until the family sold it and it became the Grapevine Restaurant . Mrs. Kopek or Jeanne Kopek as we knew her, passed away on Sunday, September 26, 2010. It was not long after disengaging from the business.

Alice McKenna Toole, Jeanne's mom, started the place in 1948 and she was actively involved in the business until her death. Alice, was always known as Mrs. Toole even to my dad, who I am fairly certain was her senior. Jeanne Kopek ran the "Queen" from that point on. In the East End Section of Wilkes-Barre. Jeanne ran the place well and was inducted into the Luzerne County Tavern Owners Hall of Fame in 1993. Both Jeanne and the Silver Queen Hotel are sadly missed by East Enders and those of us from other parts of the City and beyond, who felt a kinship to the place.

My dad loved going there to hear great music and he loved to dance to the "orchestras," as he called them. His hair was white very early in life and he loved finding some other "white hairs," as he called them in any place we went. He was especially insistent about white hairs being present after mom died at the young age of 67.

The whole family loved being with dad and he loved the Queen so we were there for every reason we could think of. There were "white hairs" aplenty at the Queen. Many female white hairs found Mr. Ed Kelly to be quite attractive, though even after mom's death, he was never quite available.

Bands and "orchestras" would play at the Silver Queen just about every weekend. It was the place to go on St. Patrick's Day and it was always festive around the holidays. I cannot remember it being anything other than a great place to be.

Eventually the McKenna / Toole family sold the big Inn, and it reopened as the Grape Vine. It opened up and looked like a nice job of refurbishing the place. Then, after a short while, unfortunately, it burned down. My dad had already passed away but it was very disappointing.

What a loss to Wilkes-Barre and the East End community. Anybody who is anybody in East End, knows of the Silver Queen. It actually had silver siding early on, and in many ways for years, it was the silver lining in a lot of people's lives. Send me a picture of the Queen if you have one and I will get it in the book.

Other East End Watering Establishments:

A few East Enders lots older than kids have been known to find comfort and solace in the other fine establishments in East End, particularly on Scott Street. There were a few elsewhere in East End over the years but not many.

Though my sister and my book designer both live on Kidder Street, along with many of my nephews, these two serve only water to their families. OK, I am not really sure. Many East Enders and others I am told, however, have seen the insides of the 112 Tavern at the foot of Scott Street in Wilkes-Barre proper, East End, more often than they can count to 112.

By the way, East Enders know that the 112 Tavern was the 112 Tavern for many years until it changed hands in the 90's to Ziggie's Pub 'n Grub. After several years, it seems like it went back under its old name of the 112 Tavern. Now, in 2022, like many things of Wilkes-Barre's glorious past; it is long closed.

Dave's Tavern was a few doors up from the 112 but located across the street. It changed hands in the late 80's or early 90's to the Brickyard, Sometime after Y2K, it changed hands again and is now Don Kasper's Watering Hole. We have no witnesses from back in the golden days of Wilkes-Barre glory to attest to its one time fare or grandeur.

A note from a concerned citizen of East End gave this inquiring writer more information than expected. He said "I believe that the baseball diamond at the end of Scott St. was an actual brickyard at one time. Parking for the Brickyard Tavern was next to (or in) the brickyard. I also believe that the nickname of the baseball diamond, 'The Brookie' was somehow a derivative of The Brickyard."

"The baseball diamond is out of commission and has been for years, but it sits right next to a very active Chacko's Bowling Alley, or, as some in East End see it as 'The East End Cultural Center.' "

Big thank you's to this concerned East End Citizen for straightening that out for all of us. PK, it was JF – RIP.

This concerned confessor also confessed knowledge that Brislin's Tavern on Scott St was Brislin's for as many years as anybody can remember. He does recall a side door where kids (surely they were over 21) could go in and buy candy and also pick up beer and cigarettes for their parents.

He vividly recalls that in the 70's he was going on a cigarette mission to Brislin's on Christmas morning on behalf of a friendly force carrying the bands "Leland Zard." Of course, that may be just East End folklore.

Not wanting to divulge much more, this same one, in his youth, who saw it all, made note of how many East End patrons he recognized in Brislin's Bar on this fine Christmas morn. No Scrooges were there for sure. This same one may have known them all, but he was sworn to secrecy as would be expected in an Irish Pub. Some candy must have been part of the reward.

There they were, pre-8 AM arrivals, comfortably sitting in Brislin's on their favorite stools or at chairs & tables, and the little hand on the big clock had yet to hit 8 AM in the morning on Christmas day! But the little hand that had shown up unexpectedly pre 8 AM ran off to home in the end with a bag of needed supplies, which included, burdensome, but substantial Christmas loot for the delivery person.

Thirst is surely a powerful agent in the war for creature comforts. Isn't it amazing how such things can happen in America as happened right there in East End, Wilkes-Barre, PA one bright Christmas morn.

Brislin's in East End, changed hands sometime in the 80's to become the R Bar. It is now "Shooters." They tell me it has become a preferred watering hole.

East End establishments are extremely resilient even if no customers are coming in—as it has been explained to your humble scribe. And, so, Moore's on Scott St. was Moore's for as long as most East Enders can remember. However, It did close for a few years and then, can you imagine this—It reopened as Moore's. From what we can see, it is still open.

McKenna's, a more recent pub, also on Scott Street, located near Weismann playground, has been closed for a while. It is now a grocery store and has been for the past several years.

The *Other Place* in East End, is near the corner of Bowman and Laurel Streets. This bar was located in a basement somewhere in East End. You had to go downstairs to get to it. It was a great watering hole used often for quenching thirst in the 1960's.

Joe & Kitty's Pizza and Bar on Kidder Street was located on the opposite end of the strip mall from Harvey's Flea, which some say was the most awesome discount store ever. The store closed many years ago after Harvey died. If you ever saw the movie, "Porky's," from the late 70's early 80's, Harvey looked and talked exactly like the guy who played Porky. This fine establishment has morphed into a Chinese take-out.

Across from Wendy's Joe & Kitty had this little "dive bar" in a back room of the pizza parlor. Joe & Kitty moved their business to route 115 in Buck Township many years ago. The original spot became a Weight Watchers.

Exercise and Sports in East End

There is a small park on Scott Street in East End at the top of the Hill by Schoolhouse Lane known as Weissman Park. It is nice with a few swings. My Aunt Marie lived right across the street (alley).

There are no pools or major athletic fields anywhere today in East End. Like many in the new Wilkes-Barre, young East Enders are trying to get Red Cross Life Saving certificates from doing the backstroke in their six foot long bathroom tubs. What happened to the pools? What happened to the jobs? Lifeguards are not needed in places with no pools.

On dry land. my truthful nephews tell me that the best ball field in East End for years always had been Jenks Lane. There is hardly ever traffic on this lengthy alley and the empty driveways give the illusion that the alley itself is much wider than it actually is.

The nephs tell me that most of the northern part of Jenks Lane is unused and can perhaps be used to help another WB neighborhood to find a place for their youth to frolic and play. They would have to be trucked to Jenks Lane of course.

The mini entrepreneurs from Jenks, I suspect would be pleased to offer an alley rental service for small "lane" games for trucked-in needy ONK's. ONK, of course is short for *"other neighborhood's kids."* Such 'hoods would be selected as long as they had none of the major Jenks Lane type facilities, such as an alley with driveways. In other words, Jenks' *"fields"* were so great, according to those who grew up there, they wish everybody has the chance one day to enjoy them.

Jenks Lane still has a hard and dusty surface

Though there have been lots of scuffed knees from the dirt road "pavement," over the years, this impediment was not obstacle enough to stop the "Jenks Lane" games system. It has always been worth playing sports, tag, and all sorts of "street" games despite these risks on Jenks Lane in East End. Jenks was a major part of the glory days of Wilkes-Barre as it is today, and hopefully with God's blessing, will continue to be in the future.

Football, basketball, and baseball, including wiffle ball were the norm on Jenks Lane. The boys felt that they ran the place. Life was a holiday on Jenks Lane, and there was always a sporting event going on. Scrappy girls were permitted to play. But since the kids could not write with chalk on the dusty road, there was little to no hopscotch. Jump rope, yes, but there was just about no hopscotch on Jenks Lane. Chalk lines were a definite problem.

Later in this research project, concerned citizen research concluded that an East End Little League field does exist. Ironically, it appears to be the result of a cross-sectional Wilkes-Barre treaty between the Heights and East End sections of the city. The field seems to exist geographically in the Heights Section at Coal Street but euphemistically in the minds of city officials, not wanting to mess with the Irish in East End, they declared that East End exists spiritually on the East End side of the Heights Park, wherever that is.

Maybe it is actually in East End but to know for sure, we would have to ask the City Sectional Boundary Mediator, who some say is still enjoying a liquid lunch at the Silver Queen.

Further Analysis is Necessary

I know my nephews will be reading this, including the Pephs – Pephard Q Whoozer, Minnard Q. Peph, and Billiard Q. Peph, along with other Flannery's, even some "bobs," pikes, larues, beans, and wees. This of course includes Jimbob, McPike, Ken-A-Larue. R-Bean, and Maywee!

So as you can surely appreciate, I am trying to be a little cute here using poetic license just for them. They are a great lot for sure. David Davidow, along with Leland K. Zard, of similar roots are indulging as I write, in some fine turkey from an unknown heavenly fridge. RIP

For those of you checking on my East End accuracy, please note that yes, I am aware that the East End 5 Points A.C. Little League Club that some of my East End nephews played in, disbanded several years ago. Another little bit of lost glory I might add. Shame!

In addition to Jenks Lane, the clear center of activity for all East End Youth, and others invited, the East End kids were also happy to play in the vacant lots. But, unfortunately, no lots were vacant, Take a run up East End, and you will see.

Can you imagine what the Jenks Lane *seventy-three* could have done with a facility like the Silver Queen parking lot if it were available to them then, instead of after the big fire?

Since the Queen was in-tact until recently, and had yet to meet its fiery demise, besides the Jenks Lane Sports Palace discussed above, the East End kids played ball regularly in various church/school parking lots. Several different yards were their favorites, especially one that was affectionately named "the big yard."

Of course, as noted, the Jenks Complex itself was always available in combination with driveways for an ad hoc sporting event or game of any kind at any time. Amen!

Now wonder East Enders have such great mettle.

An East End Hotel / Motel

In the mid twentieth century, the Host Motel became very popular. It even had a mini nine hole golf course. It was located on Kidder Street. It was one of the local pioneers of the "motel" concept once the moguls at the time began to believe the era of the downtown hotels had diminished. It was later torn down and the site redeveloped. So much for "motels!

Chapter 21 Wilkes-Barre Section: Mayflower

Mayflower 288 Little League honors all stars

The Mayflower 288 Little League recently held its annual field day and award ceremonies at which time the league's all-star team which par-ticipated in the District 16 and W.B. Recreation... Rushkowski.

Second row, Bob Mullary, Bobby Marconi, Steve Vlastaris and Brian Isopi.

Third row, Ed Jarnot, manager, Andy Gavlick

Great places and parks in Mayflower

This area is located south of uptown. My buddy Annie Demmick from the Heights who lived around the Mayflower Little League (Norb Slease Field) Joe Zalewski's tavern off Moyallen Street used to protest vehemently to me that she did not live in the Heights. Sections in Wilkes-Barre are important and I know I did not get them all right in this book. Annie would shout from the rooftops that she lived in the Mayflower. It is still tough for those of us not from any particular section to tell what section it is even if we, at the time, are in that section. Let it be said in finality, Mrs. Annie Demmick, my good buddy, lived in the Mayflower. Her Kids Carol and Joe and Joan loved her to pieces.

My great dad, Edward J. Kelly took his wife Irene and kids Ed, Nancy, Brian and the twins Joe & Mary for the walk to and from Joe Zalewski's from our home on High Street each summer for my sister Nancy's birthday celebration July 22. We all had Lobster Tails which were cheap enough that dad could afford them. Dad had Clams and a huge klupski (a polish burger) and he got a bowl of the Clam bullion which he loved. We loved Zalewski's. The twins all tried to get Brian's cole slaw and offered one of their three tails for the privilege.

The Mayflower section was once a wealthy area where the homes were often beautiful mansions owned by various "big wigs". The section is now a more affordable neighborhood, It is off Park Avenue and includes a good part of Moyallen, Prospect, Dana, Grant, Sheridan, Sherman, and Empire streets. Scholars tell me it ends at Northampton. Beginnings are a bit uncertain.

Huber Park and the Mayflower Little League are mainstay recreational areas in this section of the city. Zip Walko and Norb Slease are legendary area names. Stanton lanes is a mainstay. It was built near the end of the glory years but well before they had ended. It is still there and thriving thankfully. The A&P and Insalaco's Markets are both gone as is the ten Pin Bar. They were fine places to shop and have a nip in that order. Maybe one day nice stores like that will reappear in the Mayflower section.

There is a fine High School in the Mayflower section, almost in the Heights area, where those from Mayflower, Heights, and the Iron Triangle attended and still attend class. It is no longer a high school but operates as a middle school still. Ok, I will say it—at least until the Axe man has his way and rips GAR down. This great school was named after Civil War veterans in the Grand Army of the Republic, G.A.R. Here is a picture from the 1940's when GAR was a High School going on twenty-years old.

G. A. R. Memorial High School, Wilkes-Barre, Pa.

Living on lower Prospect Street in a sketchy area of the Rolling Mill Hill, as I did in my early married life, we shopped at Passeri's Market and later Leggieri's, and even later Thomas's on Prospect and Grove. We found bountiful snacks (even kipper snacks and blind robins) and liquid fare at the Villa Grove across the street from Passeri's. All were well worthy of purchasing. But, to do serious shopping, it was off to the Mayflower Section we would go and to Insalaco's Supermarket. It was a fine place.

We belong still to St. Patrick's Church, which technically is part of St. Andrew's Parish today. It is also technically in the Rolling Mill Hill / Mayflower area but disputes are permitted.

After Mass on Sundays, my wife Pat and I would shop at Insalaco's, almost every week. Meanwhile Pop Piotroski would take our three children over to Huber Park and push them on the swings.

Sometimes, that was so appealing to me that Pat did all the shopping herself, and I went with Pop and the kids. What a glorious happening.

My youngest son Mikey, (now a Wilkes-Barre Lawyer -- M P Kelly) while on the swings would entertain us with his own little homemade songs. There were not many words in either of them. Here they are with author duly recognized.

Lo, Lo – the Song, by young Michael P. Kelly

Lo, Lo, Lo, Lo
Lo, Lo, Lo, Lo

Bumble Bee – the Song, by young Michael P. Kelly

Bumble Bee, who's there, Bumble Bee!
Bumble Bee, who's there, Bumble Bee!

I knew you'd like those songs almost as much as I liked hearing little Mikey sing them.

It can be argued that from the high streets of the Mayflower, the best view of the Up Town skyline can be seen. Joe Zalewski's tavern in the Mayflower section was not the spot but it was close. I learned that you could just about see the whole valley from the Dana Street School.

Thankfully, the great building destroying machine, with the Axe Man in charge, had not begun its reign of terror on Wilkes-Barre, and the Dana Street School still exists. Some think the infamous Axe Man may work for the Redevelopment Authority, but for now, we will hold that thought. We'll repeat it again before we actually make a determination in City sections that have become blighted by demolitions. I suspect you all know already which way I will vote if given a vote.

The wonderfully situated Dana Street School, from which flood victims of 1972 could get a full view of the river as it was flooding the valley, was not gobbled up when the District was looking for a new school. Instead, it was sold and it now is a set of wonderful apartments overlooking the whole valley. Amen!

Joe Zalewski's at Mayflower & Grant streets, may not have been the spot where you would go to see the whole valley but Joe and company served great food. It was a lot like Bohn's on Brown Street. They were always known for the best Klupskies (Huge Polish Hamburgers) in town. Wouldn't it be nice if we found a place like that today? That should certainly be part of any well-orchestrated return to glory—don't you think? Wilkes-Barre leadership should take notice.

There was a very fine tavern on Dana and Sheridan Streets that was frequented by those from the Mayflower for many years for a long time. They were known for fine food. It was called Parada's. Years ago, the Polish Dancers danced in Parada's backroom to the delight of the clients, who were mostly from the Mayflower. Eventually as time passed, a famous realtor, John Anstett from Wilkes-Barre sold Parada's to Lenahan's when Parada wanted to get out of the business.

Anstett sold Paradas to Lenahan's according to the records After a few more years. Lenahan's was sold off to Eddy Scavone, RIP, one of the finest men who ever lived. The building later became the transplanted Wilkes-Barre Republics Club.

Eddie smiled every day as he served liquid and food fare for his very pleased Mayflower customers. His wife Betsy was always there to make sure all was well. When Eddie took over this spot in the Mayflower, he renamed it SuCaLi's and now we all know it as the new location of the Wilkes-Barre Republic Club, which has had a storied existence in Wilkes-Barre for sure. Check out the Rolling Mill Hill chapter.

Sucali's ($$)

★★★★★ See 1 Review

View Menu

280 S Sheridan St
Wilkes Barre, PA 18702 (Map & Directions)
(570) 823-6390

Hours

This restaurant has been reported as permanently
closed. Click here if it has reopened.

Monday:	Closed
Tuesday:	Closed
Wednesday:	Closed
Thursday:	Closed
Friday:	Closed
Saturday:	Closed
Sunday:	Closed

I became familiar with this shuffleboard site when it was SuCaLi's. After dinner at Jim Dandy's after Happy Hour at the Station on Market Street in years back, my wife and I found ourselves playing shuffleboard with the Roberts' brothers et ux, at SuCaLi's.

Eddie Scavone had named SuCaLi's after his daughters Susan, Carol, and Lisa. They had a really nice shuffleboard and my father learned to love to play there after the second location of the Wilkes-Barre Republic Club burned down. Dad liked this as much as any place his shuffleboard career had ever taken him. He also like Eddie Scavone and Betsy, and the kids who bartended. My brother Ed had found it before any of us.

To repeat parts of this story, it helps to know that when the Republic Club on Blackman Street burned down in the 1990's, my dad no longer had a regular place to shoot. So, bother Ed and I and Joe found SuCaLi's, and he loved it. Ed found it first. It was clean and nice and inviting, and we would bring others there often for shuffleboard, some draughts, and great dinners.

Ironically after it became our place to go to play shuffleboard after the Club burned down, just a few years ago, the Su –Ca-Li building was christened as the new home of The Wilkes-Barre Republic Club.

There were some other great haunts in the Mayflower. Pete Simakoski, for example, had a great place on the corner of Grant & Stanton streets. The miners loved it when they got off duty and some never would have even cared to see the sun again as it was never out for them.

Their wives however, like most wives of miners in those days were not so happy about the men from the mines clearing their throats of the dust with too many shots and beers. The wives were as they say in today's jargon—well let's just say they were extremely upset and they would come in to places like Pete's and find their men and drag them home so they could eat, sleep and face another day in the mines even before the next sun-up.

Frank Radaszewski had a prime location on the corner of Huber & Stanton streets. His marriage partner Josie and he enjoyed more than a few snooches from the establishment and they loved to host the same Polish Girls as those who entertained at Parada's. The neighborhood loved seeing the Polish Dancers dancing. They were great days in the Mayflower Section of Wilkes-Barre. .

Before Bucky Joseph had issues with the owners of Stanton Lanes, one of the largest bowling alleys in the state at the time, he ran a great evening tavern in the same building. However, due to PA's blue laws, Bucky's Ten Pin could not be in the line of sight from the real ten pin spotters at the bowling lanes.

So, though it existed, unless you took the outside entrance, you could never see into the "Ten Pin Bar" from the lanes. You could not watch anybody—your friends or anybody else's friends bowl from Bucky Joseph's Ten Pin Bar. These surely are silly laws but they were enforced at the time, nonetheless.

I know of a few wonderful folks who confessed years ago to having met at Harvey's Lake at a gathering. Yes Carol Anstett and John Anstett, aka Emery Hawthorn and Rhonda Bascombe, from Rutland Vermont, unknowingly had upgrades of their Ten Pin dating pictures placed in the Times Leader as if they were one of the weddings that weekend. Ever since, the Marie Mericle charade, submitters get a phone call from the paper to assure they and their subjects actually exist. OK, it was Joe and Jeanne Elinsky, who were the perpetrators but we all applauded. Marie busted a gut.

Carol A. lived in the Mayflower most of her life so she should have known better while sporting the name of Demmick. Joey, her bro, a fine baseball player from GAR now lives in Houston Texas. He disavows all knowledge of the Hawthorne's and he claims that maple syrup comes from a tree.

The Wonderful Anstetts, when spoofed and now back as regular citizens have two wonderful children Erica and Johnnie, and a son in law named Ed, who is just as nice as the other kids. Johnnie A, Director at WBRE has a significant other name Katie.

Well, the 'stetts finally got their signals straight at the Ten Pin Bar in Stanton Lanes. Bucky Joseph took no liability. Both "tea-totallers," they were there watching others and found the literary phrase: "What are you looking for... a little conversation?" to be quite appropriate. This catch phrase helped them to decide to tie the knot simply because they had fallen in love. No words were actually needed.

These are just a few of the stories from the fully-clothed city, Wilkes-Barre PA right before the glory days, which receded along with the flood waters.

Bucky Joseph, RIP, was a great guy and a great businessman. He had some problems with the Stanton Lanes management, and he took his phenomenally successful Ten Pin bar and went home.

He set up shop in the Heights on Northampton Street as you guessed it, it was "The Ten Pin Bar," and since that time, he has not given anybody any stories to top the Anstett / Demmick saga that I just told you all. I know, because my dad, my younger brother Joe and I, one day decided to go up to the Heights section to check the stories out.

Another great place in the Heights, now that Lennie moved out—that seems to have pizza just like Tommy's Pizza corner in Kingston is Norms on 275 N Sherman St. They also serve beer. It is a huge welcoming place and groups, such as the GAR class of 1965, spent many sessions there working on their 50th reunion, Norms is most accommodating, and their fare is absolutely delicious.

Norm's makes most of us in Wilkes-Barre wonder why they even permit the notion that they are like some mythical place in Kingston as a possibility

Enjoy!

Chapter 22 Wilkes-Barre Section: Goose Island

This is the area located in the southwestern area of the city between Rolling Mill Hill and South Wilkes-Barre. It is below the railroad tracks off Blackman Street and before South Main Streets. There is a lot of greenery and outright forestry in the area.

Ya gotta be tough to live in Goose Island

I lived close to Goose Island as a kid and our paper route extended well into this mystical area. If there was anything to do but search out milkweed plants and blackberries in the summer time, with my trusty 26" bike, and a bucket attached to the handle bars, I think I would have known about it. Goose Island was the place. But, other than nature, there was little to behold.

The Goose Island Pub and Grub on Division Street, which existed long enough to still be searchable on the Internet was not there when I travelled and scoured the area. In fact, it is still not there. In a later edition of this book, I hope to have gained the original name of this establishment and I will include as much as I know at that time.

Goose Island may have had some geese at one time but they are no longer registered with the gaming commission, and there is no longer any hunting permitted in Goose Island.

By the way, the hallmark of the "Pub and Grub," judging from the site I found on the Web is that it is a mere .7 miles from Pizza Hut. How about that for a claim to fame? Unfortunately, Pizza Hut as many know folded up operations in Wilkes-Barre early this month, 2015. How about that?

One thing I do remember about Goose Island, Wilkes-Barre Pa is that there were a lot of really tough kids living there—when I was a kid. I would add that you had to be pretty tough to live and play in Goose Island. I'll vouch for that!

Wilkes-Barre Section: Other Neighborhoods and Sub-neighborhoods

Of course there are other smaller neighborhoods and sub-neighborhoods, such as Brookside, which we briefly discussed, Upper Miners' Mills, Lower Miners' Mills, Barney Farms, and Riverside Park to name just a few. I think the sections help Wilkes-Barre identify where things are and the folks have a second identity. I think it would be nice if there was a map that showed all of the sections and had the streets clearly marked by section. One day that may be done as Wilkes-Barre returns to glory.

Chapter 23 Wilkes-Barre Section: Central City

Downtown Wilkes-Barre is our uptown.

The central city area of Wilkes-Barre is now referred by most today as "downtown" but to some of us, it will always be "uptown." That's what we called it until more than likely we began watching TV and the movies. Our uptown area in Wilkes-Barre business circles is our central city section. It all starts with the commercial side of Public Square.

This area is situated between South and North Streets, and bordered by River Street and Wilkes-Barre Boulevard to the West and East respectively. It is the original foundation of Wilkes-Barre—the 16 blocks claimed by the Connecticut settlers who founded the city. Throughout the City's history, the area has remained the business hub for all of Luzerne County. It is still that way today though there is a lot less business.

During the City's boom years, which we may think of as its glory years of the past, this small area was home to the headquarters of more than 100 national corporations. Today, it still houses the NEPA Headquarters for Verizon, Citizen's Bank, Blue Cross, PNC Bank, Luzerne National Bank, Guard Insurance, and a number of other smaller companies. An estimated 40,000 people live and/or work in Downtown Wilkes-Barre every day.

Since the 1972 flood, Wilkes-Barre has been in a decline in a lot of ways but it is far from dead. With some new leadership and a lot more focus, we optimists are hoping to see the oxygen come back just in time to bring our fair City back to glory.

Never a dull moment in Wilkes-Barre

We have already discussed the uptown attractions of days gone by and we have already discussed a number of current sites. Notably absent from our CYC and the YMCA uptown tour in prior chapters were the spots that younger, middle-aged, and older adults would frequent in their trips uptown. We are going to take that tour right now, and we may stop to find a spot the young would like also.

So far, in this book, we surely have discovered that there are a lot of interesting sections in Wilkes-Barre and yes, there is some overlap. For example, where does North End begin exactly on North Main Street? Does it begin after North Street or does it begin at the Square? Where does South Wilkes-Barre begin? Why are there *South Wilkes-Barre; North End* and *East End* sections but there is no West End section? In my research, I have found so far that there are no answers to any of these questions. But, that is OK!

If somebody has the definitive story of the sectional boundaries of Wilkes-Barre, we promise to print it in a subsequent volume or edition for sure. For right now, we choose to be very inclusive. Central City therefore includes North Main to North Street and North Washington to North Street etc. as does North End. The same goes for Central City and South Wilkes-Barre.

A walk from the Square through North End

GUS GENETTI HOTEL
Wilkes Barre, Pa.

Let's take a walk around this area from yesteryear to today in order to see what we find. We'll start at North Main from the Square and go just a few blocks, then we'll turn and head East towards North Pennsylvania Avenue passing North Washington Street. We'll turn and go south at North Penn Ave and eventually wind up at Gus Genetti's, where we will end this chapter. In the next chapter, we will add up the buildings and make a move back towards Public Square A few chapters from now, we'll be walking down South Main Street.

Moving up North Main Street from the Square, let's say it is the 1960's or 70's (or different dates as noted in the text.) We will hit a historical spot before we even get a few feet from the Square. It may not be in anybody's historical registry but it is in a lot of people's memories.

Some say this spot was Perugino's and some others say it was the # 1 Pub, while still others suggest that it was Perugino's # 1 Pub. Whichever way you see it, most people who were around in the 1960's know about it; and remember it well.

There have been a lot of famous bartenders such as Mickey Habib, who many know once performed magic for the # 1 Pub. Most of these tenders of Bar were in action long before I was of age—or even close.

However, there were two bartenders of fine repute, of whom I am acutely aware. They are Bob Lewis and Harry Lewis. I personally never saw them in action at the # 1 Pub because I was "too young," but I was surely close to being of age. I got to see their routine many times after they moved on to their own place on North Washington & Bennett Streets.

These two pros from Swoyersville, were at the # 1 Pub for several years. While I was going for my Data Processing degree at King's College in the 1960's, my classmates, who were all about a year older than I, found Harry and Bob serving intoxicants ferociously to keep up with the customer demands at the # 1 Pub.

Having had many business courses at King's, a specific crew of Kingsmen, including Charlie Cannon, Joe Grant, George Mohanco, Carmen Pascucci, Dennis Grimes, Gerry Rodski, Vic Margevich and other older Data Processing Majors, along with Stanley Sudo, a Business major, Stanley Benjamin, and Ron Steve—both Bio majors, and others from King's found the # 1 Pub to be simply number one in handling the needs of all majors, who were almost twenty-one years of age. Reportedly, Benjamin in his chosen military profession as a surgeon, operated successfully on President Reagan.

All you had to be was from King's or Wilkes College (not a
University yet in the 1960's) and you were automatically old
enough in the 1960's to consume. Charlie and the "boys" had
begun their trek to thirst quenching from the campus area of
King's College and from what I have been told, they were often
thirsty. During these early years at King's I had been dating a
young lady from my former high school, Meyers, and so the
"boys," did not get me to frolic much until the young lady
chose to set me free. Then, I knew for sure.

These compadres all knew about the # 1 Pub, on the corner of
the Square and North Main Street, as well as Walkers' Pub up
a bit on the left looking from Public Square, right by the Sickler
Bike Shop. They also knew about the S & W for life saving
food treatments after some liquid at the # 1 Pub or elsewhere,
and, they also knew about Senunas, when "Helen," ran it in
the old building that is now part of King's by East Jackson
Street.

Bob and Harry Lewis who were mainstays at the # 1 Pub in
the late 1960's, eventually found enough capital and enough
favor with clientele that they decided to take their bartending
magic to their new spot on East Bennett and North
Washington streets in North End. Technically, their new place
was both in Central City and North End.

Gonda's, which changed hands just a few years ago was also
on E. Bennett on North Main Street, and until the proprietors
moved to Florida, they too ran a successful business.

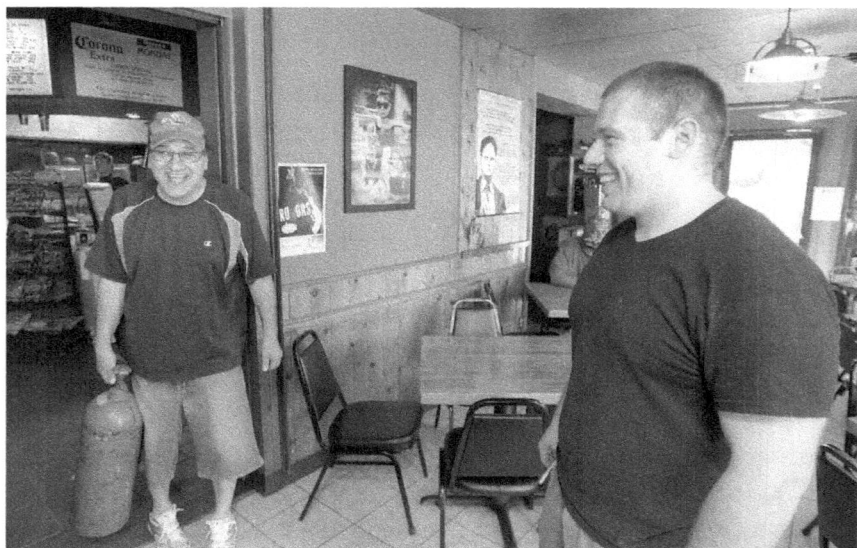

Gondas, an insider viewpoint

Bob and Harry Lewis did not care about Gonda's, Walkers, Senunas' or any other place once they sprung themselves free from just bartending to a working ownership. They simply called their place, Lewis'.

Their ad In the Wilkes-Barre Record was captivating and surely was a huge draw. It always read: "Red Carpet Service; Color TV for Viewing." Who could ask for more if you were nineteen or twenty years old—almost legal. They did have a red carpet as you walked in and they had a color TV which was often viewed. After a long day at class, or a mid-day cut, their Chile was always the best, with or without a Stegmaier.

Bob Lewis, the senior partner in the Lewis' enterprise, and my future father-in-law were great friends. Until it was too late, I did not know that. That story will never be told...Hah!

When I turned 21 at midnight on that special night in 1969, I was at Lewis's celebrating my birthday along with a number of friends already mentioned. My best friend, Dennis Grimes asked Harry Lewis if he was going to buy me a beer for my birthday. It was 12:01 AM and with the change in days came my 21st birthday. I was now legal but it did not seem any different to me. But to Bucko, who had been twenty-one for more than three months, it was a big deal. So, he asked!.

I had been a regular at Lewis's for more than a year. Harry said to Dennis: "How old is he?" Dennis looked at his watch and said twenty-one!. It was funny. Even Harry got a chuckle out of it. I was a regular patron.

Long after we graduated from King's we kept going back to Lewis's and we donated more of our incomes to Lewis's Café before we were 25 than we did to King's, though most, if not all of us, were members of King's Century Club where membership required a donation of a century note ($100.00). We hit Lewis's every Friday night that we could, even when we lived out of town. Other than on Saturday nights, when we would bring our current best girl friends to Lewis's for a few pitchers, I do not ever recall seeing a young lady in the Place. I do recall Rose, a lady even older than I am now at that time. who became a good friend to us all, watching some color TV and listening and laughing with us all.

Some of us would come from Utica, NY, and others would come from Rochester or Syracuse or Poughkeepsie NY. Many worked for IBM and others worked for Sylvania or Kodak. We did not all live locally at the time but our parents' did and so we lived in Wilkes-Barre on weekends. I never officially changed my address for the two years in which I spent time in Ogdensburg, NY or Utica.

We loved to play shuffleboard as a skill game at Lewis' in the early evening hours before we went to places like Art Stock's Colonel's Garter in prime time for some ragtime or rock music. Bob Emma and Georgiana, or Joe Kreidler and the "We Too" often were headliners there. It was a lot of fun.

There were some future notables in our crowd at Lewis's. As upperclassmen, we did not know them so well. But they did make their share of noise at the café. They included underclassmen Fatty Brislin, Scowl, Mark Ciavarella, and some in the real senior ranks such as John Jacob Gazeimis, Jacob (pronounced Yawcub), and Joe Pruller from St. Nicks. Last time I saw Joe was at a St. Nick's event in 2014. He looked great. He is now with the Lord.

Mr. Pruller was 101 and he looked like he could still play a great game of shuffleboard. Unfortunately, Joe passed away right before Christmas, 2014. I'll never forget him. He was a good man; always remembered me from our days of competition at Lewis' and he was a great shuffleboard player. All these people made Lewis' a place of wonderment of conversation and sportsmanship centered on darts, shuffleboard, and song.

My Uncle Pat Kelly from Espy St. in Parsons, and my uncle Bud Hopko who later in life lived alone down the street at the corner of East Jackson and Washington Streets, regularly played Lewis's board. Pruller, Uncle Pat, and Uncle Bud were great players and they all hated to lose. That is part of what made it so much fun to play. Sometimes we would even win. My dad took my mom out in the neighborhood each weekend so even though his brother played shuffleboard at Lewis's with his son, my father chose not to leave his Rolling Mill Hill Haunts. OK, Mom told him he could not go.

The Screamer and the Torch

Lewis' was just down North Washington from Tom and Eva's. To my chagrin to this day, in all those years I never got to Tom and Eva's. I loved Lewis' and I was always trying to win the game that I was in. Yet, today, I sure wish I had taken the time when it was apparently a really nice place.

One last story that I must tell about Lewis' stars one of my greatest friends Frannie Kurilla who died too young seven years ago. Frank had a great voice like he belonged as the lead in a choir. He and I and others would harmonize "Down by the Old Mill Stream," and other old time tunes and we'd get everybody singing at Lewis'.

One night as we left after some great song, the police were responding with the Paddy Wagon to a raucous on E. Jackson Street. We had nothing to do with it. I mean it. But, circumstances brought us into the East Jackson Street story, nonetheless.

Our exit from Lewis' was precisely the time that police were passing the Café' on their way to a called-in situation. Dennis Grimes let out a big happy yelp that was like a loud Yahoo type scream. We probably were having such a nice time at Lewis's that we should not have left. Frannie Kurilla, all full of the happiness we had experienced in Lewis' simultaneously set off a fifteen second photographic flare.

I had never seen such brightness. It lit up the whole block so brightly that it put out the photo-sensitive street lights. When the flare burned out, other than a few neon signs, the area was pitch black. I had never heard of or seen anything like that. Apparently Hollywood for years had used these flares for day shots filmed at night. For fifteen seconds, just as the police were passing, Lewis' parking lot was brighter than a sunny day.

The photoelectric cells in the street lights thought morning had come early. Needless to say, we were discovered and the Police no longer went to the call on Jackson Street as they felt the problem was in Lewis' parking lot.

I was in my car when the police got there but Frannie and Dennis were lollygagging in the magic of the moment. The Paddy Wagon took the two of these happy blokes to a Magistrate in Kingston, where we bailed them out quickly and we were on our way. Ever since that day, we refer to this as the case of "The Screamer" and The Torch."

Tom and Eva's up the street from Lewis'

Time changes lots of things. In Wilkes-Barre's glory years, there was no real problem with drugs that I can recall, and there were few unseemly people. I got word in the late 1980's, many years after my last visit to Lewis's, and several years after Bob Lewis had passed away that Harry Lewis, the other brother in the bartending duo, had also died. Lewis' building was torn down some time in the 1990's.

Tom and Eva's, 176-178 N. Washington Street, a spot I never visited to my chagrin, unfortunately ran into their own mess as the drug trade got really big in that section of town.

In February, 1995, Sascha Brodsky, writing for the Times Leader described one of the final nails in the coffin that ultimately brought Tom and Eva's down:

"They came and you would have to serve them," said Tom Bartosh Sr. "This is the worst time in all these years."
In 1995, the police padlocked the doors of Tom and Eva's Cafe, 176-178 N. Washington St. They shut down the bar and made several arrests at the location and they arrested fourteen other pushers close by. The charge was delivering controlled substances.

At the time in 1995, Wilkes-Barre detective Bill Maguire called Tom & Eva's and the vicinity, which included Lewis' as the "bases of operation" for the drug trade. The Senior Bartosh owned the building and his son Tom Jr. at the time ran the place. Tom Jr. expressed his own frustration to the Times Leader.

He told Ms. Brodsky that he had suspected drug dealing in the bar, but fear kept him from doing anything about it: "What am I going to do, go over and say `hey man, are you selling dope,'...I'd get a bottle over my head."

The tavern and the locale was getting so bad that its neighbors were very nervous as well. "I was really glad when I walked past it this morning and saw it was closed," said Winnie Pugh, who at the time was the manager of Wilkes-Barre Trophy Inc.

"It would be better if the place doesn't reopen unless they clean up their act," offered another neighbor.

Not too long after this incident in 2000, a new place emerged in town on the former site of Tom & Eva's. It is still called "Beer Boys." Everything that I hear about it, is on the up and up, and "they say" that it is a fine place to enjoy a quaff.

And so, being located at 176 N. Washington Street on the foothills of North End, Beer Boys can also be categorized as part of Central City Wilkes-Barre. This is a bar that serves great beers with over 44 on tap at last count. Their claim to fame is that many of the taps feature beers that cannot be had anywhere else in the area.

Rumor has it that the wings are good and the pizza is also better than average. This mostly beer bar features good service and a friendly knowledgeable staff. They just celebrated their fifteenth Anniversary in January 2015. Thank you Beer Boys for being part of the solution to the glory days of Wilkes-Barre and not part of the problem

Right across Washington Street from Lewis' in the 1970's was a King's College night student lounge called Gus' Inn. Somebody who lives in my house pursuing her degree at that time, would go to the study sessions at Gus.'

Working down North Washington Street from Lewis', which we often called the Café Lewie (Louie)—right by the new police building and City Hall was a "downtown" neighborhood watering hole named Ward's. It was there for years situated by the Eagle's Club Bowling Lanes. Like many things in our town, since it began its downhill spiral after the flood, many things, including the bowling alleys and Ward's simply disappeared. I suspect that few of Ward's regulars even know what happened.

Going over one more full block to the northeast, not counting State Street in the Central City / North End Section on

Pennsylvania Avenue, you would find Eddie White's Café, owned by then Councilman Eddie White, who also in the glory years was the owner and coach of the Wilkes-Barre Barons Basketball Team. White's was just down from the Thomas Buildings on Penn Ave and was within walking distance from the State Office Buildings. The office building's proximity to White's certainly helped Eddie's business.

Moving back towards East Market street, and walking briskly, we are all familiar with the fantastic Gus Genetti Hotel, now the only big-time hotel in Central City Wilkes-Barre. Years ago, however, the place was called the Hotel Redington.

Just like Gus has some fine bars within his place over the years, so also did the Hotel Redington. For example, The Redington's Bar and Grill Room was a favorite of locals and visitors.

Redington Bar & grill Room circa 1940

One day about ten years ago, I had the pleasure of being Gus Genetti at the wedding of Paul and Melissa Sabol. Gus was in a good mood and he gave me his ID card. The staff were perplexed as I tried to literally bark out orders but they gave me no special service. (I do have the gift of bark.). I had fun with it nonetheless and Gus and I had our pictures taken together. Nice guy!

With the Ramada now being King's College, the Genetti good fortune in Wilkes-Barre is now assured for many more years. At 80 some years of age, Mr. Genetti surely wants to be part of Wilkes-Barre's coming renewed glory days. After all, according to the master Innkeeper, he had read "The Power of Positive Thinking" by Norman Vincent Peale when he was just 18 and it changed his life.

Gus Genetti in interviews over the years tells everybody that he just does not give up. A few years ago, we remember Mr. Genetti doing ads for General Hospital after he had successful Heart Bypass surgery. He runs a great business of which all of Wilkes-Barre can be proud. He surely does not give up.

Before Mr. Genetti's father Gus Sr., purchased the downtown Wilkes-Barre hotel in 1963, as noted above, it had been the Hotel Redington, which itself had been built in 1906. "I don't care how many hotels they build out there," Genetti once said… "the historic downtown brings people."

I agree, and thus, we have to protect our history. Frank Pasquini, a very good friend of mine and my wife Pat's who is not giving up on his own health battles, one time queried about what Mr. Genetti put on his Cheerios every morning to remain so active and successful. Hopefully our friend Frank has that recipe now. Pasquini added in a recent interview with Denise Allabaugh of the Times Leader: "He [Gus Genetti] has been one of the prime engines of the revitalization of downtown Wilkes-Barre." When we get a leadership change in City Hall and even if we don't, I am sure Gus Genetti will be doing his best for Wilkes-Barre. He's that kind of guy.

Just a few days ago, Gus hosted a grand celebration for Frank Pasquini who was suffering from cancer rand eventually passed to the Lord in Heaven. With Gus's prime engine attitude, Frank looked like he was ready to use a page from the Genetti playbook to help him in his own fight. Knowing Frank, I know God is on his side, and I pray HE treats Frank kindly and helps him and Donna get through this. Frank is now in heaven. He does a good imitation of Dan Flood so he is entertaining friends of the Lord.

We all prayed for Frank to be well again. I recall telling Frank to look at Gus after the flood in a picture on the next page. Like you, he was not demoralized. Like you... Gus picked himself up and dusted himself off and ran again through the huge 1972 storm clouds sent by his God. See this picture of a young Gus, after the 1972 flood, working with his staff to get his place ready for business:

Gus Genetti washes pump as other employees wash office equipment.

Picture above is 1972

In the next chapter we will move around this block on East Market Street and finally wind up on Public Square. Amen!

Chapter 24   East Market to the Square from Genetti's

Functioning Central NJ Station in WB circa 1900

Same Site as the Station Restaurant, Iron Horse Saloon circa 1990.

Heights side trip up the road first

Of course, now that we are on E. Market close by Central City, those from the Heights Section are wondering why this was not flagged in the Heights Section information that we already covered. Well, we're trying to get the wondrous buildings from Central City noticed a little bit here and so now it is the right time to fully admit that Genetti's and everything else in this chapter until we reach the Square from East Market Street, is also in the Heights. We have already snuck our way out of North End.

In 2015, across Penn Avenue from Genetti's is a huge empty lot used for Gus' banquet parking. Moving further up the road is a nice Citizens Bank branch building and then a parking lot and then the remains of what was the glorious Station Hotel and Bar. Before there was such a Hotel and Bar, the site housed the Central New Jersey Passenger Railroad Station. Even before that it was The Lehigh and Susquehanna Railroad Station.

This property was a big deal long after the flood in the late 1980's and the early 1990's. It was the old Central New Jersey Station, which had grown into disrepair by then. It is shown first in its operational grandeur with steam engines and later after its demise and revitalization by the Roth Family, it is shown in the splendor of its reincarnation as a grand restaurant and hotel in the mid 1980's.

On their site, Terrastories.com talks about how magnificent the Station building was inside, but they have little good to say about the corruption and the politics that permitted it to go dormant and then fall into disrepair. Check out that magnificent double decker bus in the picture on the prior page.

"Within its walls are awe-inspiring works of original craftsmanship: hand-carved mahogany, hand-laid terrazo, and—perhaps most compelling—a resplendent, curved staircase banister, a spiral exemplar of roccoco. Just look inside this station and you'll immediately know why it earned its place in, 'Great American Railroad Stations.' "

I sure hope this magnificent structure is not ripped down as the Sterling was. We can do better.

There is no doubt that The Station, as we knew it and loved it was as good a place in all its incarnations, as it gets. When it was still in operation, with its hotel rooms built on railroad tracks in delectably styled train cars, each equipped with a modern day bathroom, people from out of town loved coming to Wilkes-Barre.

Magnificent Mahogony Steps Lead to Upscale Upstairs Dining Rooms

What a look! What a place! Somehow in Wilkes-Barre, we have a hard time hanging on to the great things from our past. The Roth family did a great job of giving us something we should have kept. Deep Thank You's to the Roth Family who revitalized the Station into a masterpiece.

Before I retired from IBM, Our Scranton location was a part of a bigger IBM Bethlehem Branch Office. The one time that the Branch meeting was to be held in Scranton, I suggested that we dine at the Station in Wilkes-Barre. It is about twenty miles from our Office to the Station, so I asked Mrs. Roth if she would send their double decker bus to our office to pick up forty of us. She was thrilled to do so. We enjoyed one of the nicest dinners ever that evening—the works on IBM.

Despite how great the place was and how great the dinner was, the highlight for many was that great ride back and forth on the Double Decker Bus. It was simply magnificent—the whole thing. What a class act! I had parked my car in the Station Lot and had scored a ride back to Scranton earlier in the day so I could be on this magnificent bus for the trip.

See more station pictures and a recount of corrupt politics that our area has been fighting for years with the help of the FBI. http://www.terrastories.com/bearings/pa-train-station

Stegmaier Brewery East Market Tracks Where Station Was

Stegmaier Brewery in the flesh!

Across the Street from the Station. Whoops, not true … across the railroad tracks from The Station was the Stegmaier Brewery, which is discussed elsewhere in this book in greater detail. Note in the picture, the railroad tower to protect the people, the horses, and perhaps a few horseless carriages from the big locomotive trains of the day. Any bets on whether a horseless carriage could power itself up Market Street?

Moving towards Public Square from Genetti's

Let's now go back to the great Gus's spot, which at the time of this picture was the Hotel Redington on Penn Ave and East Market. Let's start moving towards Public Square but let's take a respite to name the Hotels on the same block with Gus's properties.

The Hotel Hart, directly across East Market Street from the Hotel Redington, near North Pennsylvania Avenue had its own day in the sun when Wilkes-Barre was a boom town. It was on a corner with four other glory day era hotels. The Hart was doing pretty well in in its day and it competed with the Hotel Sterling quite well. At one point the property was transferred to a Mr. Mallow who represented the Sterling at the time.

Hotel Hart Across East Market from Genettis Circa 1904

Hotel Hart, Wilkes Barre, Pa.

The name Hart is big and still held in kind regard in this town as the family was quite famous in local government and in Wilkes-Barre business activity. Daniel Hart, for example was Mayor of Wilkes-Barre from January 1920 to February 1933. The Harts are a fine family and they always loved Wilkes-Barre.

Along with Jay's Hotel, and the Grand Hotel, shown on the next pages below, the Hart was demolished in the 1970s when Wilkes-Barre felt compelled to use redevelopment dollars in central city and all sections to blow away historical landmarks rather than try to help these businesses make a comeback.

How many parking lots do we need?

Unfortunately, our glory days were in the rear view mirror soon after the flood. And though many of us were looking for the easy way out from this terrible disaster, our city leaders could probably have figured out another way of saving Wilkes-Barre, rather than using Redevelopment Authority dollars to destroy the town.

How many parking lots do we need? That is why it has been so hard to make an economic comeback. Many buildings of consequence are gone, and many of those that are not gone, other than Genetti's thankfully, are looking for the Axe Man. They would love to find some money from the feds so they too can rip down their buildings—or so somebody paying attention might conclude.

The Grand Hotel was across Pennsylvania Avenue from the Hotel Redington. It is now a parking lot for Gus Genetti's. It was torn down after the flood of 1972. Jay's Hotel was not exactly on the corner but it is across East Market from The Grand. It also met its demise shortly after the 1972 flood. The four corners of hotels can be seen in the picture below. The picture was snapped during the flood of 1972:

The Kryger Family, Wilkes-Barre Glory Assets

Working back up to Public Square, on the right side of the street were some famous buildings including the Hotel Hart, that have in recent times morphed mostly into the State Office Building. Famous Band leader Brunon Kryger, who died in the early 1950's ran his Wilkes-Barre music business in one of these fine buildings, which no longer exist. Kryger was a master and a great family man. His progeny include three other music masters, two of whom have joined their dad in the Music Hall of Fame. More than likely, all four should be in the Hall of Fame.

Four Corners Genetti's, Grand Hotel, Jay's Hotel, and the Hotel Hart

Kryger chose Wilkes-Barre as a place to live in 1938 after he came to Philadelphia in 1935 from the Old World to marry his childhood sweetheart. Love is at the top of the agenda for all good people. They say that Brunon Kryger had such a great voice, he could have been an operatic tenor. When he arrived in America, he joined a Polish theatrical group touring the country.

Victor Records signed him to make a series of Polish folk songs. Many, we might call polkas. In time Kryger would be crowned as the King of Polka's in Pittsburgh Pennsylvania.

While not in America too long, and before he took off for the Northeast, Brunon formed his own music school in Phila. teaching voice and violin. Kryger then discovered an opening as a church organist and he arrived in Shenandoah, PA where he became choir director of the Chopin Choir.

His parish decided it needed a full blown orchestra, and Kryger organized his own on their behalf. In 1938, he loved the orchestra "business" so much that he chose to devote all of his time to being an orchestra Maestro and he moved to Wilkes-

Barre, a big city at the time. He brought his whole family at the time as Wilkes-Barre was reasonably close to Shenandoah.

From there, Mr. Kryger became the best in the polka field. He recorded for RCA Victor and Harmonia. He had a number of big-time hits including: "Hula-La Polka," "Accordion Polka," "Ho-Siup Oj Dana Polka," "Rock Glen Polka," "Cornet Polka," and others. He was a fine man and a Wilkes-Barre legend. His records sold well wherever they were available in every state in our country as well as in Germany, France, and England.

Kryger's family lived in South Wilkes-Barre and they operated the Kryger's Music Store on East Market Street. Lucian Kryger, a son, was just about as famous as his dad. He lived in South Wilkes-Barre until he died at home eight years ago in January 2014. Lucian P. Kryger, like his dad, was definitely a legend in the polka field, and he was known also and perhaps even better as "a wonderful family man and friend to all who knew him."

Lucian was born when the family lived in Shenandoah before his Dad, Brunon and his mom, Alexandria Wroclawski Kryger moved to Wilkes-Barre to take up real roots. Pictures of Brunon Kryger are not as plentiful as those of his famous children who formed the Kryger Brothers' Orchestra. Therefore, I have decided to show one of Brunon Kryger's albums below:

Buffalo Gals Polka by Brunon Kryger

In the early 1950's when their dad passed away, the Kryger brothers, George, "Jerry", and Bruce, established The Kryger Brothers Orchestra. When the brothers retired, Lucian continued the band as The Kryger Orchestra until 1996. He was nominated for a Grammy Award in 1988 for his "Polka Mania" album and he, along with his father & brother Bruce, were enshrined in The Polka Hall of Fame.

The Polka Hall of fame had never inducted three members of the same family. The Kryger family in my eyes are all in the Wilkes-Barre Hall of Fame, and they surely have added to maintaining the glory years of Wilkes-Barre City over many years. Wouldn't it be nice if....

For our edification, Lucian Kryger was also a member of the Blinded Veterans Association. As his whole family, he was a great American, and a great member of the Wilkes-Barre community. I am so glad to have taken the time to write about a real person in Wilkes-Barre who helped Wilkes-Barre be as good as it can be. Who'll be the next?

Down Washington Street on our way back to the Square

Now, by exploring the Kryger family store, we have moved one black towards Public Square. Let us now move down South Washington, past Gus G.'s in Central City. Let's recognize that now, before we make this temporary left, that we are on East Market, just one block from Public Square. As we make that left right now, the first building of substance on the left is the CYC, at 36 South Washington Street. It has been shepherded for years by Fr. John Terry & Tony English.

CYC Main Gymnasium Wilkes-Barre PA Scene of Many Dances

The Front of the CYC Building on Washington Street

The CYC opened its doors in 1948 and even though Father John Terry was not born yet, he oversaw the place for a zillion years. Thank You Father Terry. My kids went to pre-school there and loved it. In high school in 1963 and afterwards, I played as much basketball as I could in the gym while dancing as much as I could on Saturdays in the same gym. When we went to the CYC dances, the entrance was on the right side more than half way down the driveway. I forget how much the dances were maybe a quarter, I know they were cheap.

Yes, this is where the Saturday dances were held and where many activities for area youth were held, including many sporting events. When I first write this book in version 1, I could not find a picture of the outside of the building but the gym on the prior page was where it all happened. The CYC consumes most of this early block of South Washington when you make a left on South Washington after leaving Gus Genetti's place! It is a great place run by great people.

The new intermodal transportation facility, which I discuss in Chapter 25, is located directly across the street from the CYC.

Old Fell House

Let's sneak down South Washington a bit more before we come back to East Market Street.

Wilkes-Barre Officials Examine the Eicke Grate at the Old Fell House

At the Corner of East Northampton and South Washington in 1788, The Sign of the Buck was built. Later it was rechristened as the Old Fell House.

This great historic place in Wilkes-Barre was maintained by Jesse Fell, who is famous for developing a grate that would burn anthracite coal, thereby making possible the development of the anthracite industry. We all know, that in Wilkes-Barre's past glory days, mining anthracite and being able to burn anthracite inside was a really big deal for the city and surrounds.

Unfortunately, in what must have been an unintentional mistake made by a lot of important people, a local enterprise (reportedly a hospital) at the time had its eyes on the Old Fell

House for use as a parking lot. I still have not figured that one out.

Many of us recall that the Old Fell House disappeared almost overnight. At the time, it was a newly remodeled place run by the Mrochko family. For years after, left in its stead were weeds. At least, the famous Eicke grate shown in the picture above from the Old Fell House, is now at the Luzerne County Historical Society.

Give credit to those wanting to preserve the look of a Wilkes-Barre that once was. The Historical Society gives us a model for a Wilkes-Barre that should be. Thank them for many and Captain Clint's for many of the pictures in this book.

Isn't it nice that somebody cares so much about Wilkes-Barre's history and its future to preserve these wonderful pictures for us all? Yes, hard as it is to believe, our Wilkes-Barre officials, post glory days in 1986, permitted the Old Fell House to be razed for a parking lot, from a purchaser that really never needed the place. There was no real plan. No wonder so few trust government at any level. This historic site has remained fenced in and disused ever since.

Towards Public Square on East Market

If we turn back and come up North Washington Street past the CYC to East Market Street again, we can take a left and continue our trip west, back to Public Square. But, before we make the turn, let's look across the street. Notice City Hall!

If we had not gone down South Washington, when we were on East Market before, we would have simply moved further west by the Hotel Hart, and the Kryger Building, or now from the State Office Building, and we would have literally bumped into the magnificent City Hall Building.

When you look at the seal of the City imbedded in City Hall's entranceway, notice the honeybees. The bees are depicted in stained glass over the door of City Hall. They are emblematic of Wilkes-Barre's big boast in the nineteenth century that the city was as "busy as a beehive."

The stained glass window reflecting the seal on the next page is only one of the many striking late Victorian details that are built into this Hall, which is Wilkes-Barre's first municipal building.

Wilkes-Barre seal – busy as bees in a beehive

Wilkes-Barre's Beautiful City Hall

When built, City Hall presented an unusual combination of architectural styles. You can see at the base in the picture below the Redstone in Romanesque style; while the upper floors are Victorian banded brick with terra cotta. Why there were once even gargoyles and balconies.

At one time you could not miss the magnificent Queen Anne towers and gables at the roofline. These are shown in the original picture of City Hall on the next page. Though its towers and gables are no more, City Hall remains a building of substance, worthy of a full return to glory.

City Hall minus the gargoyles and the tower

The architects of this fine structure were William W. Neuer and Benjamin Davey, Jr. It was the home of Wilkes-Barre Mayors for well over a hundred years. Take a look at the old City Hall from the 1950's on the next page and then take a drive downtown and ask yourself if we can't do better? Glory days are not accustomed to phrases like, "I can't!"

Looking at these two pictures of city Hall, you can see how city officials saved a few bucks for their lack of concern for Wilkes-Barre City Hall's original architecture. Look at these pictures, please. Do you think this is really OK? It certainly does not work if you chinch on Wilkes-Barre's home building as a starter for a return to glory?

We all can notice what is wrong? Where is the tower and the magic in the current City Hall Building. How is it OK for us but it was not OK for our ancestors? We should fix this post haste. Somebody should want their name on the renovation and fund it for us. I like that idea. It was a remarkable building and should have been repaired.

Old City Hall with the gargoyles and the magnificent tower

Continuing the move to the Square

Various other shops and newsstands, including Baer's Variety store were on the route from Genetti's back to the Square. I think Mr. Baer was the father or uncle to Wayne Baer, one of my classmates at Meyers High School. By the way, Jim McGowan Sr., who was a great math teacher at Meyers, renamed Wayne Baer in Trig class to Polar.

Even teachers in the glory days had a great sense of humor. McGowan like the Monsignor, was a banquet speaker, and he tried out his jokes in Trig Class. He was pretty good!

Just one more block of commercial buildings on East Market Street and we are right back on the Public Square.

Chapter 25 The Commercial Square & Other Commercial sites Part I

The Paramount Theatre shown here as the Kirby Center
Public Square, Kirby Center, Luzerne Bank Bldg.

Turn left on Public Square from East Market Street for the commercial tour, The big building to its right is the Luzerne Bank Building. Moving down and today you hit Rodano's. In days of old the people of WB entered the Boston Candy Kitchen for a tummy full of treats. MMM!!! MMM!!!

Once you turn left on Public Square, you are greeted by what was the old Comerford Theatre, which became the Paramount in my lifetime. It is shown below in its current incarnation, The Kirby Center. Note the marquee lights going around the canopy.

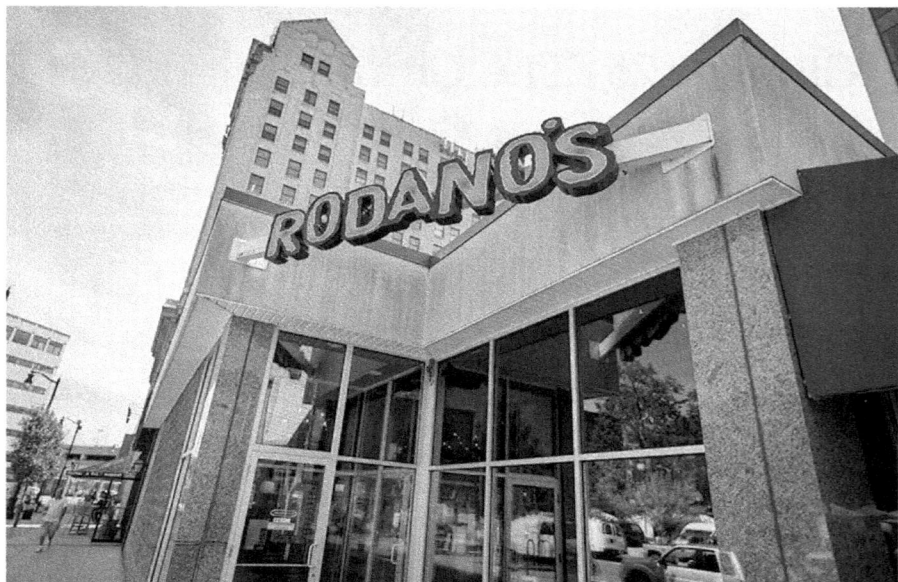

Coming down East Market Street, you make a left onto the Square- It's Rodano's

The places to be!

When we wrap up our tour around all of the Business District on Public Square and West Market Streets, etc. , we will repeat some of this if it is OK with you. To the right of the huge Bank Building is Rodano's and then comes Wilkes-Barre Center directly to the right of Rodano's. In days past the Boston Candy Kitchen and Isaac Long's store was right were Rodano's is today. The Planters Peanut Shop with the famous Peanut Man, who walked the Square with hat and cane, was on the corner of South Main and the Square on this same block. Check out the pictures and the captions below after the Kirby and Luzerne Bank immediately below.

Looking at the picture above, think about walking to the left of the Kirby. In days of glory, there were a number of multi-story buildings there, mostly non-descript, that filled the East Market Street block that we just toured in the last chapter. These were all taken down after the Flood of 1972. The Rodano's site is very new and a nice addition.

Now, imagine going up a set of steps to the left of the Kirby, to the second story of one of those buildings on East Market and the Square. You would be headed for the old Stardust Ballroom. It was on the second floor right next to the Paramount Theatre or so it seemed. Some of us imagined being on top of the Paramount when we were dancing in the Stardust Ballroom.

The Granada Ballroom was down this block of the Square and way past the Boston Candy Kitchen, you would walk left down South Main Street and it was on the left as you approached South Street. You also could have gotten there by walking from the CYC down Washington and over South St.

OUR BIRTHPLACE
WILKES-BARRE, PA
LUZERNE COUNTY

In the olden days, from the Square, you would say hello to Mr. Peanut on the corner before you went down South Main. Like the Stardust, the Granada was up a flight. A few addresses before the Granada was the Starfire Ballroom, also up a flight.

It has been so tough getting accurate addresses for things after so many years. When I wrote the original book early in 2015, my friends had convinced me that just to the left of the Kirby Center in the picture, there was a building that did not make it after the flood. They thought that its second floor was the Granada Ballroom, the scene for many fine Wilkes-Barre events over the years. They were wrong. It was the Stardust. The Granada was down South Main Street.

Is that all there is?

Most of the great stuff on the square is gone. The Public
Square in Wilkes-Barre today looks very much like the first
picture below taken from East Market Street. The picture on
the next page takes a view of the Northeastern side of the
Square as it looks today. Other pictures to follow show this
same area as it looked years ago.

Four large office structures are not quite occupied to full
capacity on Public Square. Yet, in recent years their occupancy
is not doing badly at all. These include Wilkes-Barre Center,
on the Kirby side of the square by Rodano's, shown in the 2nd
picture. It is the one time home of Frontier Communications.

Public Square Picture from East Market Street

October 20, 2008

Martz Building & Wilkes-Barre Square (formerly the Alltel Building)

Wilkes-Barre Center Building – Once Frontier

The Intermodal facility on South Washington with a pathway to Public Square in the back has helped occupancy on the prior buildings and other major office buildings on Public Square. Rob Finlay is the city's largest landlord, so he ought to know.

Back when the intermodal was coming on line in 2011, Finlay, President of Humford Equities, noted that the buildings, owned by the firm, have seen significant increases in occupancy in recent years even before the intermodal was completed. Finlay is convinced this occupancy increase has to do with a bus-free Public Square.

Intermodal South Washington Street WB Across from CYC

Not only does the intermodal provide over 700 parking spaces itself, it also gave back to the city about 80 diagonal spaces that were unavailable prior to bus traffic stops being eliminated from Public Square. "Without such bus traffic stops and pickups as a continual occurrence on the Square, Finlay said that "the intermodal, even before its opening, had resulted in over 600 new jobs having come to the downtown area." That is what we are looking for, for sure.

Finlay noted that the Wilkes-Barre Center at 39 Public Square, a 10-story office building with 116,381 square feet of space had a 45 percent occupancy for three years and it was up to 97% in 2011. Unfortunately Frontier moved out of the building in the interim and occupancy for now at Wilkes-Barre Center is just over 50%. I am rooting for Finlay to be right on the future of the City.

The Bicentennial Building at 15 Public Square—a six-story office building with a floor plan of 10,777 square feet—is just about filled. Only four thousand square feet were available as of February 2015.

15 Public Square Wilkes-Barre—Bicentennial Building

Midtown Village, which is not on the Square but important to Wilkes-Barre nonetheless, consists of three buildings with several storefronts and a courtyard in the middle. Finlay noted these are just about at full occupancy.

Midtown Village Sown South Main on the Right from Public Square

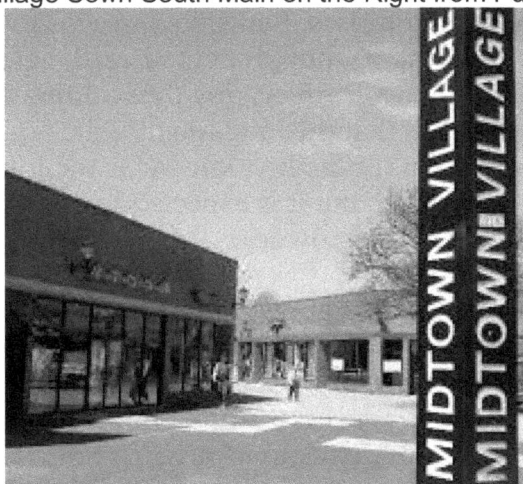

The Wilkes-Barre Square Building shown on page 206, across East Market from the Kirby, is home for the Geisinger Clinic and Verizon as well as the Comptroller of the Currency. From my research, I would conclude that the building is at capacity.

The Martz Building (just sold) is to the left of the Wilkes-Barre Square Building in the picture. After its recent ownership transfer in January 2015, it is expected to change names. It too appears to be at full occupancy. This is great for Wilkes-Barre. Now, if only we can figure out what to do about the major business corner at Franklin and West Market Streets.

Just as I was ready to close out this chapter of the book, I discovered that just last week, the seven-story former Martz building at 46 Public Square was transferred to a new owner for $4.54 million, according to a deed filed in Luzerne County Recorder of Deeds office.

The owner had been Frank M. Henry Associates, in partnership with Charles Parente and the Wilkes-Barre Industrial Development Authority. Looking at the deed filed January 9, the transfer was to PSA Realty.

The office for PSA Realty is in the Martz Building, 46 Public Square. Pagnotti Enterprises, Berkshire Asset Management, Lackawanna Insurance Group, Parente Beard, Mimmo's Pizza. and Comitz Law Firm occupy the building at just about capacity. The word is that the long-time Public Square business, operating in the facility, known as the Leo Matus News Stand, has closed; but it is expected to open in February or March 2015 with a new owner.

The Bicentennial Building at one time, contained all of PA Millers Mutual Insurance Company. When I was with IBM I was the systems engineer who was assigned to make sure PA Millers continued their success. After a number of years, PA Millers decided to move back to its original home on North Franklin Street. They moved back in the 1990's after a successful ten years in the Bicentennial Building.

The historical site on 72 North Franklin Street, shown on the next page, was built in 1935. When I was an IBM Senior Systems Engineer, ACE Agribusiness, then known as PMMIC at the time, were one of my clients. They used one of the biggest AS/400 machines that IBM made. It ran their entire insurance business at 72 North Franklin, then as they grew, they moved to the Bicentennial Building, and then, they added on to their historic building and moved back to 72 North Franklin Street.

It has always been a great company. In the 1980's Joseph Kologe was the IT Director, F.J. Gager was President. They chose IBM because IBM kept helping them be successful.

For sure Wilkes-Barre's days as a farming town are long gone. Yet, this elegant building was built to house the Pennsylvania Millers Mutual Insurance Company, which was formed in 1887 for the purpose of insuring gristmills against fire. The company insured such properties all across the United States. The first grist-mill erected in Wyoming Valley was on Mill Creek in Miners Mills.

In 1992, as noted lightly above Penn Millers chose to rehabilitate its original 1935 headquarters building, designed by Wilkes-Barre architect L. Verne Lacy in a combination of Art Moderne and Colonial Revival motifs. It joined the older historical section to a new office wing in the back. Today, the company is now called ACE Agribusiness. It continues its fine national service providing agriculture insurance policies from its new-again historic North Franklin Street quarters.

ACE Agribusiness PA Millers Mutual Insurance Co. original building.

Save the Irem Temple, Please!

Just down the street from ACE Agribusiness is another Wilkes-Barre City monument worth preserving. It is known as the Irem Temple. Many in Wilkes-Barre are supporting an effort right now to rehabilitate this grand building. The group and the initiative is called "The Irem Temple Mosque Restoration Project."

This monumental initiative is currently underway to stabilize, and eventually restore our region's national, historic, iconic landmark. The famous Irem Temple Mosque is located on 42-46 North Frankin Street in downtown (North End) Wilkes-Barre, Pennsylvania.

The Irem Temple Mosque is currently 107 years old and in dire need of funding to secure the building. Break-ins and thefts are a regular occurrence. Consequently, the building must first be secured to eliminate break-ins. Secondly, the group must secure funding to make the necessary reparations to secure an Occupancy Permit (electricity, heat, natural gas lines, working water / sanitary facilities, etc. Third, funding sources must be found for a full restoration. Items # 1 and #2 are most critical right now.

In order to achieve these goals, we need the people of northeastern Pennsylvania to make their voices heard! This author and many others encourage you all to call your state senators and tell them how you feel. We do not need another Sterling Hotel debacle.

Let your voices be heard! Thank you! Before King's College built its gymnasium on North Main Street in 1969, it used this terrific facility for all of its college gatherings including graduations. Great Rock Groups for years played in this great amphitheater. Wilkes-Barre must hang on to this historical landmark and make it whole again.

It sure would be nice if somehow King's or another great institution like King's, perhaps even Wilkes, chose to purchase the Irem Temple and restore it to glory. King's has been doing some great things like that lately. In fact, King's College is reportedly interested in buying Luzerne County's vacant Springbrook Water Company building on North Franklin Street in Wilkes-Barre, just up from the Irem. What a wonderful idea.

Irem Temple Mosque 59 N. Franklin St. in its glory days circa 1910

Irem Temple Mosque Inside—in disrepair circa 2013

Many in Wilkes-Barre do not know that The Irem Temple is the most spectacular Shriner's Temple in the world. Therefore the project to save it is very important. It will provide a substantial lift to our local economy. The main auditorium, shown in disrepair above, will be returned to its original configuration — a flat-floored hall. This would create a multi-use event space, allowing for everything from weddings to farmer's markets and ring-based sports. It would allow our community to attract the 50% of touring acts that demand this configuration (no seats on the main floor) and be synergistic with existing downtown venues. The rest of the building will be a museum that speaks to the revolutionary history (American and Industrial) of Wilkes-Barre and the Wyoming Valley. Heritage Tourism will be a broad-based driver of economic growth in this community and saving this building is the best next step.

Springbrook Water Company–Another Great Building

King's is moving along with its project to the betterment of the City. The state has awarded King's College $100,000 in tax credits to offset renovation of the Spring Brook Water Supply Company building on Franklin Street.

How, you may ask, does a tax-free non-profit use tax credits? The Spring Brook project and the renovation of an historic church on North Street are being done under a taxable subsidiary created by the school.

That complicated financial move helped the school get enough credits to pay about 40 percent of the nearly $12 million combined renovation costs, according to John Loyack, executive vice president for business and administrative affairs at King's. The bulk of those tax credits came through federal historic tax credits and "New markets tax credits" designed to help revitalize old city buildings.

Springbrook Water / King's project in process

Ending the detour

You may recall that we took this detour as we were looking at the Bicentennial Building (shown several pages above) and we recalled PA Millers as a great tenant in the 1970's and 1980's.

To the left of the Bicentennial Building in the pre-1972 Public Square on this block at the corner, there was a newsstand, a Loan company, Fanny Farmer Candies, and then the other entrance / exit for Kresge's 5c & 10c store. It represented the modern western face of Public Square.

Like the great stores of yesteryear, but not exactly, today some great spots still exist on this side of the Square; but not in those old historical buildings of yore. These include Circles, and at the corner, on address 1 of Public Square, Toscana's is rated the number one restaurant in NEPA. That's not a bad rating.

Bravo to all of the fine people who come to work every day to Public Square or close by in the uptown area. It means a lot to all of us regular folk, and to the city.

We'll come back to the Square soon after a detour down West Market Street.

Chapter 26   The Commercial Square & Other Commercial Sites Part II

Citizens Bank circa 2010 huge logo changed like they meant business.

Franklin & W. Market—WB business section

Right behind the Bicentennial Building on 8-18 Market Street on the corner of South Franklin, is what was for a short time, the Citizens Bank Building. It is one of the tallest office buildings in downtown Wilkes-Barre. On February 8, 2013,

Citizens Bank, the Bank, moved out, leaving a magnificent huge vacant lobby at a historic Wilkes-Barre corner—Franklin & West Market.

This once was the hub for most major regional banks, and major business transactions. That bank lobby looks perfect for a new exquisite jewelry store, IMHO.

I took a trip uptown today to get another look and it appears a company called The Bank, not a "bank," but a real estate firm has taken over the place. I hope this is all good for Wilkes-Barre.

When Citizens announced its departure plans, Ross Macarty, a major official for the local Chamber of Commerce expressed deep regret about this end to the glory of Wilkes-Barre's prime business district. "That corner was the cornerstone of the Northeastern Pennsylvania financial world. Now, that is going to be dead space," Macarty said:

"This is just another nail in the coffin of community banking we once knew." it makes the city's return to glory more difficult but nothing is impossible when your motto is not, "I can't."

As previously noted, I took a trip around the area again right before I put the original book to print in 2015. I wanted to see if anything good was materializing. The beautiful bank lobby had all kinds of crap in it and the windows were not covered so all of us can see and speculate that this may be good since maybe success is being staged or it may mean that it is bad because crap is simply being piled up in the beautiful lobby because nothing is happening. What business would not want to have that lobby as their lobby?

I sincerely hope that this prime, historical building in the business district will be able to reemerge from this low point to future days of glory. Over the years, these grand buildings on the corner have had their lows but each time they emerged again with a strong tenant. This is the master building for the business district. It must be successful, period.

The historic 14-story building, the tallest in Wilkes-Barre and in the entire area, was designed in 1911 by Daniel Hudson Burnham, a Chicago architect who also designed the Flatiron Building in New York City, the Reliance Building in Chicago and Union Station in Washington D.C.

When I was a kid, the Citizens Bank Building was The Miners National Bank and then later it became the United Penn Bank and then Mellon Bank. Each time the huge sign on its top that was a symbol of great Wilkes-Barre commerce changed with the new owners. See beginning of chapter.

The city of Wilkes-Barre agreed to sell the former First National Bank Building on Public Square to developer George Albert for $400,000. Exterior work stabilized the more than 100-year-old building from further deterioration, but additional investment will be required for the interior. Jerry Lynott | Times Leader

The downtown Wilkes-Barre skyline changed Friday afternoon when workers removed the last piece of the Citizens Bank sign from atop the 14-story building at the intersection of South Franklin and West Market streets. The building, designed by Chicago architect Daniel Hudson Burnham in 1911, was home to the Miners National Bank, the United Penn Bank and the Mellon Bank. The Citizens Bank moved out in February 2013. By then it had been purchased by Citi Tower LLC. The more than century-old high-rise has been remade into luxury apartments and renamed The Bank.   Jerry Lynott | Times Leader

Here we are in 2022 and it is no longer iffy as the City is going to have these luxury units in WB but the Web Site on Facebook still makes it look more than promising. Some of the pictures are below. Luxury for sure in WB.

The Bank
March 18, 2015

We have a single one bedroom unit left. Unit #806, available at $875. We have a few two bedrooms left starting at the $1600 price point. All units include water, trash, WiFi Internet and a free reserved parking space in our secure parkade. Fill out the inquiry form on www.thebankdowntown.com to setup a showing.

The Bank Luxury Living in Downtown Wilkes-Barre PA

With state-of-the-art amenities and updated floor designs, The Bank is the perfect marriage of historic charm and modern functionality.

THEBANKDOWNTOWN.COM

The downtown Wilkes-Barre offices of eBay Enterprise Marketing Solutions have become the company's new headquarters, and an expansion plan now includes the addition of even more jobs than projected..

Banneker Partners and a company owned by the Permira funds announced the successful completion of a $925 million acquisition of eBay Enterprise Marketing Solutions from eBay Inc. Right after that, eBay Enterprise co-founder Mike Jones called it "a pretty big event" for the WB Area. The skeptics will quiet down when the first Wilkes-Barre native cashes their big eBay check at a real bank in Wilkes-Barre. Hopefully soon! This is an awful lot better than they typical WB approach of destroying the buildings and then hoping for a tenant

I know that Wilkes-Barre officials are not interested in hurting the City but the Sterling experience makes us all wonder if parking lots are not preferable to history in Wilkes-Barre. Will Wilkes-Barre officials choose again to cherry bomb these historic business buildings simply because they can?

At least the kids with the little bombs would get something out of it! Will the Redevelopment Authority, a.k.a. "the Axe Man," be giving out the little cherries with fuses for the taking? One would have thought officials with $6 million in their pockets could have saved the Sterling so who knows what these folks may do?

A stitch in time saves nine

In April 2006, the Citizens Voice, not related to Citizens Bank, did a piece on the condition of all of the one-time great properties on the one time busiest business corner in the Wyoming Valley – West Market & Franklin Streets. Yes, that was in Wilkes-Barre's glory days! Over nine years have passed and there appears to be little change.

Denise Allabaugh wrote: "While landmark buildings in central Wilkes-Barre are being preserved - like the Hotel Sterling [now gone] and the Irem Temple Mosque [hopefully it will be preserved by King's College or some other group as noted in prior chapter]—major bank buildings on West Market Street, once the office hubs of downtown Wilkes-Barre—have fallen into major disrepair." She noted that the multi-story, grand historic structures from the Wilkes-Barre days of glory are mostly vacant.

Worse than that, however, the owners are reluctant to fix them because it has not been easy for them to find new tenants. I would suggest they hire Rob Finlay as a consultant. He and his positive attitude and his commercial properties on the Square, seem to be doing just fine.

Wilkes-Barre awaits its return to glory in the business district. Though it does look bad, where there's a will, there's a way. There is always hope.

Miners & Second National Bank—W. Market looking towards Square

I am not sure which movers and shakers in Wilkes-Barre helped this to happen; but there is some recent good news about the former Citizens' Bank Building.

Six floors of the historic Miners National Bank Building in downtown Wilkes-Barre pictured above in the glory days, are to be made into 72 luxury apartments. This is the same model used for the Luzerne Bank Building on the Square, and it seems to have worked there.

If there is no longer a bank there, I would vote to have the landlords change the sign to Miners National Bank again for nostalgia and historical purposes. But, that is not as important as moving towards success for Wilkes-Barre. Maybe if the City Fathers read this book, it will help.

In a full return to glory, it would be wonderful to add a few floors of such apartments or create indoor mini-malls or other commercial notions in this building or say, even the former First Eastern Building, which at least as a PNC property is lit up today. How about the same for our historic Savings and Loan Buildings on the other corners.

Wilkes-Barre officials and the Chamber of Commerce must work diligently to bring back our wonderful city 100%. No excuses will be permitted.

Lowes fed the masses

Lowes was where the cocktail symbol is in the above picture on W. Market Street next to Abrahams. Rug place. Lowes Restaurant and Cocktail Lounge for many years, was located on the North side at 35 West Market Street. It was right down from the one-time busy business corner. it was always one of the most popular places in town for great lunches, dinners and for a quench of the thirst. Ironically, it is no longer there as it got its call from the Redevelopment Authority's Axe Man!

Other than the restaurants in the Hotel Sterling when it was alive and well, and whatever Emmet Toole's across the street could conjure up, Lowes was one of the only pure eating and drinking establishments that was right next to all of the tall buildings. Those people who chose not to bring a lunch, if they were human, had to eat someplace. Lowes was the most convenient spot; and it was always a great spot to be.

Those who frequented this children-friendly, affordable restaurant found a full range of traditional Italian dishes, as well as piping-hot homemade garlic bread. Popular choices at

Lowes included the spaghetti marinara, cheese ravioli and brick-oven pizzas. For lunch, their hamburgers were among the best.

For Happy Hour, when they were really looking for business, you could get filled up so much on free food that you might even choose not to wash it down

When the business buildings were occupied, Lowes had a great lunch crowd (try to get in) and a great happy hour contingent of regulars. Even City officials from back thirty years or more frequented this great haunt in Wilkes-Barre's glory days.

Unfortunately the fewer the tenants in the business district, the less opportunity there was for Lowes Restaurant & Cocktail Lounge to survive. Actually, the same goes for why Wilkes-Barre itself is not doing as well today than yesterday.

Lowes, a great establishment, that would have made it if the Sterling ever did come back, was forced to close its doors just a few years ago around the time that hope for the Sterling was waning and Citizens Bank was having really tough times. Maybe we can contract with the Lowes people as we return to Glory to show some new restaurateur how it is done. They sure did it well as Lowes.

Signs of Decline

One of the most poignant reminders of Wilkes-Barre's recent decline from its days at the top is the startling absence of the once venerated Hotel Sterling from our skyline. Originally, when I wrote this book, I was convinced that The Hotel Sterling was right down the street from Lowes and across the street from Emmett Toole's. I was wrong on Emmett Toole's, corrected by Bernie Hummer of St. Conrad's Club.

Emmett Toole's Bar & Grill was located on 22 N. Washington Street. The politicos from the City kept it busy for years. West Market was also a busy place with watering holes and eateries galore. Lowes' was at 35 W. Market; Treasure Island was at 59 W. Market; and Rooney's Seafood Restaurant and Grill Was across the street where I thought Toole's had been. It's address was 40-42 W. Market Street. Those were the days. Thanks Bernie & John Rose.

Some might call this a symptom of politics-as-usual, but we have got to believe the prior Mayor was very disappointed that he was not able to avoid the demolition of such a historic building (Sterling), and an opportunity for a Wilkes-Barre revival. Rooney's Treasure Island and Toole's were long gone for the saving but Lowes packed it up just about five years ago.

And so, yes, right across the street from Lowes on West Market was a tavern by the name of Rooney's. I could not find much more information about it but it lived there for years before it was torn down for the betterment of the city, or so I suppose.

Emmett Toole's will therefore never play a major role in Wilkes-Barre's return unless of course, we learn that it is really Emmett Kelly, the famous Clown, and he has been reincarnated to run the place.

In the "not worth admitting" category, I had friends who could not figure a nickname for my first name of "Brian," so they found something to hang onto by remembering my last name was Kelly. Nobody called me "Grace," but a few felt it OK to call me Emmett. I am always happy to be called—anything.

Wilkes-Barre loses when the wrecking ball wins

We all need to reflect on what we lost with the demise of Hotel Sterling and the most fabulous chandelier in all of Wilkes-Barre if not the whole Northeast. The Hotel Sterling was Wilkes-Barre's largest and most luxurious hotel while its population reached 88,000. Such a small city geographically had so much to offer. Today's young adults would pay dearly for that opportunity. It has passed but some of it is back, but not enough. We can and must do more!

I am very skeptical about politics and politicians and their intentions. If I were given six million dollars, as I understand was turned over to CITYVEST, I would have fixed the roof of the Hotel Sterling first. Of course that is only if I did not want the building to decay away, which in fact, it did.

In searching for appropriate commentary and for appropriate pictures, I stumbled on one, source unknown. I do not know if this is real but one thing is for sure. Both the six million and the Sterling are gone. Can this picture be real? If it is, it tells us a lot. Can you imagine a casino where the Sterling once was? Did CITYVEST have a lot to gain?

CITYVEST Hotel & Casino????

The Sterling's guests from the time it opened included movie stars and nationally known politicians, who at the time at least, were not thought of as "bad guys." As commonly known, the Hotel Sterling stood at River and Market streets for more than a century. Wilkes-Barre politicians let it die.

JFK's Motorcade in 1960 Passing the Hotel Sterling on River Street, WB

The Sterling hosted weddings, proms, and welcomings for dignitaries including President John F. Kennedy—shown above, Louis Armstrong and Danny Thomas. Its attractive marquee on River Street was an inviting mainstay for those entering the city from the West side and all others.

By the way, the Kelly family from High Street were also guests of the Hotel Sterling. On our mom and dad's 25th Anniversary, my two brothers and two sisters and I had the pleasure of taking our wonderful parents out to the Hotel Sterling's Sunday Smorgasbord. The Sterling was famous for this treat. Wow! I never saw so much food, and at 15 years old, when it was all over, I felt that I had eaten my share. Wilkes-Barre had it all. It was a great town for old and young. Such dreams need not ever die. Wilkes-Barre has more to give and then more to behold.

The Hotel Sterling opened the first time for business on August 14, 1898. It was a grand experience. Its first guests enjoyed a once in a lifetime treat. They experienced the biggest, most luxurious hotel Wilkes-Barre had ever seen. The property was named after businessman and investor Walter G. Sterling.

This grand hotel was seven stories tall and had a spacious, columned lobby that made it look as nice as the great metropolitan hotels all over America. Eventually, a huge tower was built. It was ripped down a few years before the main hotel was ever seen to be a potential casualty of political impropriety. The 14 story Plaza Tower had made the place the tallest building in Wilkes-Barre.

Wilkes-Barre was busy as bees in a hive in the early days of the twentieth century for sure and the new building was a reflection of just how well the city was doing economically. It had charm, and growing wealth and investor confidence. Everybody seemed to want to spend their precious bucks in Wilkes-Barre PA.

The coal industry, upon which the whole area's economy was based at the time, was booming. I mean booming! Other industries followed to supply the needs of the miners and those making a big buck in this industry. Look at the huge homes in Scranton, and those in the sections of Wilkes-Barre close to the river. Most of these mansions are now part of Wilkes University, a school with a beautiful campus right on River Street. Wilkes itself began as an adjunct location to Bucknell University.

It had to be fun being in Wilkes-Barre when it was a boom town. Would it not be nice if we could arrest our tendency to stay on the other side of boom and bust back into a boom cycle for the city? Of course in the coal boom areas, industries such as railroading, manufacturing, and of course the selling of products as in the Hollenback store across W. Market Street from the Hotel Sterling were all rolling strong. It was a great place to live, work, and shop.

Bucknell Predecessor to Wilkes University Pre-1950's

<<< Bucknell, For years before it was torn down, there was an apparent attempt to save the Hotel Sterling. Many of cannot get over the fact that over six million dollars of taxpayer dollars were invested in saving the Hotel Sterling. Somehow, Wilkes-Barre gave up the dream of a revived Hotel Sterling! I hope it is the last dream we choose to give up on our way to glory.

By the way, the Hotel Sterling was not the first magnificent edifice to be torn down on this site. In 1870, before the Sterling, there was a wonderful Music Hall built on this site. It was the Wilkes-Barre Music Hall. I bet you did not know that. Look no further than the Sterling. Some of the old Music Theatre's original walls were strong enough to make it into the "new" Sterling as it was built.

The Sterling, Market Street, Hollenback Building, Wilkes-Barre, Pa.

Wilkes-Barre Music Hall 1870 to 1895

We already peeked at Wilkes when it was Bucknell. Wilkes University was founded in 1933 as a satellite campus of Bucknell University, and became an independent institution (College) in 1947. In January 1990, the institution was granted University status.

Moving down River Street to the Wilkes University property today, we find one of the most beautiful campuses in all of Pennsylvania. Wilkes is also a very highly regarded university in Academic circle.

Wilkes-University – A very pretty view from River Street.

WILKES COLLEGE
Wilkes-Barre, Pa.

You can still see some of the grand buildings though some
were destroyed in the 1972 flood. They once housed the well-
oiled finery—the top citizens; the elite, and the best business
people in Wilkes-Barre. From the huge mansions on River
Street, these folks, who made life much better for all of the
people in Wilkes-Barre because of their perspectives and
investments, did not have too far to travel to attend great
concerts at the Wilkes-Barre Music Hall.

There was another notable hotel set up even earlier in WB
history right there by the Music Hall across West Market
Street. This too was there when the Sterling was built. In 1831,
The Phoenix Hotel was constructed on South River Street right
near West Market. At four stories, it was the area's first large
hotel. In 1866, it was torn down to make way for the
Wyoming Valley House, which itself was also a hotel.
Historians who discuss this era suggest that there were lots of
hotels; but there were not a lot of bricks at the time, and so
large hotels were uncommon.

The Wyoming Valley Hotel River Street Wilkes-Barre

The Wyoming Valley Hotel,
Wilkes-Barre, Pa.

Old Wilkes Barre Hotel River Street

The old George. M. Hollenback dwelling and store was
situated on the corner of the block on South River and West
Market Street was. It is pictured opposite the Sterling on page
229. Perhaps the Hollenback Golf Course in the Parsons
Section bears the name of this gentleman. Like the Phoenix

Hotel, right nearby, which by the way had a nice bar called the Phoenix Tavern, the Hollenback place was a brick building. So, we know it was special.

It was one of just four brick buildings in Wilkes-Barre at the time. The ground floor of this corner spot was a famous store for its day. In fact, it was a leading store in this part of the state. As noted previously, where the Valley House stood—a spot where musicians and actors would practice their art, and live within their means, it had been originally occupied by what the locals called the Phoenix Tavern.

I found it funny that I have found fewer historical references to the Phoenix Hotel in early Wilkes-Barre times than to the Phoenix Tavern. But, isn't that just like Wilkes-Barre. Are we not a town, where hard working people, often miners, from day one liked to enjoy themselves, and then some. Is that not one of the key notions to bring back a great Wilkes-Barre that the folks in this town will love. Why should it not be also a place where those from elsewhere might wish their own towns would emulate?

The Hotel Sterling, at West Market and North River streets. or the Sterling as we called it, quickly supplanted the Wyoming Valley House (Hotel) across the street and down a bit, for size and luxury and it lasted well into the late 20th century when, as we all know, it deteriorated and had to be demolished. The picture below is how the Sterling once looked.

It was neglect that brought it to its ruin. The neglect came from hoteliers taking too much profit as well as for City Officials not realizing the treasure in their midst. Here it is in all is glory. Would it not be nice if we could have a structure like this back again that merely needed repairs. Notice in the depiction, there is no dike system

Unfortunately, the Sterling itself was not represented by its own counsel at the time (about 2013) or it would have complained about its untimely destruction. Nonetheless, it was permitted by its poor hotel managers and also by inattentive Wilkes-Barre City officials to fall into major disrepair. Eventually they all cried despair for city managers like to create crises so the public will forgive them. But the people were not in synch and we the people, most of us at least, wanted the Sterling saved.

Hotel Sterling With Tower, the Picture of Grandeur

Hotel Sterling, Wilkes-Barre, Pa.

Regardless of the wishes of the people, City Officials, in an ignominious move, eventually declared that this monument of the hard work of miners and others who loved the city, had to be torn down. Yes, as hard as it is for me to write, the facts do not lie.

Demolition of this magnificent original 1897-built building began on July 25, 2013 and finished on July 30, 2013. Amen! Before this of course, the city annoyed us all with barricades and one lane traffic to help us accept its version of inevitability.

King's College Has Helped

Many know that in the 1960's as the Sterling's Hotel Business was not doing as well as in the glory years, King's College was really growing. The College rented the top two floors of the Hotel Sterling, and used it as an adjunct to their dormitory facilities. Later, King's rented even more.

King's College, formally The College of Christ the King, is a liberal arts college located in Wilkes-Barre, Luzerne County, Pennsylvania, United States. Accredited by the Middle States Association of Colleges and Schools, King's has been ranked among the best colleges in the nation by U.S. News and World Report for 16 straight years. Despite its founding in liberal arts, the college has strong science programs in Computer Science, Business, Biology, Chemistry, etc. It also offers a Physicians' Assistant Masters' Degree Program.

Many know that King's got itself going in 1946 but few know that the good priests from Notre Dame did not pick the Lehigh Valley Coal Building at 133 N. River Street. Instead, King's College began holding classes in 1946 in the same building where Wilkes got its start on Northampton Street. While I was a student, King's was pleased to be growing faster than it could handle new students. They brought back Northampton Hall in 1968 at that time.

Before Bucknell Junior College / early Wilkes and then King's
and now Luzerne County Community College, most men in
the area went to Penn State or Bucknell Universities—if they
could afford to leave home in the first place.

My long-time friend, Bob Ell, 88, of Wilkes-Barre, was the first
registered student at King's College. According to reports this
is because of a generous aunt. I'll have to ask Bob about that.
By the way, in the heyday of the Station on East Market Street,
I came across three generations of Bob Ell's and we enjoyed a
fine conversation. The 1st registered King's student is Bob II,
and his son of course is Bob III. I saw the two surviving Bob
Ell's at Frank Pasquini's benefit just last week. Both are doing
well and look great.

On the King's College Alumni Home Page (BTW, I am
pleased to be a King's Alumnus—BS, and a Wilkes Alumnus,
M.B.A.), King's recounts briefly its history. In 1841, Blessed
Father Moreau sent Father Edward Sorin and six brothers to
the United States. In 1842, they founded the University of
Notre Dame du Lac, the first permanent foundation of the
Holy Cross Congregation in the United States.

In 1946, the Congregation of Holy Cross accepted the
invitation of Bishop William J. Hafey of Scranton to begin an
independent four year college for men in Wilkes-Barre. It
opened on Northampton street but soon thereafter moved to its
permanent address of 133 North River Street.

Many think King's had originally established itself in the old
Lehigh Valley Coal Company building, down the road from
the Sterling at 133 North River Street. Though not 100% exact,
it is pretty close. The building was designed and built in the
1920's. Soon after 1946 King's moved into its new building. By
1965, when I first attended class, King's had already built a
Science Wing, was about to bring on a second high rise
dormitory building, and it was planning the new gymnasium.

The Bishop was pleased to have these Notre Dame priests
begin to teach the children of the many miners in our era how

to gain a lot more than just a high school education. King's has been very successful in educating those of us, like me, who otherwise would be really poor. Thank you King's College for all you've gone for all of us.

King's campus extends well beyond the picture on the next page, but the picture does capture the essence of the early campus. The original Lehigh Valley Coal Company Building is in the center of the picture facing the river. You can just about make out the stature of Christ the King, several stories high, mounted on the top front of the building. This is a magnificent sight to behold. I show a picture of the original building from 1916 when King's was not even a consideration.

King's College Facing North River –133 N. River St WB PA

When the mines were gone, King's persisted in helping poor people like Brian Kelly (me), and my two best buddies, Dennis Grimes and Gerry Rodski, and others who needed a boost from God and his infinite knowledge, to progress in life. King's offers many majors including at the time Data Processing (IT), Business, Accounting, Biology, and Chemistry, or whatever. Thank you again King's.

Lehigh Valley Coal Company Building pre-King's 1916
Notice the later addition of Christ the King had not been completed.

Long after King's assured my dividend in life, my wife, carrying our first born marched unabated to the King's stage in 1980 to claim her King's College degree. Bravo King's. Two additional possible "Kingsmen" emerged from this union.

Just recently, King's showed its interest in hotels again with the purchase of the Ramada Inn. It was at one time the Sheraton-Crossgates, and before that until after the Flood, it was Bartikowski's Jewelry store and the Pizza Casa, on Public Square. The hotel structure was built after the flood of 1972.

King's opened the building in September 2014. The first floor now houses classrooms and office space for the college's physician assistant studies academic major. It also has a public eatery, called Zime, and the Sue Hand art exhibit: "Anthracite Miners and Their Hollowed Ground," is displayed along two first-floor hallways. The sixth, seventh and eighth floors have already been remodeled for student housing. The capacity on those three floors is about 200 students. The second through fifth floors will be used for offices, labs, and classrooms.

King's College New Building on Public Square Wilkes-Barre

I remember like yesterday that my tuition at King's in my first year was $950.00 for the whole year. It went up a few hundred each of my four years. I had taken a big scholarship test early on when I was in High School and I must have done well. One day, I saw my picture, along with Pete Gill's and Joe Grant's together announcing our King's Academic Scholarships.

Our high school pictures were grouped together and we were featured on the major pages of the Wilkes-Barre Record / Times Leader. That was neat. I knew I could not afford college and so this boost from King's really affected my whole life.

We each got a $400 per year King's scholarship, and a $500.00 National Defense Student Loan. Pete Gill and I also got a job at King's in a work-study program, which paid $1.25 per hour. This permitted me to pay for my books and the $50.00 that was left in tuition.

For my pay, I got to clean floors, ceilings, steps, and light fixtures, blackboards, and yes, erasers. I worked 40 hours per week in the summer and 15 per week during the semester. Joe Grant and I later joined the IBM Corporation to begin our careers in Information Technology. Pete was Valedictorian and had many offers for additional schooling and for work.

Across the street and up just a few blocks from King's is the
magnificent Luzerne County Courthouse, the picture of which,
is shown on the next page. . The fact that this structure is right
here on River Street, a few blocks from the Square meant that
in the first decade of the twentieth century, about 1909,
Wilkes-Barre's Public Square had a Courthouse building that
was vacant. We all know the rest of that story because it was
one of the first chapters of this book.

That concludes this section of the tour. Now, we will move our
tour back to Public Square

Luzerne County Courthouse 1909

Chapter 27 The Commercial Square & Other Commercial Sites Part III

Pomeroys in the 1950's before the Façade "Lift"

Start with Pomeroy's / now LCCC uptown

Let's now move from King's backyard back down River to the Sterling, and then let's go back up Market Street towards the Square. On the left corner, you would find Pomeroy's, one of the finest stores in its day. In the 1970's they relocated their business to the Wyoming Valley Mall.

This great Pomeroy's structure has been restored and is now occupied by Luzerne County Community College as its "downtown campus."

In the 1958 time frame, turquoise-colored panels were added to the Pomeroy's building, rather than giving it a nice facelift for its age. In 1994, Pomeroy's was out of business and the building needed help and it got it big-time–an almost $5 million grant to completely redo this Wilkes-Bare monument which turned 154-years old in 2014.

Pomeroy's purchased the building from businessman William MacWilliam, who had bought it from Jonas Long's Sons early in the 20th century. Founded in 1860, Jonas Long's Sons was affectionately known in Wilkes-Barre as "The Big Store."

Until 1917, the building thus was operated as Jonas Long's Sons. It was Wilkes-Barre's first department store. When the Pomeroy's façade was removed in 1994, it revealed an original marking chiseled in stone above an arch entrance, denoting Jonas Long's Sons ownership. Neat!

Saving Pomeroy's skin—maybe it was a joke

You can please some of the people all of the time and all of the people some of the time. I chalk the SPS (Save Pomeroy's Skin) initiative to one of those two different or similar points of view. A lot of work went into the saving of the Pomeroy's building and I am glad it succeeded.

At the time of consideration in 1993, the building was 133 years old. The Times Leader archives tell the story best of a group that wanted to save the old 1958 façade of the building rather than bring it back in original Victorian style.

"The idea came with the punch of a wrecking ball; Wilkes-Barre's downtown renewal needs solutions that are creative, not destructive. That's why I'm (writer of the article -- Joe Butkiewicz) hoping the populace will do some soul-searching, dust off their protest placards and picket on Public Square to save an architectural curiosity from demolition."

"Before it's too late, we can save the facade on the Pomeroy's building. Call it the 'Save Pomeroy's Skin Delegation' (SPSD); a lost cause with a lousy acronym. Obviously we're in the 11th hour on this rescue, what with construction to remove the facade set for spring and Gov. Casey having already made the trip north to present a ceremonial, oversize check for the project."

I do not agree with Joe Butkiewicz, who was doing quite well with the Times Leader until about the time the Sterling met its demise in 2013. The paper wrote about Editor Butkiewicz: "Times Leader Executive Editor Joe Butkiewicz, a journalist with the newspaper for the past three decades, announced his resignation on Wednesday July 17."

By looking at this beautifully restored building that was once Jonas Long's Sons, and then Pomeroy's, I for one am so glad to see the 1958 skin long gone. For the architects in charge of the remodeling, it had to be like taking an aged piece of My Brothers' Place paneling of an aging wall and finding columns of oak in restorable shape underneath. Looking above at the beginning of this chapter, you can see how Pomeroy's looked like before its 1958 façade-lift.

Below, you can see both the 1958 façade that the folks were still staring at in 1993 along with the fully transformed building that looks better than the pre-façade and, perhaps even better than the Long Building from 1860.

Pomeroy's with Façade—left; Redo with no façade as LCCC--right

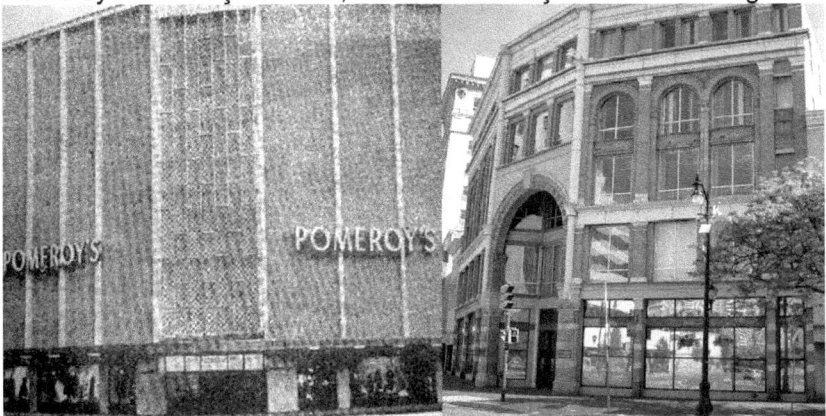

Luzerne County Community College, which now uses the former Pomeroy's building as its Wilkes-Barre campus, was itself created on December 15, 1965. Luzerne County Commissioners adopted a resolution agreeing to act as sponsor

of a two year-college under the Pennsylvania "Community College Act of 1963."

Before moving to its permanent campus in Nanticoke, LCCC was a happy resident in Wilkes-Barre right in the old Hotel Sterling Annex, which by the way, still exists. Here is what it looked like circa 2013.

It is not nice to second guess Mother Nature, but it is OK to second guess city and county leaders who do not always have our interests at heart.

Darryl Moran's picture of the Hotel Sterling Annex, LCCC's First Building

I have a big problem with the Axe Man showing up whenever anything nice has been neglected by supposed caretakers. Typically the neglector wants to destroy it, have taxpayers pay for its destruction, and then wants to profit from its destruction as he or she gets it back as a vacant lot.

July 2022 – Sterling Annex Reborn with a new clean face-- Empty Sterling lot next door

Somehow we the people have to learn to lighten up to help save some history and create construction jobs, not demolition jobs, and give businesses a chance to come back to Wilkes-Barre to create permanent jobs. It is OK for the Redevelopment Authority to save something every now and then—don't you think?

The latest vestige of the Hotel Sterling is about to fall to the Axe-Man. The Hotel Sterling Annex, right next to the now vacant Sterling lot on the corner of West Market and West River Streets is in the Axe Man's sights.

Admittedly, this four-story building shows no visible signs of renovation since a Bear Creek Village man bought the property more than two years ago. His name is not important. What is important is that he got a two and out sentence. His property is now on the Luzerne County back-tax auction list.

I fear seemingly trustworthy county officials would like nothing more than for a bunch of kids to buy cherry bombs and take this building down to the ground so nobody has to pay for its demolition. Actually, I really do fear that they don't care if you and I have to pay as taxpayers as long as one of their buddies gets to make a killing when it is down. Am I being too harsh on the political class?

It ain't cheap to bring down a building

For its own reasons, Wilkes-Barre officials budgeted $1,000,000 to bring down the Hotel Sterling but the lowest of 14 bids was just $419,000. Brdarik's Construction Company of Luzerne got the contract. This small business completed the high-profile demolition of the Hotel Sterling in July, 2013. Now, the Annex, the little brother of the Sterling, may itself have to come down. Nobody is stepping up to say it is a historical asset for the city and must be preserved.

Here's the rub: The back taxes on the Annex are $49,000 and the guy has had the property for just over two years. How is that? The Sterling was worth zero and the City paid $419,000 to bring it down. When the city gets its bucks back from CITYVEST, the taxpayer loan will be paid off...Right!

In June 2014, the City won its fight against CITYVEST, but the lien filed was undeliverable and returned. I wonder if they skipped town. Six million dollars of federal money did not get them their casino. $569,112 (the amount of the WB win) is a lot of bucks. Perhaps a few sharp attorneys can be contracted to find the source of CITYVEST and go after them individually to pay the City for their poor work.

It really seems like both city and county officials were snookered for real and despite it being wrong, CITYVEST still pulls in income from the swindle. How stupid can we be?

Well, when we expect people to represent themselves truthfully, in this day and age, the honest folks most often pay for dishonesty out of their personal hides.

Although Wilkes-Barre's judgment was smaller than the county's $6.5 million judgment against CITYVEST, the city filed its liens first and bumped the county to second in line. Good work WB! Now what? Who are these people wanting to destroy Wilkes-Barre for their personal gain? Where is the FBI? There were federal dollars involved.

Right now it seems the Sterling went down at taxpayer expense. Why should we all not give the Annex a chance? Why not find out what can be done to help the entrepreneur, who obviously has become disenchanted with county and city officials so much so that he'd rather have the property taken from him. Then what if we foreclose? Do we get a $200,000 tax bill (half of big brother's cost) to tear it down to make an even bigger parking lot for CityVest to run? Who does this help? Why not give the Bear Creek guy $200,000 to help remodel it? Put him in jail if he steals it instead!

Back to the Square at King's College

Later in that Pomeroy's / LCCC block in the "College Block" of Public Square," you will find the New King's building that we discussed in the prior chapter. A nice touch for the public is that the former Ramada Inn's Tiffany Room has been transformed into Zime Bistro. The focus here is on feeding students who will live in the dorms upstairs; but the bistro is also open to the public seven days a week. Now, that is great!

Although like many, I did not like the idea of having King's on the Square, I am really softening to the idea. Now, I think it is great. Without college's in our town, can you imagine where Wilkes-Barre would be. It is our # 1 industry. Thank you King's, Wilkes, LCCC. and your student body. Many of us in Wilkes-Barre were students at all three, including me.

Moving past the Pizza Casa side (King's) we continue

Moving down the Square on that side in the 1960's and long before, we would find the Pizza Casa which pre-1972 had been operated by John and Pauline Bettelli. Right before the Flood, it was all done-over by Rex-Craft. What a loss. John passed away early after he had moved the family business to the beautiful Bettelli's Villa on Kidder Street. Recovering from a flood is not easy as most folks in this valley well understand.

Pauline Bettelli, passed away December 26, 2014 in Wilkes-Barre. She was a wonderful lady. She and her daughter Donna [Sheehan] and granddaughter Jessica, ran the Villa for many years. They worked very hard and every Friday for nostalgia, they served Wilkes-Barre's original Pizza Casa Pizza. They are still ready for business on Kidder Street across from the Mall.

Also on that side of the Square in the pre-flood days, we would find Bartikowski's Jewelers. That is where I bought my wife's engagement ring. My cousin Rich Knaus, RIP was with me when I bought it and it worked. Pat and I are married forty-seven years this year.

John Anstett bought his wife Carol her engagement ring there also as did many young men, who fell in love with their sweethearts over the years. Back then, most such men chose to get married. After the flood, Bartikowski's moved to the second block of South Main Street and just recently, they closed their doors for good. Another shame. This store was good for Wilkes-Barre.

In 1886, The Luzerne House on Wilkes-Barre's Square, right where King's college is now located was the place to stay. The "House" had largest commercial trade of any hotel in the city.

There is very little other information about this old hotel on Public Square other than that it surely existed, and it was a mainstay of trade in the city.

Bartikowski's Public Square WB

The Luzerne House finished the Northwest block at the corner of North Main and Public Square. Across the street was the # 1 Pub and then Leo Matus' Newsstand. Also in this next block of the Square was the Comerford Theatre.

The Luzerne House – An Early Wilkes-Barre Hotel on the Square

The Exchange Hotel opened in this block on Public Square in the late 1800's. This property was once owned by James Wheeler, who was Sheriff of the county at the time. Later, Major Helme took over as proprietor. Many of the conventions held by Luzerne County in its infancy were held at the Exchange Hotel. It was succeeded by the Hotel Durkee, which stood for a long time and was part of Wilkes-Barre's heyday.

Fort Durkee Hotel on Public Square, a beauty, circa 1930

FORT DURKEE HOTEL, WILKES-BARRE, PA.

There was a bar in the basement of the Hotel known as The Fort Durkee Bar on the square. It was on the Comerford side. You walked down steps from the Square to get into it.

Three young and talented musicians got their start there. Joe Devine on Drums; Frank Killian on Accordion and Gerry Rodski on Guitar. This group played polkas and old standards like Twilight Time, Tara's Theme etc. It was a lot of fun and they got paid too. They were actually pretty good.

They were not playing at the Granada or the Stardust but the Durkee, What makes this so special is that Wilkes-Barre was doing great and these guys at the ripe old age of 13 or so (around 1959) were doing this as kids. Their parents came religiously every week to chaperone them. Later in life, Mr. Rodski played with the Cobras and the East Coast Blues Ensemble, who were regular performers at King's dances.

Like everything else in town, The Durkee was severely damaged by the flood of 1972 along with Mal's Men's Shop, the Astor Restaurant, the Taxi Stand, and everything else on that side of the Square including the Comerford Theatre, which was once the Capitol.

In the late 20th century the Hotel Durkee and everything else on that part of the Public Square was finally torn down, and the block now hosts only of the Wilkes-Barre Square Building on the right, and the Martz Building, which just changed hands in January, 2015 on the left side.

Durkee Hotel, Astor Restaurant, Mal's Men's Shop Public Square after the Flood

Current Martz Building & Wilkes-Barre Square (once the Alltel Building)

Public Square With Capital / Comerford Theatre & Durkee on left

Public Square, looking towards East Market Street, Wilkes-Barre, Pa.

After 1949 the Capitol on the left above, changed its name to the Comerford because an anti-trust suit led to the newer theater, located on the block straight ahead, which had been known as the Comerford, to change its name to the Paramount. It is now the F.M. Kirby Center.

After the disastrous 1972 flood the Comerford, formerly the Capitol, survived briefly. Like the partitioned theatres in the new cinemas of the day, the Comerford Theatre was divided into 3 houses: Barre East, Barre West & Barre Loge. None of us liked the change—at least I did not.

This Theatre survived only until about 1977, when it closed for good, and it was demolished not long afterward. Technically, there is no Movie House in Downtown Wilkes-Barre today, though we have a phenomenal theatre—The Kirby Canter, and occasionally, they run a movie.

The second coming of Comerford

Because this is confusing unless you lived it, permit me to go through this again differently. The Capitol Theatre, whose marquee you can see in the picture on the prior page was designed for the Comerford Chain by Leon H. Lempert Jr. of Leon H. Lempert & Son.

It opened to the public on October 11, 1920. When there was a major controversy about the original name of the Paramount (Comerford), the name of the Capitol Theatre took the name of the Chain and became the second Comerford on the Square. Both Comerford's were never open on the Square at the same time.

The new Comerford was thus the old Capitol and it was situated to the left of the Hotel Durkee and Kayo Bock's Tavern on the Square. It was demolished as noted several years after the flood of 1972 along with all other buildings on that section of Public Square. Somebody thought they were doing Wilkes-Barre a favor. Somebody other than me. The Axe Man prevailed and they are now all gone.

The original Comerford became the Paramount

The old Comerford was and still is extremely opulent compared to the much more modest Capitol/Comerford that did not make it long past the 1972 flood.

It was way back in August 18, 1938, when Wilkes-Barre's business and its population was booming. On that day, the original Comerford Movie Theater opened its doors showing Alexander's Ragtime Band, starring, Tyrone Power, Don Ameche, and Alice Faye. I have a friend who swears *Gone With The Wind* was the movie that night; he is the only one who believes that. I surely do not know other than what I have researched and so, Alexander's Ragtime Band it is.

Ironically over the years, as noted, the Comerford was re-made on the East side of the Square where the Fort Durkee Hotel had been. Coincidental to that, the 1938 Comerford Theatre became the Paramount in 1949 as the result of an anti-trust lawsuit. The ownership of the Comerford Theater at that time was transferred to the Penn Paramount Company and the building was renamed the Paramount Theater.

All of this was the beginning of a rich and colorful history for what, after the 1972 flood in 1977, right as the "new" Comerford (formerly Capitol) closed, the Paramount also closed. Later the Paramount became the F. M. Kirby Center for the Performing Arts. When the building was originally erected in 1938, it was to be the grandest of movie houses.

Comerford Theatre Became the Paramount

It had replaced a bus terminal, a printing company, a stonecutter and a drug store, and Wilkes-Barre has been benefitting ever since. Ironically just in the last few years, the Martz Bus Company relocated its terminal from the Square to the intermodal facility on South Washington Street. Most people my age have never seen the Paramount with a Comerford Marquis.

Luzerne Bank Building is Huge

Now that we have completed our powerwalk around most of Public Square, examining both the old, the new, and the newer, let's stop at the Luzerne Bank, the tallest building in town right now, shown on the next page, and remember it is home to the Luzerne Bank Luxury Apartments.

The Luzerne Bank building is from the past but it is so strong that it has made it to the present as well as the future. There are two more great old places that were close to this bank building in the glory days of 1972. They were right at the major bus stop. Many have reminded me of the Isaac Long Store, which the ladies really liked. I especially liked the Boston Candy Kitchen. Dorothy Mossbacher, who worked for the "Kitchen" for 55 years offered her simple summary: "It was sad when they tore down the Boston Candy Kitchen.'

Kirby and the huge Luzerne Bank Bldg. on Public Square

There was nothing like a C.M.P. or a banana split or some great candy back from "Boston," when in my life at the time, such amenities were very scarce. People of Wilkes-Barre never asked for much of anything, but if we could come up with a dime or a quarter to have a feast uptown. that itself was glory.

I wish I could, but I cannot find a picture of the square with either the Boston Candy Kitchen or Isaac Long's. Hopefully someone will give me a number of pictures for the next edition.

Two new places have replaced the Boston Candy Kitchen and Isaac Long's. We have already talked about Wilkes-Barre Center.

Rodanos where Isaac Long's & Boston Candy Kitchen once stood

Rodano's moved its pizza / food, and beverage act from North Main Street by King's Margaritaville to a huge facility on this sacred candy kitchen ground. It is one of the best locations on Public Square.

They run a fine business there and they are very successful. Let's do our best to keep them successful.

You may recall from earlier chapters when we took a walk down Memory Lane from the CYC and the YMCA that we discussed these spots as well as the Stardust Ballroom. This was to the left of the Kirby Center, We also discussed the famous Granada Ballroom. This was on the second floor in the open area to the right of Rodanos that precedes the entrance to Wilkes-Barre Center.

Now, that does it for Public Square. It was so great, we came back twice, and we may be back... time to move on to South Main Street.

Chapter 28 Walking Down South Main Street—the Real Uptown

Great stores – All inviting!

Let's take a walk down South Main Street. I know you all have been waiting for this walk. Me too! But I typically came uptown on the sidewalks in my youth and never got to the Square. South Main was Main Street USA to me for sure.

South Main Street from Public Square circa 1900

Most of us in Wilkes-Barre, though we loved the Square with Isaac Long's and Pomeroy's, and the great restaurants, Embassy, Astor, and Boston Candy Kitchen, most of us non-adults at the time, felt that South Main Street was the real uptown. Not kidding! We called it up town. I am not sure what the adults at the time thought but the South Main Street venues were well frequented.

Thanks to Captain Clint's on the Internet, and other great picture sources, we are about to present some great shots of South Main Street real early in the glory days and then again right before it all ended with the flood. I hope you enjoy these as much as I.

South Main from Public Square circa 1960

On the left side of the street not shown in the pictures, stood the Planters' Peanut shop. It was on the corner of the Square and South Main St. The Peanut man was always outside except in the cold of winter. The ladies crossing the street in the picture seem like they were headed there. You can see all the bustle on the Square and South Main St. on this day that the 1960 era picture was taken. Wilkes-Barre was a great town and uptown was a busy place. And, would it not be nice if...

When I was pre 10 years old besides my 26 inch bike, I got to the square via the Grove & Brown Trackless Trolley and then when the WB Transit Co. went gas, we took the converted gas busses.

You can see Fanny Farmer Candies on the right side and next to it was a newsstand. The next building down was SS Kresge & Company or as we called it, Kresge's. Aunt Clara's Toy Shop was there. To the Right of Fannie Farmer's was the second entrance to Kresge's. You could go in on Public Square and come out on South Main Street. It was unique.

Moving down the South Main block, you would come to Woolworth also known as the F.M. Kirby 5c & 10c store. You can see some of the affiliation of the Kirby family and downtown merchants.

Right next to that was Fowler, Dick & Walker, the Boston Store. When the Boston Store closed its doors after the flood, another owner who was in the car business as I recall took it over. We were all happy that he stepped up. He was not a retail professional and annual sales dropped to $6.5 million. The store and the uptown could not have made it without a messenger and benefactor from God.

In 1980 Albert Boscov RIP from Reading, already successful with a chain of stores in Reading and elsewhere, took over our most famous store and brought Boscov's Boston Store to life. He added a lot of zip to a number of Wilkes-Barre residents who were still dying from the devastating flood. Annual store sales quickly eclipsed $40 million.

I don't remember the sequencing of all the stores moving down to South Wilkes-Barre but there was the Europa Lounge, Neisner Brothers, Frank Clark Jewelers, and Lazarus' on the way down to Northampton Street on the West side of South Main Street.

Across the Street in the first block of S. Main on the east side from the Square was The Spa, a great restaurant, Thom McAnn a shoe store, the Hub-- a classy men's clothing, John B. Stetz Tux Rentals and men's clothing. There was also a big Rea and Derick Drug store that every now and then sold trains at Christmas time.

After all the stores from the past, in the past, the spot to go after crossing Northampton Street was a long thin night club named McDermott's. It was for adults. The parking lot across from Percy Browns, now the new Cinemark 14 Theatre would permit easy entrance into McDermott's Pub.

Percy Brown's was a mainstay in Wilkes-Barre. It was just a few doors down from South Main Street on Northampton Street before you crossed the street.

Looking at the fabulous Percy Brown's in its worst day below, we are now very close again to the CYC but even closer to Wilkes-Barre's fabulous YM/YWCA building that we should show before we go back to the second block of South Main Street. From South Main, we would cross Northampton, where Percy Brown's was located and then go down to the corner with S. Franklin Street, and there it is—the rendering in the second picture of the next page. It is still a classy looking building.

Percy Browns was a place everybody from the 1950's remembers

Percy Browns, Wilkes-Barre, empty of food gets ready to begin again.

YMCA Corner of Northampton & S. Franklin

Moving from Northampton & Franklin, let's go back to South Main Street and pick up a few notable spots before we reluctantly conclude our tour of South Main Street & vicinity.

As we pass McDermott's if we keep going through a bunch of spots that once were wonderful, we will eventually come to the Marquis Art & Frame company, the former site of my favorite spot in uptown—The American Auto. My good buddy Mike Grant and his cousin Joe Grant's family, (Joe shared the scholarship picture with me in 1965) have run Marquis for ages and moved to the American Auto site when it became available.

Up one address from American Auto back towards the Square, and you would find in the 1960's at least, Bushels of Bargains. I loved that place. It had to be the model for Dollar General and Dollar Tree stores of today. It was great for me as a young shopper with little cash.

Also in this block was the exquisite Poli's Theatre, 131-137 South Main Street, built in 1908. It was used for Vaudeville Acts in the twenties. It was renamed as the Penn Theatre in 1931, at which time it became one of the major movie houses in Wilkes-Barre.

Moving down to the third block of South Main, the stone G.A.R building from the late 1800's as well as the fortress-like South Main Street Armory were there for years before being adapted for other uses and then torn down. Pictures of these two fine buildings are included Chapter 32.

The greatest fine restaurant in town is in this block also. It is Ray Hottle's Restaurant, which for 73 years served the finest of the finest and people would cram in to get it.

Hottle's closed in October 2010 and many have been awaiting a return. Thankfully in this day and age, the building was saved from vandals. I drove by the other day, and I saw it was opened again on January 23, 2015. Now, that is great news. Additionally right up the block from Hottle's Donohue's Hour Glass has reopened under Hottle's management.

Wilkes-Barre seems to have a lot of little beginnings but few
sustaining. Because of our successes, we cannot stop. The new
Hottle's has a lot of folks biting at the chomp (if that is a proper
phrase), waiting to be able to return. Many have already come
back to the finest eatery in Wilkes-Barre. Not sure if she will be
there officially to greet us but I have great news. Janice "Olex"
Brizgint (she does not use Olex), who I spoke to in the original
version of the book, a one-time regular waitress in Hottles' over
the years, is now healthy again. I say let's praise God on that.
She looks great!

Hottle's is back at the same spot and the food is as great as ever!!

Sneaking way down South Main Street to almost the end,
across the street from the old Acme, was the Gerstein family's
General Radio & Electronic Company. They started off across
Wood Street in a much smaller building. My high school
buddy Bruce Amos's dad worked there and took care of me
when I needed help with my Hondas.'

By the way Alan Gerstein, who recently passed away, son of Ben, who moved the store across the street into the old Wood Street Acme for bigger quarters got the company involved in selling small motorcycles (Hondas). He frequented the Ovolon just up the street from his store. I saw him coming out of the place just one time when I was 17 at his Honda Shop. I never had to promise not to tell.

A handsome man, I am glad Mr. Gerstein found the Ovolon to be worthy of his trade. The Ovolon looked like a great place. My dad and I bought a Honda 50 in 1965 from the Gerstein's Both Ben, the founder and Alan, his son, treated us very nicely. My Honda never broke...well, not exactly! My Meyers classmate Bruce Amos's dad worked at General Radio and he always took care of me.

General Radio & Electronic South Main Street WB PA

When they moved across the street, the Honda spot was to the left of this picture. Across Wood Street was the American Clothing Company... later to become Torbik Locks. In the same vicinity of South Wilkes-Barre – right across the street, I think I can still smell Parlenti's fantastic Chicken Francaise so it too must have been close. Their Pizza was great also! Gone but not forgotten.

Chapter 29   1972 Flood-- As the Glory Days Were about to End

Back to SQUARE ONE (Public Square)

A Clockwork Orange – Last Paramount Movie Before the Flood

As we noted in several previous chapters of this book, The Comerford Theatre was between Market and North Main streets and the Paramount Theatre was between Market and South Main Streets. The last show that I saw at either of these theatres was on June 22, 1972. I was on a date with my wife to be (though neither of us knew it at the time). We were married three years later in 1975.

Pat and I saw the worst movie either of us had ever seen—Stanley Kubrick's "*A Clockwork Orange*.' Kubrick's *2001: A Space Odyssey* was exceptional and exciting. This newer movie at the time, from our eyes was simply sick. It was the right movie to usher in Hurricane Agnes on June 23, 1972, however. It was the last movie shown at the Paramount before it became the Kirby Center. It was frightening.

The Paramount did come back somewhat as a spot where companies such as Mountain Productions would run concerts.

The Lady of my dreams 47 years later and still beautiful

It had rained for about a week before my date with Pat. I was waiting for nice weather so I could take my motorcycle license test. The nice weather did not come until everything in Wyoming Valley had changed, and to this day, I never went to get my motorcycle license.

On this day, and for a week before and several days thereafter, the folks in Wilkes-Barre were "Singing in the Rain." Anybody who saw this movie knows that the villain loved to sing that song. It was a sickening irony to a tragedy that was just beginning.

There is much written about Hurricane Agnes and the Wyoming Valley so my intention in this chapter is to show just a small part of what was happening from my eyes. However, the eyes of many, who lived through it also saw what my eyes saw, and perhaps even more. Again, I will not tell the whole story as it has been told many times before.

Despite that after the 1936 Flood, Congressman Daniel J. Flood from Pennsylvania Avenue in Wilkes-Barre, had reportedly proclaimed that "the next Flood you see around these parts will be me," Agnes's rains and floods came nonetheless. Though the Congressman's words stood for 36 years, his proclamation would not last through the night of June 22, 1972 and on to June 23. The Valley was about to be flooded again, and this time much worse than 1936... and this time we actually had a levee system. It did not matter.

Dan Flood, however, did not weep about missing it. He was affected like everybody else. His very humble abode on Pennsylvania Avenue was flooded. His proclamation of 1936 had been nullified by God. Instead of whimpering as politicians like to do today, the Congressman dug in with the rest of us, and he helped all of us, as we all were affected. He helped us dig out of our misery as well as any public official could possibly have helped.

As a side note to this story, June 22, 1972 was one of my first "dates," as we called them with this young lady from Cummiskey Street in Wilkes-Barre. We were both about 24 years old at the time.

And, in case you were wondering, she is the same girl that looked at my curly crewcut, and my large blooming bathing suit at the Parish Street Pool and had declared me off limits from her life for all time. Thank God she had forgotten as we have almost forty years of marriage and another load of years before marriage as the best of friends.

I admit that I tricked her. I had just gotten out of boot camp and I had a thirty inch waist, and my crew cut was replaced with thick hair that was still a bit curly and was just becoming grey. She did not recognize me from the Parrish Street Pool. Hah! For me, those were the glory days of Wilkes-Barre, and here we are almost fifty years later still together, and still in love. The flood, of course was a big setback for everybody.

402nd Military Police

By the way, back then in 1972, I was a member of the 402nd Military Police. On Friday June 23, 1972, the next day after Kubrick's A Clockwork Orange, as I heard about the rising river, there was a frantic request on radio and TV for everybody to help in filling sandbags. This was to help avoid the potential devastation. I thought I might be more help working officially.

I put on my fatigue shirt, my field jacket, and my MP hat and boots, and of course, my trusty whistle. I then drove to the Reserve Center on Route 315 in my 1970 still pristine Chevy Camaro to see if I could help in any way as an MP or otherwise.

I kept my jeans on, rather than wear OD green fatigues, as I was not really on duty that day and I wanted to protect my options. I looked good enough as a soldier that the unit commissioned a jeep for me and my job was to find out just how bad it was and report back. The Army was very concerned.

I can recall being at Lee Park Avenue and Oxford Street on June 23 with my jeep, after the River had already come over its banks earlier in the day. Nobody knew what was next. I had been other places with the jeep that day and my heart was sick.

I recall being with many others watching the waters come up Horton Street slowly but surely. Then, as the water got deeper, we left and I drove the jeep down Oxford Street and stopped before Lee Park Avenue. It seemed there was no end to the water. There were no plans from headquarters other than to make sure everybody was safe. My action was voluntary and unofficial.

Everybody in Wilkes-Barre and surrounds was worried and scared. We had no walkie-talkies or cell phones so my information from the unit command was no better than theirs. None of us knew how far the river would go. It got worse before it got better. After learning what I could about the situation, I went back to the command center and eventually went home to High Street.

On Saturday June 24, I put on the full regalia, with my OD green pants and again, my official boots. I was commissioned a jeep again. I lived on High Street at the time and few thought our home would be affected (It was not). For us to be flooded, we were up so high on High Street, that it would have to be the end of the world. So, unlike a lot of my buddies, who lived in the flood zone, I did not have to protect my home. I do not recall much about that day but I remember the next.

The floodwaters finally had begun to recede on Sunday, June 25. I had a jeep again. As the water disappeared, what was left for all to see was a muddy, stinking mess. The citizens Voice in 2012 reported that "about 80,000 people were homeless and 11,000 were out of work. Five bridges were damaged or, like the North Street Bridge, destroyed; 38 churches and three synagogues were damaged and a million tons of debris accumulated and couldn't be carted off to a landfill for months."

"People in Wilkes-Barre had no power for 13 days, while in other parts of the county, flood victims went without electricity for up to 104 days."

"It took years for the Wyoming Valley to recover from Agnes, and the landscape would never be the same again." Some say that we have yet to recover from the devastation and then from all the businesses being torn down and not coming back.

When the Army chose not to activate our MP unit immediately– even those of us who were already volunteering on duty status, Wilkes-Barre was basically shut down.

Many of us went back to work to keep our jobs. After a few days of helping relatives the following week, I went back to IBM in Scranton, which was unaffected. Since I often played shuffleboard on Friday nights, while there was no Wilkes-Barre spot like Lewis' on Washington Street, a number of us for a few weeks found a place in Dunmore called the "I Go Inn," to practice our game. It was not the same. It could not be the same, and it never was the same again. But, over time, everything got better.

The Flood took its toll in central city

Back to Sunday June 25, 1972

Though Saturday was uneventful as far as taking any action was concerned, it was the day that the big flood was at its peak. Eventually the waters began to come down, and knowing this I went back to the Reserve Center on Sunday the 25th of June. Somehow, though just an enlisted man, with even more volunteers showing up, I became part of a jeep crew. I was a licensed truck driver in the Army so that may have been why I got to drive the jeep that day.

I recall making the first tire tracks around Public Square in Wilkes-Barre early in the morning with my MP jeep. Because the sight of my tracks was so pristine and because at the time, there was no looting to report, or protect from, I circled the Square just once.

I was disheartened as you might imagine. This wonderful magical place, Public Square, where I had just seen a movie on Thursday night at the Paramount looked devastated. The mud was about two to three inches thick. The asphalt on the streets and the sidewalk delineation was not visible. After circling just once, I remember like yesterday looking back and gazing at these huge tracks that the jeep had made in the brown silt and dried mud.

Uptown did not get a ton of water but it got enough to create major devastation. You can see the water in the picture at the beginning of this chapter. It got just enough to put most of the stores out of commission for a long time. For many stores and businesses, it was the end, but nobody knew then for sure. The stores all had basements that were part of the shopping scene. The basements, including Neisner's were destroyed.

To me, it all looked like a scene from the old west when there were no paved roads. I can't get over the sight of the sidewalks being indistinguishable from the roadway as the whole area was covered with light brown mud.

Everything after that as I write this account is a semi blur. I do recall that after just a few weeks from June 25, my unit, the 402nd MPs was formally activated.

Clean-up was tough

Before that time, with my father, I helped relatives in their clean-up. I took as many days off from IBM as I needed. IBM, my employer based in Scranton, was not functioning 100% at the time. Most businesses were stunned and had not figured out how to operate with so many trading partners out of business. People were not permitted back in their flood homes or businesses right away.

Our IBM office in Scranton was unaffected but a few of our customers in the Wyoming Valley needed help from our Field Engineers (those who fix the machine hardware), to get back in business. I was not part of the IBM repair team. I was mostly a designer. Nonetheless, it was an unsettling period for everybody in Northeastern PA. Nobody really seemed to know the right thing to do.

I can recall several homes of close relatives—all on Horton Street whose limited dreams at the time had been shattered by the flood. One of my cousins had just remodeled his basement and he had not even had the family over to see it yet. My dad and I worked together and we all went in and cleaned out that house and the houses of all relatives. We never finished working with the relatives and so we did not have much of a chance to help many friends.

Eventually, I did make it to Hamilton Ave in Kingston where I helped a good friend, Al Teufel, who had a number of small children, clean out his home. I had met some people from the Civil Air Patrol who were in our area helping out, and I asked them to visit my friend's home. By this time, water was back on. They were giving out plants for people to replace some of their landscaping.

Anything that anybody did for anybody during this time, was most appreciated. Lots of people were helping lots of people. My wife Pat took on the job of cleaning the toys that could be salvaged. Adults were crying it was so bad.

Decisions had to be made about whether to rip out carpeting— even carpeting that had just been installed. We realized eventually that we had to rip it all out. Nobody knew what toxins were in the flood waters. Think about that for a while, and you can get a feeling for the feelings. Everybody was glad that only a few had perished, but nobody was sure what would happen to their disrupted lives.

Would you rip out this carpeting?

In one home as I recall, while my dad and I were still working with relatives in Wilkes-Barre, we were the first to open the refrigerator. Electricity had been off for days. It was hot. The stench was overpowering. Nothing, including the refrigerator itself was kept. As I recall, there was no water yet, so we had to bring our own. Eventually power and water were restored as much as 13 days later. It sure did take a while.

Everybody had to decide to risk disease or throw out carpeting

When water was all turned on, a big hose was one of the best assets a person could have. The curbs were laden with one-time magnificent pieces of furniture, clothing and all sorts of artifacts that had been used daily before the flood; yet when on the curb, they looked like they had been in somebody's cellar for fifty years. It was ugly and it was sad.

Despite it all after the first tears, and there were many, there was an aura of optimism over the people in their quest to come back stronger than ever. It is the finest manifestation of the human spirit.

Going home the first night after working as long as we could about 6:30 PM, my 57-year old dad, had no work those days because the Stegmaier Brewery, where he worked, had flood issues also. On the way home, he used his favorite word to describe how he felt. He told me he was "pooperdooped."

Going back up the Horton Street Hill from where most of the flooded McKeown cousins lived, was a tough chore and after about ten or twenty feet, I wanted to help my father. I did not ask. I just put my hand in the small of his back and literally pushed him up Horton Street.

A very independent man, I thought my dad was going to tell me to stop. He did not. When we reached the top, he thanked me. It was the toughest type of work anybody could do. My dad was as good as it gets. As I recall we were back at it again the next day but after that first day, the sequencing of all the Agnes days for me are now a blur.

Back at the Reserve Center

Our MP Reserve Unit was uniquely qualified for traffic detail as we all had training to perform the traffic mission. Yet, as a POW Camp MP unit, our training was mostly directed at how to manage prisoners in a POW camp, and not how to handle normal MP duties.

The camp to which we were scheduled to go for training that year, Camp McCoy, was in Wisconsin. Despite the trauma in our home town that many members of the unit were having, and the need for more "police" to stop looters and direct traffic in the valley, the Army took a while to react to what could be done. They were prepared to send us out of town to Wisconsin for two weeks.

A Great Congressman Helped the Valley!

Congressman Dan Flood was on duty during the entire flood period. His help was priceless. One of the littlest known things that he did was that he stopped our unit from being deployed to Wisconsin. They did not need us in Wisconsin. The Congressman used his influence to have our unit deployed right in the Valley, where we were needed.

I may be mistaken but I think he also got the Army to forgive those severely hit who were working on their own homes. They were permitted to continue in their personal missions. They got credit for camp by working on their own homes. It went down the way it should have. Dan Flood was an angel.

When I got to the Reserve Center after being activated, it was not long for all of us to be dispatched. The officers were on duty and so the jeeps were not as available for enlisted men, such as I, as they were once available when I helped out as a volunteer before being activated.

So, we all received assignments and military vehicles dropped us off at our posts and they picked us up at the end of our twelve hour shifts. We were on traffic detail. We would add an hour on to our shifts each day for a few beers; but we were tired at the end of each day and we needed to rest to be able to go out the next day fresh. Periodically we would have visitors from the unit while on our posts; but mostly we were on our own.

I held posts at North & North Main and then Kidder and the bridge. At North and North Main, I had the good fortune of working with Wilkes-Barre Policeman Ben Victor who was as good a guy as it gets to work with. At Kidder and the bridge, the traffic was a lot lighter, and I was 100% on my own.

My sister and her family lived a few houses from Kidder and the bridge and she made my stay in the blistering sun of July / August 1972, much more pleasant than any of my commanders might have thought. It is amazing how much liquid one can store in a military sized canteen.

Stegmaier could have made it!

I know I have said this many times in this book. My dad worked for the Stegmaier Brewery. The Brewery never really came back after the flood but it was able to survive a bit until October, 1974. At that time, brewery operations ceased.

In many ways, the business known as Stegmaier Brewery died right after the flood, but they had been dying from absentee ownership for years before that. The company had been suffering a cash shortage that was plaguing it before the flood. My dad told me at the time of the closing that before anything could be bought, the profit checks (real profit did not matter) had to be sent to California to the owners.

Consequently, no supplier in 1974 would give Stegmaier any more financial credit. In other words, without cash, nobody would ship them disposable products such as bottles and crowns.

Since beer is brewed and then stored to age, the company still had lots of beer at the time, ready in vats to be bottled. But they had no way to buy bottle tops, known as crowns to those who speak brewery jargon. They had returnable bottles, which could be washed but they had no NR's (non-returnable bottles) or cans to fill. Not being able to bottle beer that was ready, put this brewery out of business.

Yes, a great brewery of historical proportions actually had beer to bottle but had no money to buy bottle tops. After 115 years in business under the Stegmaier flag. What a shame!

One hundred fifty workers got put out on the street on this day. I know I repeat myself when I say, "What a shame!" But, the look on my father's face after 31 years of hard work to be left out on the street, was a lot to take.

I am sure if some of the noteworthy people of our city were aware of the plight of the Brewery, and how easy in October 1974 at least, it was to avoid; they would have all chipped in to save such a wonderful testimony to our glory days.

Stegmaier could have been saved; but it was not. Another notch was taken from the Wilkes-Barre tree of glory. The final payment went to California as I was told and it was for the sale of the label of the company, not anything else. The building was not part of the deal. It was basically abandoned for a number of years.

You may know that part of Wilkes-Barre's legacy is that Stegmaier, a huge brewery was able to pipe beer under East Market Street from the vat/keg side on the left side of the street (looking up) to the other side. The main building there is now a Federal Building.

The other side was known as the Bottling Shop. Today it stores records for large corporations under the Diversified name, and there is no scent of barley, malt, or hops. You may also know that Stegmaier was a gold medal beer as it called itself. It was not a euphemism for anything. It was for real.

Stegmaier had won eight gold medals at expositions in Paris, Brussels and Rome. It was worth saving as much as the Hotel Sterling was worth saving. Wilkes-Barre cannot afford to keep making such mistakes, permitting our legacy and future to be destroyed at the same time, as we move forward. The end of such a pattern is that there will be no historical Wilkes-Barre, and perhaps no Wilkes-Barre at all. One hundred fifty jobs in Wilkes-Barre is a big deal. They should have been saved.

Most of the main buildings were saved, but the brewery as a brewery never operated again. This is lots better than what happened to the Sterling, but it still was a big shame. It did not have to happen.

The Stegmaier Brewery split in half by Market Street Wilkes-Barre

Stegmaier was the little brewery that could!

When America lifted its prohibitions of the twenties, this little brewery in Wilkes-Barre PA became one of the largest independent breweries in North America. By 1940, its output had reached over a half million barrels, and it shipped its brew from Maine to Florida.

On the way back from Florida, oranges were in the beer trucks saving on overall transportation expenses. By the time it closed, the company was putting out 800,000 barrels.

With the cash issues and the significant capital drain from the flood loss of 1972, the brewery was known to be in financial straits. However, the sudden announcement in October 1974 by Edward R. Maier, the great grandson of Charles Stegmaier, that the Stegmaier label was sold to Lion, Inc. of Wilkes-Barre, was like hearing the death knell for yourself.

It put most of the loyal members of the brewery's work force, including my dad, out of a job. Edward J. Kelly Sr. after 31 faithful years on the job was one of the casualties. He had his brewery career cut short at this time. He was as they say, *out on the street.*

The Lion Brewery at the time had been doing business as Gibbons, and they felt no reason to take the older union men from Stegmaier, such as my 57-year old father, though both were union shops. The union made excuses but in the end it supported the Lion's choosing not to hire these men, like my dad, with the greatest seniority.

And so, those with the fewest years at the brewery got jobs, and those that had been loyal forever to the union and the Brewery, lost their jobs. This is just another chapter in how Wilkes-Barre has separated itself from the notion of glory. How was this dissolution of such a grand city asset and edifice a glorious event for anybody?

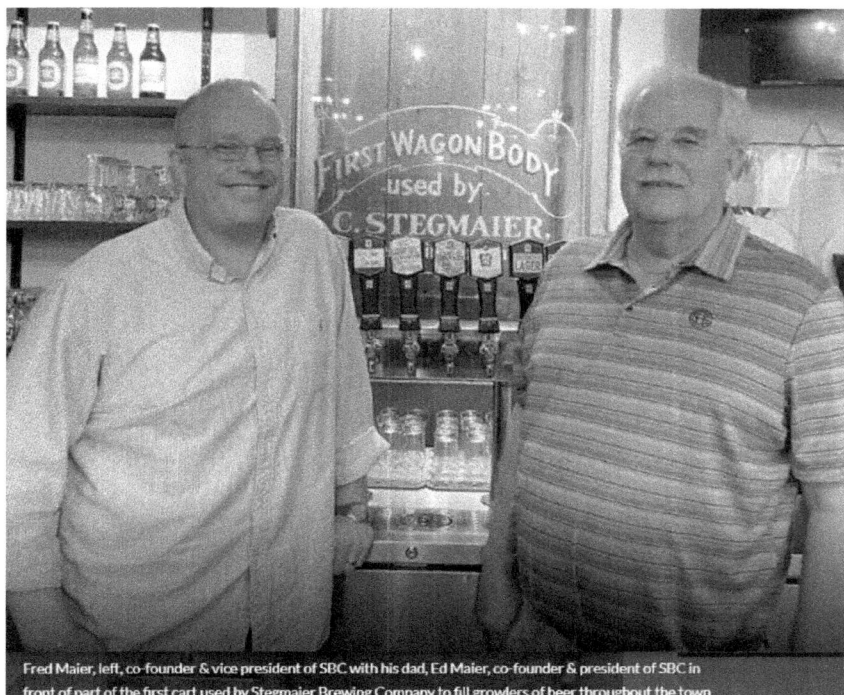

Fred Maier, left, co-founder & vice president of SBC with his dad, Ed Maier, co-founder & president of SBC in front of part of the first cart used by Stegmaier Brewing Company to fill growlers of beer throughout the town

The Stegmaier Legacy is Back

The Maier family finally bought the Stagmaier label back so watch out for an even better Stegmaier brew coming shortly.

In the next chapter we begin to look on the bright side again.

Chapter 30   Wilkes-Barre Lives on Both Sides of the Susquehanna

Kirby Center – A great Wilkes-Barre addition

The Kirby family loves Wilkes-Barre

Wilkes-Barre has forever loved the Kirby family, and we certainly should. Residents and officials of the City are and have been grateful to the Kirby Family for a very long time.

Dear Kirby Family, thank you for being so nice to us. You have helped Wilkes-Barre so many times, even though you did not have to do so. Wilkes-Barre appreciates it for sure. Thank You again to the Kirby Family for all of your help.

To some of us, it is a surprise to discover that all of Wilkes-Barre is not located on the east side of the Susquehanna River. Most may have known at one time or another that Kirby Park is "owned" by Wilkes-Barre as our major celebrations, such as 4th of July, are conducted there, but it is much more than that.

Kirby Park is an integral part of Wilkes-Barre City, just as South Main Street and Public Square. There just happens to be a river running through Wilkes-Barre itself. Moreover, Artillery Park on Northampton Street in Kingston, connected by land to Kirby Park, a Wilkes-Barre landmark, is also part of Wilkes-Barre.

Our magnificent Kirby Park is situated on 700 acres of land that were donated to Wilkes-Barre by the Kirby family. It adds immensely to the city's portfolio of recreational spots. Thank you again to the Kirby family. Can you imagine of Kirby Park were a strip mall?

Please note that I am not asking the people to thank the AhhhGGG family or the ZBhhhDDff family or the QUdddgggrrgh family, as they have chosen not to be as beneficent or even as munificent as the Kirby Family has been to Wilkes-Barre, PA. Thank you again, Kirby family.

I can tell you that it certainly would be nice if the AhhhGGG family or the ZBhhhDDff family or the QUdddgggrrgh family chose to donate land or other assets to Wilkes-Barre to help us as the Kirby's and the Charles Miner family have done over the years. It would be a big help if a big donor stepped up to help Wilkes-Barre in its quest to return to glory.

The Kirby Health Center

Wilkes-Barre residents are all welcome to Angeline Elizabeth Kirby Memorial Health Center.

Located in Wilkes-Barre, Pennsylvania, the Kirby Health Center offers state-of-the-art laboratory services in the environmental, clinical, toxicological, and consumer product testing areas. Clients for the laboratory are found locally, nationally, and worldwide. Another gift of the Kirby Family.

Wilkes-Barre Municipal Zoo

There is a great story, and as all great stories, it is a true story about Kirby Park in the peak of Wilkes-Barre's glory days. In 1932, Wilkes-Barre opened up a Municipal Zoo in Kirby Park. Yes, it was like Nay Aug Park Zoo in Scranton. It was located on the west bank of the river close to the river, where the nature area is located today in Kirby Park.

The Zoo featured monkeys, bears, deer, buffalo, wild game birds, and several other small animals. There was no elephant as in Nay Aug Park of old, when even Scranton thought it was something. The zoo was located right by the Susquehanna

River but it extended into what is now referred to as the Park Area.

The Zoo had been incorporated into the original design of the Kirby Park along with other parts of the original design—a cottage, a reflecting/wading pool, sand boxes, and walking/bridle paths.

Kirby Park was reflective of a grand and glorious and prosperous Wilkes-Barre. It is still a wonderful place to visit. Yet, whether we thank them in our secret thoughts or not, no family has ever been as nice to Wilkes-Barre citizens as the Kirby Family. We should find out one day that they have been so kind and ask: Why? Maybe others in Wilkes-Barre with means, or those who gained from business in Wilkes-Barre can choose to be like the Kirby's and help us all.

In just four years after its opening, in 1936, a great flood, similar to Hurricane Agnes in 1972, wiped out most of the area in which the Municipal Zoo was contained. For years, animals had a tough time surviving there and over the few years from its opening, some animals had unfortunately died. Without the devastating flood of 1936, most of us would have called these issues growing pains. But, the 1936 flood was devastating to the WB Municipal Zoo.

Though it was a really nice place and a really nice idea, after the devastation of the flood, there was not much left to save, and many were disheartened. And, so it did not take too long for Wilkes-Barre City Officials, as the Zoo's financial caretaker of the gift, to realize that the banks of the Susquehanna were not friendly enough for a municipal zoo.

In 1941, the City began the abandonment of its zoo with the sale of the bears. The monkeys were last to go. They were given to the Nay Aug Park Zoo, when this longer lasting Scranton area zoo and park facility was in its heyday.

The Zoo was part of great dreams for Wilkes-Barre in its glory days. Sometimes, even in the best of times, nature gets the best of it all. Sometimes good things do not always work out.

During this period after the 1936 flood, with the construction of a major dike system, Kirby Park had to be split into two areas with a portion on the "park and sports field" side of the dike, and a portion in the nature area on the "river" side of the dike. Nobody knew what to expect if God sent another flood. Yet, until 1972, it seemed like the levee system built after 1936 was keeping us all safe, and so more than likely, it would continue to do so.

Ruins of the Kirby Park Zoo circa 2000

Like many parents, long after the 1936 devastation, my dad took the five Kelly kids a number of times to Kirby Park and the River in the early to mid-1950's. I can recall being amazed at the nature side of the dike with all its winding pathways and interesting ruins. Perhaps they were part of the bridle trail. Maybe not?

I can remember on the river side, we could go right under the bridge into what is now Nesbitt Park in Kingston. I still recall seeing these huge stones embedded into the dike itself. There was grass growing in between them. You could not tell they were stones until you were walking on them. My father told me they had been laid after the 1936 flood. The 1936 flood victims unfortunately had no benefit from such a levee system.

There was so much mud and dirt and grass around the stones over the years since 1936 that to me they looked as if they had been cemented neatly by a skilled mason. They appeared to be flat against the ground. Watching the crews repair the dike by Barney Farms in South Wilkes-Barre, several times over the years, I noticed there were no masons. The stones, laid well or not were to keep the river from blowing away the dirt that composed most of the dike.

In Wilkes-Barre, after 1972, they merely dumped huge rocks and stones over the river side of the dike and leveled them off with a back hoe or "Steam shovel." Again, there were no masons involved for sure. So, they either did things differently in 1936 or things were different than they appeared when dad and the kids were checking it out in the 1950's.

Nature / Bridle Path on Nature Side of Kirby Park

On our many trips to Kirby park, my brothers, sisters and I were introduced a number of times to the nature side of Kirby Park on the river side of the dike. It is still in its natural form with some great bike and pedestrian paths. I love taking my bicycle there as much as I like to walk there. Lately, I do not feel as safe, however, and I would prefer to be on my bike for a quick getaway. I wish it were not so. Wilkes-Barre officials can and should make that better.

Looking back to the nature side of the park

When I was about ten years old, my older brother Ed took me bicycling there in the old west wilderness by the river on the other side of the dike. Later on as I got even older, my younger brother and I rode our low-cc motorcycles back there over the same paths our dad had taken us years earlier.

From when I was a kid, all those ruins of the old zoo park really caught my imagination. I never knew they were from a zoo. It was surely lots of fun exploring the back area of Kirby Park, back then and even now.

When my kids hit the age when they could ride bikes, I returned the favor that my father and brothers had given me. On one of my days off, several times a summer, we would collect as many kids from the neighborhood as we could. Mom would pack some waters bottles, some Gatorade, some snacks, and some "sammiches," and she would dust off her blue bike for the adventure.

As the dad of a number of the bicyclists, I would lead this pack by bicycle along the back way of Wilkes-Barre through Pickering Street to Riverside Drive by the trestle. After some work, we would emerge on South River Street on the red ash, before the latest river rebuilding, until finally we could ride on the huge sidewalk over the Market Street Bridge. What a treat for the kids, and I admit I loved watching them all smile.

From there, on the west side, we would find and quickly go down the steps to the "underworld" of the Kirby nature area. It was still a thrill for me, and the kids were in awe of the majesty of it all. None of it was especially pretty, but it was "majestic" or as the kids would say, *awesome.*

Yeah! Just like me when I was little, the kids were just a little scared of the "Sleepy Hollow" look of the place, and so we chose to eat our picnic lunches on the park side of the dike.

Since my legs, thank God, are still working, thanks to a new knee installed by Pittston's Dr. Thomas Meade, and some great chiropractic tuning by Dr. Louis Guarnieri on Wyoming Ave in Forty Fort PA, I suppose that I should get that ole bike out again and make the trek with or without my adult kids or the neighborhood kids. BTW, Dr. Meade, and Dr. Guarnieri were classmates at Pittston High, the "Healing High School," or so as it should be nicknamed.

I think sometimes about how nice it would be if there were a safe way from Wilkes-Barre proper to get to the nature area of Kirby Park without having to cross so many streets. That is part of my Wilkes-Barre dream. But, when I get my bike out this spring, I am going regardless. Maybe I can get my dear wife Pat to join me?

Chapter 31 Sports in Kirby Park & Wilkes-Barre

Kirby Park: Play Ball!

Lots of Sports History

Kirby Park is the home of a number of softball fields and tennis courts and other goodies that Wilkes-Barre residents and others, male and female still enjoy.

At one time in the back of the park, there was even a picnic grove. My first year playing minor league ball in St. Therese's at eleven years old, after not being picked for a Little League that year, found my team, People's Laundry winning the championship. We were honored in that Picnic Grove at Kirby Park. What a treat!

My team was coached by Mr. Charles Romaine and his son Chuck Romaine, with Lex Romaine as catcher, and Brian Kelly as pitcher. We were pretty good. Bernie Hine, RIP a Wilkes-Barre Dentist, was the best of us.

Bernie was "picked up" by a Little League team after our first game. In our second game, I played short stop and I felt like Ernie Banks after I hit two home runs out of the park in the same inning. Believe me, I was not bad in baseball but I was no Ernie Banks. Hah! Regardless, I'll never forget that. I never hit another home run that year until I made the Little League the following year.

Even without Bernie Hine, our team was still a very good team and we were well coached. So, our team really enjoyed the picnic feast in the Kirby Park picnic grove. We got T-shirts that were filled with letters proclaiming our good fortune—St. Therese's 1959 Minor League Champions. The letters covered the whole green shirt.

Each of us also received a trophy. I wore my green T-shirt almost every day for a year or more at least until it had multiple holes where the letters were attached. The letters were still there so I loved wearing the shirt. One day after asking me many times to give up that "holey" shirt, my mother had enough and she tossed it, someplace. I never saw the shirt again.

We were all thrilled to have played for People's Laundry, which, by the way is another Wilkes-Barre business no longer active. I still remember that fine picnic in Kirby Park.

My good friend Bill Eydler convinced me to play organized baseball. He made the Little League his first time out. Later, he got really good at Tennis. For years, he took care of the Tennis Courts in Kirby Park. Bill was a fine athlete in many sports and he eventually became the Varsity Tennis Coach of King's College

Artillery Park, Home of the Wilkes-Barre Barons

There have been few, but all notable tenants of Artillery Park, which is close to Kirby Park and is part of Wilkes-Barre City. Artillery Park once provided the stadium for the famous Wilkes-Barre Barons Baseball Team, when they were in their heyday. In 2015, this magical park is the home of the Wilkes University Colonels Baseball Team, successor occupants to the Wilkes-Barre Barons. You can see the whole shebang with a nice trip through Kirby Park today. If you care to go, please note that Artillery Park is on the right as you reach the end of Kirby Park proper.

When the Barons were the Wilkes-Barre Barons, a semi-pro baseball team like those that play in the Lackawanna stadium off route 81 in Moosic, Artillery Park is the well documented location of Babe Ruth's longest home run.

Before Wilkes, the park was formerly the home stadium of the Wilkes-Barre Barons of the New York-Penn League and later the Eastern League. The experts note that the B*ambino's blast in an Artillery Park Stadium exhibition game traveled about 650 feet over everything and well into Kirby Park.*

Sultan of Swat, the Great Bambino Clouts Longest HR in Wilkes-Barre

When Wilkes University brought in its own expert, after substantial work with interviews and newspaper accounts, and a trusty tape measure, the expert declared this Artillery Park Home Run as the longest Home Run in Babe Ruth's career and the longest in baseball history. Have you heard about this tribute to Wilkes-Barre?

It is reported that Babe Ruth told people right after he hit it, to measure the home run in 1926. He felt it was his best blast ever when he hit it in an exhibition game not long after the Yankees season was finished. The Babe came right from the World Series to Wilkes-Barre, PA, where he liked to hunt and fish and frolic, and swat huge home runs.

It all happened in Wilkes-Barre Pennsylvania. May I repeat? Do you remember coming into Wilkes-Barre from any of the highways and byways and seeing an inviting billboard or other greeting in which the great Bambino is immortalized for having clouted the longest home run in human history in Wilkes-Barre PA? Neither have I. Shame on US! Maybe we should do that? What do you think?

A very good friend of mine, John Anstett tells me that you have to shine your own light in life. Obviously, nobody else is going to boast about this one of a kind event. It did not happen in their town. We need to shine the light on Wilkes-Barre's proud relationship with the greatest baseball player of all time. Why not?

Wilkes University now occupies Artillery Park in Wilkes-Barre. Their season kicks off this year 2022 in early February down in Virginia and then Florida. They'll be back home at Artillery Park about mid—March. Why not go watch a few of their games in this historic park?.

Wilkes-Barre had its share of native born baseball stars over the years from when baseball statistics began to be kept. Considering that there are about 30,000 incorporated cities and towns in the United States, having sixteen stars great enough to play pro ball in the major leagues is a lot for one small community such as Wilkes-Barre, PA.

Wilkes-College Colonels have Artillery Park looking sharp

I was never really a star baseball player, but I did get to play catcher and pitcher for Meyers and I played catcher and pitcher for King's College for three years. While at King's, the best baseball player I ever saw played short-stop for our team.

The late John Dorish, a great athlete himself was the coach. James "Jimmie" Kobi was like a cat at shortstop and he could hit all pitching. He graduated before me. While at King's, I heard that Jimmy had gotten picked up by the Detroit Tigers the year after they won the World Series Championship.

I researched and found that he played for the Lakeland Tigers in 1969 and he did fine with the team. There is another reference for when Jim Kobi was at King's in 1966 as he was drafted by the Houston Astros. One thing for sure. If Pittston and Wilkes-Barre's Jim Kobi did not make it big in the major leagues, it is unbelievably hard to do. He was the best ball player I had ever seen close-up in my life.

Even today with expanded teams it is a major challenge to be a major leaguer. I have a list of Wilkes-Barre born ball players who made the big time, and played at least a part of one season. That is pretty good. Jim Kobi was not born in Wilkes-Barre but he sure played enough for a Wilkes-Barre College team. If it were up to me, Jim would have been in the major leagues and he would have a great pro record. He was that good, and he was a nice guy to boot!

Before I show you the list of major league ball players from Wilkes-Barre from the 1880's on, you may recall that King's College's baseball coach for years was the late John Dorish, who died way too young. He was also King's Athletic Director. John and his uncle Fritz, even better at baseball than Coach John, were not from Wilkes-Bare; but they loved Wilkes-Barre as I do. Fritz Dorish, a very popular local athlete, made it to the local Hall of Fame. That too is a difficult task for any athlete.

Harry "Fritz" Dorish was an American professional baseball player. Born in Swoyersville, Pennsylvania, he was a right-handed pitcher over all or parts of ten seasons with the Boston Red Sox, St. Louis Browns/Baltimore Orioles and the Chicago White Sox. If you are interested in finding any more Pennsylvanians who played major league baseball, take your favorite search engine and look for "Major League "Baseball Players Born in Pennsylvania"

In the meantime, enjoy the chart that I put together below, after days of research. Wilkes-Barre has lots of talent for sure.

Major League *Baseball Players Born* in Wilkes-Barre, *Pennsylvania*

Player	DOB	Debut	Final	Team(s)	Position(s)
Dave Pierson	8/20/1855	1876	1876	Cincinnati Reds	Catcher/OF
Dick Pierson	10/24/1857	1885	1885	NY Metropolitans	2nd base
Billy Goeckel	9/3/1871	1899	1899	Philadelphia Phillies	1st Base
James Francis "Kid" O'Hara	12/19/1875	1904	1904	Boston Beaneaters	OF
John Walsh	3/25/1879	1903	1903	Philadelphia Phillies	3rd Base
Al Klawitter	03/29/1889	1909	1913	NY Giants, Det Tigers	Pitcher
TyTyson	06/01/1892	1926	1928	NY Giants / Bklyn Robins	OF
Ed Cole (Kislauskas)	3/22/1909	1938	1939	St. Louis Browns	Pitcher

Mickey Haslin	10/25/1909	1933	1938	Phillies Bos. Bees, Giants	SS 2B, 3B
John "Red" Davis	7/15/1915	1941	1941	NY Giants	3rd Base
Pete "Piccolo Pete" Elko	6/17/1918	1943	1944	Chicago Cubs	3rd Base
Tommy Hughes	10/7/1919	1941	1948	Phil Phillies, Cincy Reds	Pitcher
Joe Murray	11/11/1920	1950	1950	Philadelphia Athletics	Pitcher
Hal Woodeshick	8/24/1932	1956	1967	Tigrs, Inds, Astros, Cards	Pitcher
Don Schwall	3/2/1936	1961	1967	Red Sox, Pirates, Braves	Pitcher
Kevin "Groundball" Gryboski	11/15/1973	2002	2006	Braves, Rngrs, Nationals	Pitcher

Eastern League Basketball etc.

Though they did not play exactly in Kirby Park or Artillery Park, Wilkes-Barre also was home to Big Bill Spivey and the Wilkes-Barre Barons Basketball team. For the most part, the Basketball Barons played in the "Kingston Armory" right next to Artillery Park and Kirby Park. The Barons were a great basketball team from a great city, Wilkes-Barre, Pennsylvania. I am not sure if the Armory is technically part of Wilkes-Barre like Artillery Park.

I remember the Barons as a kid as they lit up the Eastern League as semi-pros. Wilkes-Barre was never big enough to attract a pro team but the semi-pro Barons played between 1933 and 1980, in several different American leagues. Various Wilkes-Barre venues were the team's home court including the Kingston Armory, Coughlin High, and King's College.

WILKES-BARRE BARONS
DEFENDING LEAGUE CHAMPIONS

The Barons won 11 titles during this time, including their time in the American Basketball League and the Continental Basketball Association. The team was owned and coached in later years by Eddie White, Sr., who was once a Wilkes-Barre

City Councilman, and well-respected by Wilkes-Barre folks and those near and far.

The Sunday Independent, which was always my favorite newspaper as a kid, with Lou Rauscher as its Sports Editor in Chief ran great stories about the Barons' escapades. I loved grabbing the Paper's Sport's Section before my dad saw it on Sunday mornings. It would always highlight the Barons games as if they were being played in the Independent Building itself. There was a lot of fan support, especially for the best player in all of basketball at the time, Big Bill Spivey. For much of his semi-pro years, Spivey was a mainstay for the Barons.

Mr. "Big Bill" Spivey was the University of Kentucky's (UK) first 7-foot-tall player. As he grew up, he had dreams of playing for the National Basketball Association. He would have been one of the best for sure but his NBA career was not in the cards. You are going to love his picture from his days at UK.

Nobody was seven foot tall at the time. Unfortunately, Mr. Spivey had been implicated (not convicted in any way) in a point-shaving scandal in the early 1950s. A number of folks on his team admitted they had accepted money to shave points. Spivey took no money and he admitted no guilt. It cost him his NBA career.

Big Bill Spivey, who was indicted for perjury in the case, was ready to die rather than to lie. He could not admit any part in attempts to fix college games because he had not done so. A New York trial jury voted 9-3 for acquittal, and the district attorney's office said it saw no use in trying the case again. Yet, Spivey's career in the NBA was done!

Unfortunately, the damage could not be reversed by normal means. Big Bill Spivey was simply a victim of being associated with bad guys. I bet many in NEPA remember how good he was, and what a fine man he was, and how he kept the name Wilkes-Barre on the map. Take another look at this picture of

Spivey at UK. Everybody expected him not only to be a pro but one of the best there ever was.

Mr. Spivey was never found guilty of any wrongdoing. Yet, trying to be pristine, this seven foot skill player was barred from the NBA for life even before he had a chance to play his first professional NBA game. His obituary says that he "went on to play for some minor professional teams, including a stint with a team opposing the Harlem Globetrotters." Surely, one of those teams that they were speaking about in the obit was the Wilkes-Barre Barons.

Wilkes-Barre Pennsylvania loved Big Bill Spivey. None loved him more that Eddie White Sr., owner and coach of the Barons, who, himself, was one heck of a man.

Big Bill Spivey, Famous WB Barons Pro Player at UK

A great devotee of basketball once said of Mr. Spivey:

"He was the first big man that could just fly up and down the court. He had extremely good agility as a big man."

"He was one of those guys that loved to live. He played hard. He worked hard. He lived hard. He just loved life."

Big Bill Spivey was selected as top player in the nation by the Helms Foundation, and he was the UK's 29th all-time scorer with 1,213 points although he never got to complete his final season due to what I would say were lies about him.

A very young Bill Spivey, one time scored 22 points and collected 21 rebounds in the UK's 1951 NCAA championship game.

In his obituary it noted that "But the point-shaving scandal left him a broken man, his former wife Audrey Spivey said. 'He never got over it. Bill could not let that go. He was just devastated. He was probably the best basketball player in the country at that time,' "as she said. She was right!

Big Bill Spivey of Wilkes-Barre fame was in fact, the best basketball player in the country at that time,' " as Mrs. Spivey had said. Too bad somebody in Wilkes-Barre had not taken up his cause.

I read intensely the Sunday Independent as a kid, and as an adolescent, and as a teenager—about how well the WB Barons did on Saturday night. I still followed them when I was in college and when I came home to live before I got married. Many did.

The Barons were a big success story for Wilkes-Barre. As I read his obituary, though I did not understand politics at the time, I wondered how city officials, other than Eddie White Senior could have permitted Big Bill Spivey, a Wilkes-Barre Hero way beyond many more—he played for Wilkes-Barre as a pro—to die on the vine without any support from Wilkes-Barre City Officials. Nobody from Wilkes-Barre wrote an epitaph that I could find. Next to Bob Sura, Wilkes-Barre basketball knows nobody else who comes close to being the best. What a shame!

Most Wilkes-Barre people at the time loved the Barons. Eventually, when they were playing at the new King's College Gym in the late 1960's / early 1970's, I had the pleasure of seeing the Barons play. Unfortunately, by then Big Bill Spivey had retired.

I would like to take the time to show these quotes below, which come from Big Bill Spivey's obituary. Bill Spivey died May 8, 1995. I know that I will never forget him. He was phenomenal. I remember Rauscher headlines like "Spivey scores 49 as Barons crush ..."

Besides Babe Ruth's longest home run never being attributed to Wilkes-Barre, Wilkes-Barre can claim the bulk of the career of Big Bill Spivey, but we choose not to do so. If Mike Tyson were born here, would we be praising him or condemning him? Obviously praise! I say Spivey was clean and he was persecuted by the NBA for some other reason. What do you think? At least he never took air out of a basketball!

"Everybody thought he would have been a great big man in the NBA, had he gotten the opportunity to play," said Cliff Hagan, a former teammate and past athletics director at UK. "I'm sure he was very disappointed that he didn't get an opportunity to play in the NBA."

"I really felt bad about him, because I think since the scandal that he really had hard times," UK teammate Bobby Watson.

"I always felt like he should have been given the opportunity to play. . . . I don't remember that they ever really proved that he did anything wrong." Said former teammate Frank Ramsey: "He was a tremendous basketball player . . . he was a 7-footer that could run . . . he had a good hook shot . . . good rebounder."

"It was very unfortunate he did not play pro basketball to prove just how good he was. I think it (the scandal) had a very definite effect on his life emotionally."

"After his trial, Mr. Spivey sued the NBA. The suit was settled out of court for $10,000. He passed a lie-detector test that cleared him of wrongdoing, a news report said at the time."

"Mr. Spivey is survived by a son, Dr. Cashton B. Spivey of Isle of Palms, S.C. [Wilkes-Barre should send him a sympathy card, and a commendation and thank you for the good his dad did for our City.]

"A memorial service will be held later. His wish was that his ashes be scattered in the Pacific and Atlantic oceans. Kerr Brothers Funeral Home is in charge of arrangements."

We owe this Wilkes-Barre Legacy much more than we as his city ever gave him... Wilkes-Barre ought to be proud that this giant of a man who played his heart out for us, when there were almost zero seven footers playing basketball, that he played for Wilkes-Barre, and he was great!

NBA pro basketball players from WB

There is only one name on the NBA list, and he is so young still that one cannot claim that Mr. Bob Sura is part of Wilkes-Barre's old time glory years. Yet, he was as good as it gets in his playing days. Sura is part of a new wave for Wilkes-Barre's return to glory.

He learned his game in Wilkes-Barre playing hoops with his buddies in Huber Park in the Mayflower Section. Rob Brody, the Webby Twins, George Webby & Leo Webby, NFLer Greg Skrepenak, and others from the Heights and Mayflower sections all became better basketball players playing with Bob Sura right by the Mayflower Little League. Sura was all basketball...fun came later. Sura of course was in a league of his own.

Born March 25, 1973 in Wilkes-Barre, PA, Bob Sura more than made it to the pros. He was a real star. At 6'5" tall, he last played for the Houston Rockets in the NBA. He played his high school ball at GAR. He had a game high of 69 while leading GAR on a remarkable streak of 86 consecutive league victories.

From GAR, Sura played for Florida State University, with standout teammates NBA players Charlie Ward and Sam Cassell. Yet, despite all the excellent players in his own university, Sura was named the ACC Rookie of the Year his freshman year at Florida State (1991–92). He was picked 17th overall by the Cleveland Cavaliers in the 1995 NBA Draft.

He had his best season with the Cavaliers in his last season with the team, 1999-2000, averaging 13.8 points per game. Think of how many points you would have scored as an athlete in your prime playing in the NBA. What if they kept you in for both halves, would your point accumulation be higher than zero? I know mine would not. I add this because in his last season with the Cavs, Sura put in 13.8 points per game. Phenomenal!

Bob Sura was traded several times in his career. Who would trade more than a brick or a head of lettuce for you or me? Bob first was traded to the Golden State Warriors, then the Detroit Pistons, followed by the Atlanta Hawks and finally the Houston Rockets. In the 2004-05 season, his last season due to injury, he averaged 10.3 points, 5.3 rebounds and 5.5 assists. I rest my case. Like Bill Spivey, Bobs Sura gets little to zero recognition from Wilkes-Barre. Why?

Wilkes-Barre's Bob Sura was honored again by Florida State as the school's all-time scorer when the school retired his jersey in 2007. My championship minor league shirt was retired by my mother sometime around 1960. These two are not equal. Where was Wilkes-Barre with an opportunity to claim Bob Sura as one of our own?

After a great career in the NBA, on October 29, 2007, Sura was cut by the Rockets. He spends a lot of time in Northeastern PA and someday, you may bump into this fine athlete, unexpectedly. We wish him well. Wilkes-Barre City should do a bit better than that.

Pro football players from Wilkes-Barre PA

Pennsylvania itself has been well known for football for years and years. At one point Pennsylvania's All Star football players were so highly touted that PA played a team of All Stars from all across the country in what was known as the Big 33 game.

Wilkes-Barre is the town of birth for fourteen former professional football players and another nine born elsewhere, graduated from one of Wilkes-Barre's three high schools. None are active in the NFL right now. The last player to play pro ball was Meyer's Quentin Harris, who retired from the sport in 2006.

Those who went to high school in Wilkes-Barre and those born in Wilkes-Barre are included in the chart on the next page. *WB denotes those born in Wilkes-Barre. Bruce Kozersky, Ron Solt, and Notre Dame great Joe Perkowski were not born in our City, for example, but went to high school here. Seven NFL players on the list were born in Wilkes-Barre but went to high school elsewhere.

Two other adopted Wilkes-Barreans are included in the list even though they were born in New Jersey. "Rocket" and "Missile" Ismael were quite famous at Meyers, playing for Coach Mickey Gorham in the 1980's. Before I release the chart, let me tell you a little story about the Ismael Brothers and the game Mickey Gorham lost or Teddy Jackson won. Jackson pulled a Belichick long before Deflategate.

Meyers traveled to Dallas for the game. Meyers, with the two track star high speed Ismael brothers ready to rip up the sod, was expected to exact a big toll on the much slower Mountaineers of Dallas, and coached by Hall of Famer Ted Jackson. The word is that Jackson gave the grass crew a few weeks off and when Meyers came to play, the grass was about knee high. There are no pictures.

Neither of the Ismaels' could grind out any quick yardage in such conditions, and Jackson's ploy gave Dallas the win. It was the only loss on Meyer's record that year. Now, that is a good story. Ted Jackson, who I played baseball with in Senior Teener's for Kranson's Clothes may or may not admit to this story. I say Jackson won, and as much as I liked Mickey Gorham and Meyers, my alma mater, he lost.

Here is the list of players born in Wilkes-Barre, identified by *WB in the High School column. As you can see in this chart, a lot of folks moved from Wilkes-Barre after their pro footballer was born but most stayed close by.

NFL Pro Football *Players Born* in Wilkes-Barre, PA

Player Name	Years	Position	Gms	Team(s)	High Schl
Albert Bedner	1924 - 1926	C-G-T	20	NY Giants	*WB WB High
Rudolph Kraft	1921 - 1921	C-G	2	Tonawanda Kardex	*WB WB High
Isadore Weinstock	1935 - 1938	FB-HB-QB	24	Eagles, Pirates	*WB Coughlin
Peter Stevens	1936 - 1936	C	5	Eagles	*WB, Pitman
Joseph Koons	1941 - 1941	C	6	Brooklyn	*WB, *NA
Chester Pudloski	1944 - 1944	T	10	Rams	*WB Coughlin
George Young	1946 - 1953	E	48	Browns	*WB FF
Ray Yakavonis	1955 - 1983	DE-NT	21	Vikings, Chiefs	*WB Hanover
James Katcavage	1956 - 1968	DE-DT	165	Giants	*WB Phila RC
Joseph Hergert	1960 - 1961	LB	19	Buffalo Bills	*WB Daytona
William Lopasky	1961 - 1961	LB	10	San Francisco	*WB Lehman
Joe Perkowski	1962 - 1962	B, K	Injury	Chicago Bears	Coughlin
Thomas Woodeshick	1963 - 1972	DB,FB,OB,RB	114	Eagles, StL Cards	*WB Hanover
Mark Duda	1983 - 1987	DT-NT	55	StL Cardinals	*WB Wyo VW
Ron Solt	1984 - 1992	RG	116	Colts, Eagles	Coughlin
Bruce Kozersky	1984 - 1995	C	172	Bengals	Coughlin
Gregory Manusky	1988 - 1999	LB	178	KC, Wash, Minn.	*WB Dallas
Gregory Skrepenak	1992 - 1997	G-OG-OT-T	68	Panthers, Raiders	*WB GAR
Qadry "Missile" Ismael	1993 - 2002	WR	137	6 teams 10 seasons	Meyers
Raghib Rocket Ismael	1993 - 2001	WR	116	Raiders, Pthrs, Cows	Meyers
Paul Greeley	1997 - 1997	C	6	Panthers	*WB Coughlin
Phillip Ostrowski	1999 - 2000	G-OG	28	San Francisco	*WBMeyers

| Quentin Harris | 2002 - 2006 | DB | | 60 | Cardinals, Broncos | *WBMeyers |

The bottom line for Wilkes-Barre is that many fine athletes grew up in our town, and the city can be proud of their accomplishments. We are definitely a sports-minded community in Wilkes-Barre and of course all of Northeastern PA

Chapter 32 The Road to Glory Must Be Built

Train at Sans Souci

Right by the old pool at Sans Souci was the swimming pool that swimmers from Wilkes-Barre used after the City pools were disabled and/or ripped down. The book below was in Hanover Township but not the Hanover Township by Sans Souci. But it looks a lot like it. It was big. It was right by the Wild Mouse

Wilkes-Barre, A city ready to better itself

The "shoreline" of the eastern bank of the Susquehanna River has been known as the River Common for some time. John Durkee, the man who gave Wilkes-Barre its name saw the area as a place of beauty, and wanted it to be preserved for common use—for all the residents.

When he put his plan together for Wilkes-Barre City in 1773, he was quick to designate this beautiful area along the bank of the Susquehanna River as public ground; a.k.a. common ground. And so, the area by the river, long before any dikes were built, became known as the River Common. We still know it by that today.

As candidates, including myself were running for Mayor in 2015 and Congress in 2022, a recommended initiative for them to execute should have been to help Wilkes-Barre return to its days of glory. One of the ways to do that among many is to recreate Wilkes-Barre as a clean city.

Scum and dirt, unnecessary garbage, and unseemliness must be no more. Though nobody would be interested in Wilkes-Barre becoming a monitored nanny state to make sure nobody crosses the line, for sure, none of us want Wilkes-Barre to be unattractive.

To the notion of a "clean city," we must add "and a beautiful city." Sometimes all it takes is a little paint but it always takes a lot of pride, desire and strong will to make anything happen. Betsy Summers, the spunky lady who the Times Leader endorsed in her attempt to unseat entrenched politician State Representative Eddie Day Pashinsky, a guy who ran against a tax break for all the folks, and is loved enough to still get reelected, agrees with me but it has not been close to being his #1 priority for sure.

Summers says in the Independent Gazette: "I will again be raising the clutter cleanup issue to our city council this month, along with negligent street cleaning." Bravo Ms. Summers. "A clean city is the first step to restoring the pride that our community once demonstrated." Amen, Betsy!

Years ago, there was more attention to clean and beautiful. As I write this chapter, I still can remember the beautiful flowers every year placed at the memorial at Miner Park. It was opposite Hanover Street on Old River Road in Wilkes-Barre. Nobody in City Hall can tell me whether it was Charles Miner who donated Miner Park or not, and what the stipulations were. I ask myself: "Why is there a public school in Miner Park if a Wilkes-Barre prominent citizen donated land for recreation in Wilkes-Barre?" Is Miner Park a myth?

After the flood, somehow the very attractive and well-appointed Kistler School emerged on the property and the Miner Park memorial shrine to a member of the Miner family was moved, and I have not seen flowers since. Worse than that, Miner Park Swimming Pool, with its magnificent center fountain, disappeared forever. Look how much these kids in the picture below enjoyed the pool. Was there no other place for a school?

I am sure there were good intentions for things like a new school but overall the good intentions have been setting Wilkes-Barre back, not moving us forward. Kistler School could have been built in a blighted area of South Wilkes-Barre or on stilts, higher than the dike before Barney Farms was ever built. Why take away space donated for a park?

Miner Park Swimming Pool South Wilkes-Barre

Hollenback Swimming Pool had been around forever and then it disappeared. Back in 1938, there was a debate about the pool's filtering system. Some urged that hard coal would make a better filter than sand for the Hollenback swimming pool. Why is there no Hollenback Pool?

I have a friend who one time was my manager at IBM before we both retired. After living in beautiful Burlington Vermont and seeing how the well-to-do took care of things for everybody without raising taxes, he was amazed at his observations of Northeastern PA.

Hollenback Pool Parsons Wilkes-Barre – A Fun Place

Surely the Miner family, mentioned often in Wilkes-Barre's yearly almanacs, along with the Kirby family are few and far between. For their own altruism, they have really helped and always seem to help whenever they can.

By the way, about Burlington Vermont. It should be a place that our public officials ought to try to emulate. It actually comes as no surprise to me that Burlington VT recently caught national attention for its quality of living. They are ranked #2 in Kiplinger's 2013 "10 Great Places to Live" Without dreams, there are no ideas; there are no plans; and there are no positive actions.

I am concerned that those with affluence and real wealth in their time of prosperity in Wilkes-Barre, unlike the Kirby's and the Miner's, and more than likely some others, for their own reasons have not looked back at Wilkes-Barre even if it were the source of their success. It seems like when they had their fill, and they have taken enough, they move out of town and knock the dust on their sandals back onto our City.

My friend from IBM wondered why garbage and crap would be coming into NEPA from areas all across the East Coast, and few of the obvious "elites" stopped it at the gates. When his observations had turned him into a cynic, he was surprised that the town bosses did not insist that Wilkes-Barre take the garbage from all of the East Coast cities and simply let them back their trucks up and dump it all, toxins and all, into the old Wilkes-Barre mine shafts.

Just drop it down the mile or more deep shafts and never look at it again. Who would know? Maybe some have even done that. He wondered why the prominent families in Wilkes-Barre / Scranton and surrounds seemed to care so little about the hoi polloi in the area. He wondered why the people left behind put up with the corruption, and in fact come out at election time and seemed to cheer for more of it.

He wondered why IBM located in Endicott, NY rather than Wilkes-Barre PA. I had no answers. Why did Miller Brewery not locate here. Why was industry kept out in the mining days? But, I know the answer now, I had not thought about it as you may have not. He felt that the more well-to-do have a gain and run philosophy in a community, then once they collect their gains, they are gone.

I hope he is wrong for the long-haul as sometimes just a friendly reminder can make somebody see the error in their ways. Unfortunately I see tons of evidence as you do that that he is spot on! What do you think? Like Scrooge in Dickens' A Christmas Carol It is never too late. Can we talk these people who have used their privileged status to pillage Wilkes-Barre and other NEPA cities to come back and help bring our City back to glory? Do we know their names?

In its glory days, you may recall that in addition to the City Pools, many Wilkes-Barre playgrounds had these one-size fits all wading pools with a fountain in the center for kids to play and then cool off in the summer. By the time I was old enough to see my first playground, they were still there, but all were all dysfunctional, and there never was any water.

While I was growing up Wilkes-Barre had three major pools, Hollenback, Miner Pool, and Griffith Pool, which eventually was replaced by Coal Street Pool, which is no more. My sister often walked me from High Street down Hanover to Old River Road to Miner Park Pool. It took a while but it was a nice adventure.

Griffith is gone as is Hollenback along with the most glorious of all the pools, Miner Pool, which was built on donated land? Even the two pools in the basement of Meyers High School used for sporting events and swim classes are gone. An indoor pool does open up every summer religiously in Kistler School apparently so the City Officials can brag that Wilkes-Barre still has a swimming pool in the city. What a shame!

Our City can no longer afford to have the big winners in Wilkes-Barre dump on the city and have the taxpayers buy huge rolls of Charmin to clean up their mess. It is not time to rob from the rich for sure. But for all the models our forebears in America and in Wilkes-Barre put together, they surely did not anticipate the level of greed that exists today. It's time to think of others for a change. I think things can change for the good as people's hearts soften. Look how many trips the spirit had to take to convince Scrooge to do the right thing. It did not happen through taxation. It happened because of a big heart that was finally opened.

Surely as the people who made it big in Wilkes-Barre get older, they think more of eternity. Chances are they either are or once were Christians. NEPA is mostly a Christian Community. More than likely, like the rest of us, they love and worship God.

You and I know that Christians and Jews and Hindus and others are taught to care about people. I would like to see all people come to grips with their eternity and consider how they

might help others without government getting in the way.
Everybody decides what charitable acts they choose to make.
Helping out Wilkes-Barre City will help all of the residents
here and will help stage the city to be an even better place to
live.

I am definitely not talking about taxation. Taxation should be
used only for necessities. I am not talking about tithing or
anything anybody must do. The taxation system is not meant
for reconciliation with the Lord so Wilkes-Barre officials
should make no demands on anybody per se.

With a positive change in attitude about Wilkes-Barre, I would
like to see a lot of committees forming so that people can help
people. I would like to see many volunteers coming forth to
help this City in the future. If you happen to win the Lottery or
you made your fortune here and you would like to give
something back or simply want to help us out as we return to
our glory days, You can bet we will most appreciate your
generosity of time and resources.

If you have a nice business, consider a branch in Wilkes-Barre.
If you want to build a new facility, there are lots of nice places
all around this town. There are a lot of unoccupied buildings
that are begging for you to come in and set up shop. We will
help you be successful as you help us return to glory.

City Beautiful

Before the demise of many wonderful public structures, back in
the early 1900's, Wilkes-Barre leaders wanted the City to be as
good as it could be. They formed a City Beautiful movement,
which is a good idea even for today. They were not selfish
leaders; in fact, they were selfless.

Through this movement, the area by the river was further
decorated. The City Beautiful movement was a reform
philosophy that aimed to beautify urban cities such as
Chicago, Detroit and Washington, D.C. The movement swept
through Wilkes-Barre when the city council permitted the

Town Improvement Society to plant new trees on the common and to carve a footpath through it.

Wilkes-Barre leaders at the turn of the 20th Century understood that a beautiful City would help bring about a prosperous city for all. They were not in it for what they could get.

In 1906, Wilkes-Barre's first Park Commission was created. Again, the river bank was the object of attention. This time, the river bank was filled in, new footpaths and beautiful gardens were laid out and gas lamps were installed. This commission did not think that everything in this and other projects needed to be done with taxpayer dollars, and so they encouraged local people of means to donate to the city. Land was the preferred item.

And so, that is why to this day we see such nice parks as Nesbitt Park (Kingston) and Kirby Park (Wilkes-Barre), as well as the River Common, which we must remember was not always part of a levee system. And, of course there is Miner Park, the origins and stipulations of the gift from the Miner family created a marvelous park.

At this point in its glorious history, Wilkes-Barre was a booming city. Its newly landscaped common area sans dikes, gave inhabitants a most wonderful and spacious place to escape the city while still being in the city. The recent improvements on the same area by the river on the east side are also beautiful, and we are very thankful for the results of this fine work, but all was paid by taxpayer dollars, and we are running out of those quickly.

For all the good work that was done in making the City beautiful, there were always those who, for their own reasons, did not care as much about its beauty and wanted beautiful areas to be replaced for commercial reasons. Over the years, Public Square Park for example was always at risk of being ripped out and replaced with roads and buildings.

How about no Public Square?

In 1930, for example, The Wilkes-Barre Almanac documents
the attempts of City Councilman John Nobel to extend Main
and Market Streets through Public Square. At the time G.A.R.
Members had been proposing a monument be built where
Nobel wanted the new road to go.

Thankfully more insightful minds than Nobel's were making
the decision though Council did entertain destroying the
Square for this purpose. Without the criticism of the G. A.R.
members and veterans of many wars, today, there might not be
a Public Square.

In its glory years of beauty and commerce, which lasted
actually a long time until several years after the flood—about
1980, both sides of the Susquehanna River were beautiful. The
fact that there were no dikes on either side of the river before
1936, made the eastern side of the River in Wilkes-Barre even
more beautiful than it is today after the recent restoration.

East Side of Susquehanna River Wilkes-Barre Central City

The homes on Riverside Drive for example, prior to the 1936
flood had riverfront lots. It was beautiful. They were beautiful.

Some liked their views so much that they could not be convinced that the 1936 disaster was not just the one flood of a lifetime.

So, they never expected another flood. Consequently, the residents first complained when the dike system was initially built, because it destroyed their unimpeded view of the Susquehanna River. It certainly did ruin the view but it also protected them and many other residents of the lowlands from normal river flooding until Hurricane Agnes came and surprised us all in 1972.

Mansions on South River Street Wilkes-Barre 1917

View Looking West, from Miners Bank Building, Wilkes Barre, Pa.

Over the past fifty years, many of Wilkes-Barre's prominent citizens have in fact moved out of the city proper into the suburbs. Just looking at the pro-football players list of players born in Wilkes-Barre, I noticed that a number graduated from high schools close by, but not in Wilkes-Barre itself.

I think we can figure out how to get more citizens of prominence to move back if we make the City worth their return. Would it not be wonderful if we had some societies in town who wanted to bring back gardens such as those by the

Palm House in these pictures or the gardens in the Miner Park of the 1950's.

People do not forget their roots. John Durkee, the founder of Wilkes-Barre was able to get land and other amenities donated to Wilkes-Barre City in its founding years and even afterwards. I would bet that if we had a good plan to make the city clean and beautiful, safe, and affordable, and if our city officials made it known that Wilkes-Barre would accept donations— just as John Durkee did—from property to cash to the moon, we would see them come in beyond expectation.

Three Pictures on the next page of the Palm House on North River Street in Court House grounds Circa 1940 are shown on this page and the next. Look how beautiful this greenhouse structure by the Courthouse was, What happened? Our forebears saw beauty in the city as necessary. That is a good maxim for the future.

BIRD'S-EYE VIEW OF PALM HOUSE AND GARDENS, WILKES-BARRE, PA.

Palm House, Wilkes-Barre, Pa.

PALM HOUSE AND GARDEN, WILKES-BARRE, PA.

But, before we can expect that we can see beauty like the Palm Gardens above in Wilkes-Barre again, we first need to accept that we must plan. We'll take all donations from those that are glad we stand in the center of a community ready to reestablish its glory. We need everybody's help.

We certainly need a good plan but we must also put an end to the carnage in order to gain this opportunity. Wilkes-Barre has ripped down too many buildings in its time and replaced them with Plasticville factories, hotels, and monopoly houses. Does anyone recall the old South Main Street Armory? It was built as headquarters for the Ninth Infantry Regiment of the Pennsylvania National Guard in the 1880s.

South Main Street Armory – Third Block of South Main Street

This huge, fortress-like drill-shed was supplanted in the 1920s and turned to other uses, such as a boxing arena, a dance hall and a roller skating rink.

Then somebody got the bright idea to take it out and replace it with a parking lot. It is gone nonetheless and poorly built commercial structures and parking lots have replaced this great building and others like it. It is tough to have a glorious city with the Axe Man being so busy tearing things down. In my youth I was at this Armory regularly, roller skating. Others were there for boxing matches. Others were there for Weekend Drills.

Though I could not roller skate today for sure, I skated formally indoors for the first time in this grand edifice. It is gone forever. The same Axe-Man plight fell upon the magnificent G.A.R. Building down the street from the Armory.

Grand Army of Republic Building on South Main Street by the Armory

Wilkesbarre, Pa. Grand Army Hall.

This magnificent building was constructed in the late 1800's after the Civil War. Over 2500 men from Wyoming Valley fought in the Civil War. Over 1100 of them were members of the group that met in this armory-like building which disappeared from the scene after most of these veterans passed on to their eternal rewards.

That is the fate of all buildings that were masterfully built, and indestructible in their day. These buildings would be thriving today if it were not for the carelessness of their caretakers.

But shame on us but mostly those we left in charge... The buildings got a little dirty and needed a new roof, and were not respected over time. No cheap structure built to replace these huge pieces of stone will ever last as long or be as respected. What do you do when you need a new roof? Do you buy the property next to you and tear it down hoping incessant rain will not affect your property if this one is gone? No, because you are not stupid!

Civil War Veterans at the GAR Building circa 1912

In the 1970's when I visited Europe on a student fare, I got to see first-hand the neglected Roman Coliseum standing in Rome. Yet, it's been there for over 2000 years and nobody is clamoring to tear it down. It is not about to go anywhere unless some uncaring human, someplace chooses to rip it down

Chapter 33   Stop the Axe Man— Demolish Three City High Schools?

Special landmarks do not have to be destroyed

Throughout this book, as we have explored one neighborhood after another, we found a lot of holes in our City. There are many vacant lots where once magnificent buildings stood. The latest of course is the Hotel Sterling, but our history is replete with the Axe Man delivering damaging blows to our future, and the City agreeing to take down one monument after another that can never be replaced.

We have two more monuments that are about to come down if they are not cared for—The Irem Temple Mosque, and The Hotel Sterling Annex. This must be stopped. Irem Temple seems to be addressed now thankfully but the Hotel Sterling is gone but not forgotten. .

Additionally, the Wilkes-Barre Area School District, whose mission is not to care about Wilkes-Barre per se, wants to rip down our three high schools and put up Plasticville buildings that may or may not last thirty years, to replace them.

I am 100% against this and I wrote a letter to both papers about it. The Citizen Voice printed it on the day before New Year's Eve, 2014. Here it is in its entirety as printed. It says it just as I meant it. Many in Wilkes-Barre have thanked me for writing it as it represents the feelings of those of us who care.

LETTER TO EDITOR
Published: December 30, 2014

Editor:

The fixes required for Wilkes-Barre Area School District high schools have been depicted as unaffordable by taxpayers regardless of the approach — fix it or demolish and build it again cheaper. I don't think so. I don't buy it. It would have been interesting if the numbers and "plans" had been presented at Wednesday's meeting along with the impact on millage. We all know the school district has not been a tax bargain for local taxpayers. More importantly for all of us living in Wilkes-Barre Area, the question should be, "Do we really want to destroy historically important, well-built school buildings and replace them with cheap quality 30-year models?"

Wilkes-Barre High was established in 1890. It later was renamed Coughlin High after GAR opened in 1925. This old Coughlin school building is in fact the oldest public high school building in Pennsylvania. Can you believe some people want to tear down the oldest public school building in the state? The Coughlin Annex structure was built in 1952. The original Coughlin building was occupied in 1909 though construction had begun much earlier. Citizens of Wilkes-Barre Area need to get involved and think about what is being proposed and we must ask ourselves if there are not better ways to solve this problem without doubling our already unaffordable school tax burden.

In March 2005, Clif Greim wrote an excellent piece titled "New Construction vs. Renovation for Older School Facilities." Though 10 years old, it still covers the issue quite well. It is available for all to read online.

Greim offers readable counsel on the big decision for Wilkes-Barre Area:

"Generally, schools built in the 1950s or earlier have impressive architectural character and often are fixtures in their neighborhoods. They are structurally sound and can accommodate new systems. In addition, there is often strong sentiment to keep them in some form.

"Newer schools built in the 1960s and '70s generally lack architectural character, are not energy-efficient and are constructed of cheaper materials. These get torn down more often or become hand-me-down conversions from high schools to junior highs or from junior highs to elementary schools."

All of the buildings in question were built before 1950 other than the Coughlin Annex, which was built in 1952. I think it is safe to say that the same logic Greim discusses for post-1950 buildings applies to the Coughlin Annex.

I admit I was taken back by board members who said, "It's going to cost a lot but it's something we have to do." I would ask whether they would vote to tear down historic Independence Hall if it were within their responsibility back in 1860? It helps to know that at that time, this famous Philadelphia structure was about the same age as Coughlin is right now. We all know that Independence Hall is the birthplace of America. We also know that the Declaration of Independence and the U.S. Constitution were both debated and signed inside this remarkable building. Independence Hall was built between 1732 and 1756 to be the Pennsylvania State House. It still stands and thrives.

Originally, this building housed all three branches of Pennsylvania's colonial government. Yes, it was built even before the U.S.A. became the U.S.A. It is now two and a half times older than Coughlin High School and it has a lot of life left. Think of the famous graduates of Coughlin, GAR and Meyers, and think of all the memorable events at those schools. These buildings are special landmarks in our home area, and they do not have to be destroyed.

GAR is almost 90 years old and Meyers is the baby at 85 years of age. Why would we give up these historically significant, well-built structures and replace them with 30-year throwaway, square buildings made of sheet metal, plastic, and other cheap materials? We have historical buildings with grand designs, granite and limestone interiors, and exquisite stained glass auditoriums. Who are we to cast this all away so that in 30 years another study like this can be done as we rip out the structures to be built and go with even cheaper buildings with 20-year lifetimes or perhaps a modular school or a few trailers?

Where there is a will, there is a way. Somehow we lost our will with the Hotel Sterling after spending $6 million without fixing the roof. Let's keep our will and our wits as the board tries to shove a huge millage increase our way ... for a less desirable outcome than the status quo.

One off-hand suggestion I have is to budget about $1 million or more if we can afford it. We can bring in a great building contractor from our area to allocate five or 10 artisans just for Wilkes-Barre Area, to begin work on these buildings, one year at a time, one objective at a time. Let's get the hazards out of the way first. When real emergencies occur in the other buildings, we can dispatch this crew of experts along with Wilkes-Barre Area maintenance personnel to fix the problems posthaste.

I would also use our political representatives to get waivers for the beams that can withstand lateral forces. This is a very costly undertaking and should be ruled out immediately. Clearly all of the Wilkes-Barre Area buildings in question have not been blown over by big puffs of wind in the 85 to 105 years in which they have been standing and they are not going to be blown over tomorrow or any time soon. I would also try to get waivers for increasing the physical size of the classrooms. They seem big enough to have been able to be used for conducting classes for many years and surely they could continue to be used. Waivers would save a lot of money and they are practical and safe.

I would bet that the local and state historical societies would help in gaining the waivers. How can we consider destroying such history for a promise we know will be broken 30 years from now? After all, citizens make the laws. If the laws do not fit, waivers are a good way to save money and still have the benefits of a safe school.

When all the emergencies are fixed, I would put the new team of artisans to work on one floor at a time of one building at a time. I would use as many vocational students to help in the effort as possible. Think of the training they would get. Additionally, Wilkes-Barre Area also has a lot of maintenance personnel, who I bet would love to learn new skills working with the best artisans in the valley in building, plumbing, electrical, carpentry and other endeavors. Where there is a will, there is a way. Nothing in life truly worth having is easy. Why give up the best for a solution that may not even be good enough to be second-best?

Brian Kelly

Wilkes-Barre

Chapter 34 Working in Wilkes-Barre

Get a Job! Try 'n get it!

As small geographically that a town as Wilkes-Barre may be; there was a busy time in our history. During this time, it appeared that there was more industry in town than there were people. There was no problem getting a job in most of these glory years. Of course there were issues during the depression, but even then, the mines were still hot. People had to keep warm.

There was lots of work in Wilkes-Barre for anybody who wanted to work. Those manufacturing jobs are gone from here long after the mines stopped functioning. If there are some officials trying to bring back light industry to Wilkes-Barre, and being paid to do so, they are not being very successful. Wilkes-Barre may have a few spots in which we can support heavy industry. Don't forget the Vulcan Iron Works once made huge locomotives.

Look at the vacant lots on major streets where there was once industry or stores, or even car lots with cars. This explains why the city's per capita income is much less than anywhere else in the state. There are no high paying economic sector jobs any more. The biggest payers are the public sector in government and school districts. We can do much better.

Wilkes-Barre once had lots of industry

I can remember even as a kid, many manufacturing and distribution industry plants and factories right here in Wilkes-Barre, PA. When I was in my early twenties working with IBM, there was still a lot of industry here. Did local policies and union favoritism cause these industries to bail to other industry favorable states?

Ask the one time owners of Muskin Corporation in Miners Mills their opinion of that? Did all of Wilkes-Barre and our politics contribute to Muskin choosing Midway Georgia over Miners Mills in Wilkes-Barre?

I worked with IBM Marketing Representatives, who other companies would call salesmen. My job was to assure the installation of some of the biggest computers in the larger businesses in Wilkes-Barre and surrounds. IBM knew Wilkes-Barre had potential and its businesses responded to the new computer revolution by spending a minimum $100,000 at the time to become technologically more capable.

You may remember Klein Candy and the Key Stores, in the 1950's on the first or second block from the Square. My dad would stop at one of those places with me in the Christmas season to buy good candy at the lowest price possible.

Klein engaged in other endeavors such as distributing convenience store products such as candy, canned soup, lettuce and vegetables, cigarettes and soda.

Klein's customers were anybody in business that would buy what they were selling. They even found gas stations who otherwise would not be interested in anything but gas and oil proceeds to sign up for convenience goods.

Pantry Quick's, Quick Mart's, Orloski's and the like were all served from Klein's huge warehouse. These stores most often sold gasoline in most cases and they still do.

Klein eventually bought the old Economy Store Warehouse in Hanover Township, just outside of Wilkes-Barre and they continued growing as a company. They expanded their business and became a billion dollar enterprise. They were doing business in about eight states in the East. They felt they were invincible.

Unfortunately, for a lot of professionals who worked for Klein in technology and accounting, the company could not make it as it approached invincibility, and they had to sell the business. This all happened in the last ten years. Perhaps it was bad management? Perhaps it was too much debt? I choose not to judge. The new company though not American, is doing quite well, but without a lot of excellent NEPA jobs that were once there.

So, even Klein Candy, a very successful enterprise found they could not make it because they grabbed too hard at being big. So, with their huge debt, they were still able to sell the whole deal to a Canadian Company, Core-Mark.

Core-Mark as most businesses cared about one thing—the ability to sustain the business at the least possible cost. Therefore, as one of their first actions, they fired just about all of the professional people. As a side show, they got rid of their huge IBM computers and they hooked themselves up to their home office in Western Canada. The home base was using the same IBM technology as Klein so the adaptation was less costly.

The Phone bill had to be enormous but they got rid of a lot of workers, who lived mostly in Wilkes-Barre. That's what we in the US, call competition, but in this case, Wilkes-Barre and Hanover Township lost while the Klein owners gained.

Maybe tomorrow, these same people will consider lending a helping hand to Wilkes-Barre in one way or another. Perhaps establishing a business in Wilkes-Barre would be a good idea.

Unfortunately for Wilkes-Barre, the Klein story has been repeated in one way or another for far too long in Wilkes-Barre and throughout the Wyoming Valley.

Let's look at another major company, Kay Wholesale Drug. They were originally located just outside of the City right next to the former Leslie Faye building. Leslie Faye of course is another story. When Kay got bigger, they were too big for the Route 315 facility so they moved to the former Alta Footwear plant on the Sans Souci Highway. They had grown their business from $10 million to $300 million by using IBM technology properly.

When larger competitors began to invest even more in their technology infrastructures and their marketing teams, Kay was taking in some profits for the owners, and so they fell behind their competition. When they could no longer sustain the business, they were $50,000,000 in debt.

After work on September 27, 1994, 121 otherwise happy Kay Wholesale Drug Co. employees chipped in for an "it's-all-over" party, and afterwards, they all went home for good. The 54-year-old firm, which sold drugs wholesale to pharmacies in an expanding number of states, shut down and began a liquidation process. There are too many endings like this in the greater Wilkes-Barre job market. Where is a countervailing force to help companies like this to stay in business? We need to create an industry support group to help companies stay successful.

We need an industrial comeback

When I was in my teens, people would walk or take the bus to work or even ride a bike to work in most months of the year. Stegmaier Brewery, Gibbons Brewery (open for a while under a new name Lion, Inc.). **At the end of 2019 the Lion Brewery was purchased by Encore Consumer Capital**, a San Francisco-based private equity firm. In early 2022, the Lion Brewery sold the Stegmaier labels to the Susquehanna

Brewing Company, a company owned by descendants of Charles Stegmaier. We'll see what happens to Stegmaier now that it has a reprieve.

Other spots such as Carter Rubber aka Carter Footwear, Craft Associates, who made fancy furniture were among the many Wilkes-Barre plants that hired hundreds and thousands of residents. They are all gone. Now, for all intents and purposes, Klein is gone, and Kay wholesale is off the radar. Hundreds of jobs are gone for Wilkes-Barre and surrounds. That's why people who stay in the area do not make a lot of money.

There are remnants of possibilities but try to get a job in manufacturing. I dare you. Try to find some place in Wilkes-Barre that makes something other than a pie or a cake. Even the Old River Road Bakery, and its successor, Boulevard Bakery, as well as the Barney Street Bakery, Kornblatts, and Keystate, are all gone. They were great but it did not matter. We have to figure out why?

The major industry in all of Wyoming Valley in the 1970s was garment manufacturing. These shops made ladies dresses, pants, suits etc. Leslie Faye, originally just outside of Wilkes-Barre by Miners Mills had a billion dollar company headquartered right there on Highway 315 that went south sometime in the 1990's with hundreds of employees displaced. The company survived and moved to the Hanover Industrial Complex, but then what? Was any of this good for the garment worker?

There were literally hundreds of small cut and sew shops in NEPA. There were also other big-time apparel manufacturing companies such as Rex Industries and Carter Rubber. There was a huge Silk Mill on high street making textiles and just down Blackman Street a bit was the Atwater Throwing Company, who also made textiles. So, what happened?

Planters Peanuts and the infamous Peanut Man were also a big part of the landscape. They of course were bought out and were moved from Wilkes-Barre. There was a time when all you had to do is want to work, and there was a nice job.

This job more than likely was in Wilkes-Barre and it was probably fun, and it paid well, just waiting just for you. Purvin and Woodlawn Dairies—Dolly Madison ice Cream, were in town also and they all contributed to the economy, and their employees were tickled for their paychecks. Yes, they enjoyed working there!

There were also lots of lumber houses and there was lots of building buildings and homes though much of the action was in the suburbs of Wilkes-Barre. Places such as Wickes, Ryman Lumber, and Scouton-Lee Lumber, and others had their day in the sun. And, of course there was International Color Corporation, and the Sunday Independent helping the newspaper industry.

Mining had its great days here for years headquartered by the Glen Alden and the Lehigh Valley Coal Companies. Miners worked in the Red Ash Mine, Prospect Colliery, Pine Ridge Breaker, Stanton Colliery, and the South Wilkes-Barre Colliery. Other industries included General Cigar Company, Penn Tobacco Company, and E A Roos, etc.

The Railroads were here big time in Wilkes-Barre with the Wilkes-Barre and Eastern Railroad and the Delaware and Hudson. Coal always needed rails for shipping.

Sports figures made a few bucks in Wilkes-Barre. Eddie White may be the only sports industrialist that I know about. In addition to entertainment, the sports teams such as the Baseball Wilkes-Barre Barons, and the Basketball Wilkes-Barre Barons were sports employers in our area until they disappeared. It was lots easier in the former glory days to get a good job. Remember, not all employees in sports enterprises are athletes.

You may have heard of the Vulcan Iron Works, which I noted earlier in the book. They were right in the middle of South

Wilkes-Barre. They were not into small stuff. They made train locomotives. They were a nationally known manufacturer of railway locomotives from 1849 to 1954.

The Delaware & Hudson RR Freight Station, its Round House, etc. Wilkes-Barre Coal Company, Wilkes-Barre Stove Factory. Selltex Factors , Hazard Iron Works, Wilkes-Barre Carriage Company, Ma's Old Fashioned Bottling Company, Eagle Bottling Works, Star Beverage, and many others. People worked there and they got a fair wage in Wilkes-Barre's glory days. They are all gone.

So, how do we ever get back to the glory days. My best answer is that we take it up as a goal and every goal has a shot at being achieved. We dream; we come up with ideas; we plan; and then we take action.

We do not elect slouches who simply want a piece of glory and when we get out best leaders in place we follow them. If not, we choose to lead.

All things are possible but not when none of them are on anybody's agenda. Let's put the return to glory days of Wilkes-Barre on all our to-do lists.

Let's all stop saying "NO" to everything just simply because we live in Wilkes-Barre. Let's start by saying a big "YES" to everything simply because we live in Wilkes-Barre. When we think that we can, our return to glory will be right around the corner.

Chapter 35   Safe Biking, Jogging, & Walking-

A dream, and an idea for Wilkes-Barre

For a long time, I have had and still have a dream of getting Wilkes-Barre City out of its temporary rut. While working to do that, I think we can at the same time be making our city safe, affordable, and clean. But, that too is not all. Among many ideas that would help the city prosper, this idea would help our city become a city that is desirable by those people, such as entrepreneurs, who might fall in love with Wilkes-Barre as we all have, move here, and have some great opportunities for exercise and fun.

Why not make the City better than it ever has been by making it accessible and friendly to biking, jogging, and walking from point A to point B. To be able to stay fit and healthy is a critical part of being an asset for any community. And, so it is incumbent upon any mayor and council to want to be sure that there are bike paths, well-maintained sidewalks, along with walking and jogging paths to encourage a healthy lifestyle in safety. It would also make our city a lot more fun, and what is wrong with that?

So, let's examine the notion of safe streets and bike paths for both biking and walking. Wilkes-Barre is not a large city geographically and therefore mostly everybody in this City is within a half-mile of what could be interconnected bicycle facilities. Such facilities should be able to take those people on bikes or walking from very close to where they live to work, to shop, and to green space without fearing for their safety.

There are many gaps in today's pedestrian network though many sidewalks and handicap curb structures have made the situation much better over the last ten years or so. But, the job is not yet done.

Clearly all of this is not in the Mayor's sole purview as there is a City Council involved, which in the past admittedly had been a rubber stamp for the Mayor's whims. Any mayor must develop a good working relationship with City Council to work as a team.

First, there would be community meetings to assess needs. Then, officials would need to develop long-range plans to address those needs, while being consistent with funding availabilities and land-use requirements.

Would it not be nice if Wilkes-Barre adopted an enhanced bike sharing program that put say, 50 bikes in operation in 2023? Yes, we had the beginning of such a program but it is gone right now: http://wilkesbarrebikeshare.com/. For some this is not such a new idea. Is it not appropriate that Wilkes-Barre's # 1 entrepreneur, Gus Genetti is behind the bike share idea in Wilkes-Barre? It is nice of Gus to help out. Another Link is https://wbdcp.org/maps-directions/alternatives-to-driving/. Somebody wanted this to happen but whom? Like many good things in the city, this great idea had some roots but they are gone. Ask the Mayor, why?

With more pick-up and drop off points, the program could be much better than the original idea. There are many programs in other cities such as Pittsburgh, which added 500 bikes in 2014. Biking is good for a lot of reasons and if we make it safe, it can also save the expense of gasoline.

Sponsored by Highmark and Allegheny Heath Network, Healthy Ride is the name of Pittsburgh's bike share system which is owned and operated by Pittsburgh Bike Share, a non-profit organization. Similarly, the non-profit organization

Midwest BikeShare operates Milwaukee's Bublr Bike Share program.

Major cities are placing more focus on biking and walking as a means of getting around with less focus on recreation. It is a great idea. In order for Wilkes-Barre to do this, we would have to examine our streets, and help quickly redesign those, with minimal costs, to be amenable as much as possible to both bike and pedestrian traffic. Perhaps designating allies as bike zones would be a start.

We have some great parks and we have a huge bridge connecting parts of our city with recreation areas that are also part of our city. We can do lots more than we think. We have the path on the dikes which are blacktopped and as nice a path as any, anywhere—and with a great view of the Susquehanna.

Even here, it would help to have pedestrian and bike lanes so that neither are injured from not knowing the "rules of the "road." And, we need to come up with a better way to permit pass-through when the top of the dike seems to end.

Where needed, we might try to carve out a special one way or perhaps wider two way bike path in the dirt away from the asphalt on the dikes. We need to use our heads properly. Some things will work and others will not. When the cost is not prohibitive, we can test out ideas and see if they work. But we first need dreams, ideas, and then plans, before we take action.

The objective would be for our city to have significant, well maintained, bike paths, park bike paths and wonderful walking areas that can be shown as a commitment to encourage biking, jogging, and walking. And yes, of course, we would need to monitor this use so that it continually works. Having a citizen committee interested in pedestrian and biking activities would help make this even more feasible. How about that great public servant John Maday as Captain of the Wilkes-Barre Bike Share.

Leading cities for bicycling are implementing innovative bicycle infrastructures (a.k.a. cycle tracks, green lanes, intersection enhancements, bicycle boulevards, etc.) to encourage people who are interested but concerned to ride a bike. We should examine ways to implement these types of innovative bicycle facilities to attract even more Wilkes-Barre residents to ride bicycles and to be assured that the chances are low that they will be harmed by cars or that they may harm pedestrians.

Clearly in our city as in others, in just about every neighborhood, besides the idea of safety period, one of the top concerns is drivers simply going too fast, driving aggressively, and/or not yielding to pedestrians. We need a plan in Wilkes-Barre to calm traffic and make our neighborhoods safer and more comfortable in which to walk and bike?

We first must identify the problem areas and then put forth workable solutions. Have you ever heard a city official talk about making the city safer for pedestrians and bicyclists? It all starts by making the public aware. Police can be counted on to do their jobs and to keep us safe. All of us can drive more safely—but we could also use friendly, yet firm reminders.

Of course this program would involve more focused police enforcement of existing traffic laws. I know the police are stretched thin, but we may be able to use them to lead volunteer emergency police that could be used in problem areas. These extra people can be used in similar fashion to the school crossing guard system.

They would be self-policing, with the authority to issue warnings to drivers that become part of their unofficial driving record. Local citizen patrols could be formed and they could be asked to help create greater citizen awareness. After all, it is our City!

The Chief of Police must be intimately involved in the safety of cyclists and pedestrians as we permit people free access to streets designed now only for automobile traffic. Bicycle and pedestrian safety should be a city priority. Hopefully, in due time, the City will hire a Public Safety Director reporting directly to the Mayor.

The Public Safety Director would continually work in operational matters with the Police Chief and would also help codify and explain any new regulations needed so that Council can get them passed for the good of the City. When Council needs to approve them, the Director would present them to Council for that approval.

The Director would "direct" that the Chief apprise his officers of the City's priorities. They would need to look closely at jaywalking and gridlocking and to create awareness of potential problem areas and to alert motorists to requirements of giving bikers proper clearances.

If there is a will, there is a way. A nice billboard about bicycle safety factors may help our out-of-town driving guests as to how serious we are about protecting our public.

To the extent it is possible with the problem of street parking today being the most efficient form of parking in our City, open streets would surely be wonderful. Even periodic open streets can be enormously popular events as we have seen in nearly 80 cities and communities throughout the U.S.

Open Streets temporarily restrict motor vehicle traffic on one or more streets so that people can use them for physical activity—walking, biking, running, playing, or even a block party with street dancing. The Mayor could work with community stakeholders to make Open Streets Wilkes-Barre a reality?

The City of Wilkes-Barre, must act as a cheerleader in the implementation of a comprehensive education program that is pervasive in its ability to increase and maintain a constant positive awareness related to traffic safety, infrastructure, and way-finding. It is one of our basic jobs

382 Wilkes-Barre: Return to Glory

Wilkes-Barre residents want the Mayor to take the scarce resources of our City and use them for the most benefit of all the citizens. Citizens want a Mayor that has always been an advocate for common sense quality of life issues, which certainly include bicycling and walking. Even our fine Police, who make Wilkes-Barre safe for us all, can be more visible on City Police bikes in our neighborhoods.

As I discussed with you in prior chapters, I do bike myself but not as frequently as when I was a kid. I can recall taking my three kids and a zillion neighborhood kids through the maze of South Wilkes-Barre over the Market Street Bridge, and into the most desolate "nature" areas of Kirby Park right by the river. They loved it. I loved it. But, today it is not as safe to do this. It must be safe as it is such a great adventure. The path from here to there should also be safe.

I make it a point to frequently walk the dike and sometimes even the streets in my neighborhood. I admit, I also use my recumbent bike and treadmill when it is cold like many days in NEPA winters, and we have been warned numerous times about an expected "storm of historic proportions" arriving tomorrow. When the weather prevents it, exercise indoors or at the Y or at physical fitness centers but most of the time. we can have streets usable for biking.

I understand how our open spaces, bike trails, jogging paths, and bike paths have been utilized where they exist. I have personally seen the difference when a road does not have a bike lane and I have come dangerously close to being hit by passing cars. This is not good.

If we can make it better, we should make it better. Over time, almost all identified issues can be solved. But we must identify and track them, and then solve them. Those that appear unsolvable may even be solved at a later time, as we get better at what we are doing.

I understand the prioritization and seriousness of bicycle/walking related issues. I know that safety is number one but let's start thinking about what we can do once we feel safe rather than wringing our hands wondering if that will ever be.

Our police are great. With the proper leadership, they will make our city as safe as the safest cities in the country. If there are not enough police, the Mayor should be able to figure out how to give them better tools and if we need more police, we should get more.

Wilkes-Barre's Mayor must provide a comprehensive long-range plan, which would build on current assets. The administration must also vigorously respond to new solutions. Public initiatives, undergoing constant review, should be brought forth, and examined, and implemented as appropriate.

Lyft's Revamped Bike-Share Ebike Is Sleek—and Beefy

I would expect that a Mayor could do this seamlessly but nothing worth having is ever easy so there are always some lumps and bumps. I would expect that Mayor Brown or whoever the next Mayors are over time, would agree that before we see any smooth roads, we would encounter a lot of bumps on the way to a lot of great solutions.

I am not naïve enough to believe that Wilkes-Barre citizens can ride bicycles all the time as an alternative to nice warm transportation. But there are lots of times that we would be able to do just that. I know this from experience.

When I went to King's from 1965 to 1969, my dad forwarded some cash to me and "we" bought a Honda 50 for me to go back and forth to school from the Rolling Mill Hill. It was a two-mile ride or so. The Honda 50 traveled a little faster than a bike, and it looked like a moped without the petals.

A real Honda 50 looks like a Moped..

When I reached King's after two miles for class in December and January of my first two years, with my multiple layers of hoods and masks, I literally had ice forming from my watering eyes. Yet, I took the little Honda, because it was easy and inexpensive to get where I needed to go, and there was no problem parking it. Since bicycles go slower, and since the rider does not always have to get to an 8:00 AM class, perhaps less icicles would form.

You may have heard of Somerville, a small community adjacent to Boston Massachusetts. It is at the top of the game for bike commuting in the Northeast, so says the League of American Bicyclists. Other top areas include Cambridge, New Haven, Philadelphia, and Pittsburgh. Maybe one day Wilkes-Barre can be on such a list. Everything good starts with an idea. Massachusetts, by the way is not a warm state.

Somerville is dedicated to bicycling. The city has 14 miles of bike lanes, 6 miles of bike paths, and 25 miles of shared roads marked for bicycle travel. With all that in place, the city went forth and completed its first cycle track as a protected bike lane. A cycle track is in fact, a bike lane that is separated from the roadway and traffic by some form of physical barrier. Beacon Street, which runs into Boston, has never looked better.

And so, we have Wilkes-Barre Pennsylvania and Boston Massachusetts (Somerville), two cities with little more in common than long cold winters, and the hardiness of its people. The only objection I could think of to the utility of making Wilkes-Barre more bike friendly would be the cold weather we share with Boston.

Yet, Boston has proven it can be done and that the people love it. Soon, if we choose to move on this, other communities in NEPA would want to be involved.

How about a nice bike / walking trail adjacent to the "cho choo train" that one day may be circling the Square two-blocks out, each day in the future. How about extending a train from Wilkes-Barre past Eighth Street and right on into Pittston PA, the home of the greatest Tomato Festival in the world. I see there is a lot of track already on the side of the river bank. A bike path right next to it sounds like a great idea.

Since a train around the city is more than just a little project, if we gain the interest, we can surely create a bike path along the same route. Even without the train, which I know is a dream, and not yet an idea, why not be able to ride a bike, reasonably unencumbered from Wilkes-Barre, along the river to Pittston? Now, there's an idea. While others say, "Why?" Let's help Wilkes-Barre be known as "the City that says 'Why Not?' "

In June, 2005, many of us recall that Mayor Thomas Leighton suggested to Wilkes-Barre residents and friends: "The biggest obstacle that we must overcome, is the negative attitude of a small, but pervasive, segment of our population. We must reverse this negative attitude. We must be taught how to believe again." At the same time, the Mayor unveiled a new slogan for Wilkes-Barre, "I believe." The slogan turned up on buttons, key chains and signs distributed by the mayor's office. Mr. Leighton's Pep Talk to the City was a good idea, no buts about it.

I believe we need to believe we can, but we also need to dream, to create ideas from our dreams, discuss those ideas with city leaders, decide what are our priorities; plan to achieve them, and then get the job done.

Believing we can, is a great start in forming a great attitude. Those who believe they can, do! Those who believe they cannot are always 100% right.

Every four years, Wilkes-Barre embarks upon another election cycle in which, because we live in America, it gave all citizens of the city the opportunity to bring in the leadership of their choosing. This leadership is now in place. After twelve years of hard work by Mayor Tom Leighton and his administration, a new Mayor and Council have had a chance to become comfortable in their new positions. Now Mayor Brown leads out great city. Let's ask him to move on both the "Choo" project and the pathways project for biking, jogging, and walking. Wilkes-Barre does not have to be number two in anything.

Of course, we will hit some potholes along the way for sure but we can look to the future now that local elections are behind us and we can see the opportunity for some great improvements. We should thank Mayor Leighton and his administration and our prior Council and Mayor George for their service and move on with our new leadership, Mayor Brown and the new Council towards the renewal of our glory days. Mayor George Brown is just the kind of guy to make Wilkes-Barre #1.

With effective leadership, there will always be new dreams and new ideas. Whatever the composition of our political officials, we must remember they work for us—each and every one of us. And so, it is up to us to help our leaders make the right decisions about our future. We have to engage the system until we correct it. We can achieve a better Wilkes-Barre one step at a time. We all want better for Wilkes-Barre?

We live in America. In our country and in our state and city, the people run the government. We often forget that and we get stuck voting for politicians when we should be voting for representatives of the people. Public officials may think that they run the government but that is not true. It is the people. We are in charge. We determine the government we get, and we determine the government we choose to keep.

By having a vibrant city, when Mayor Brown finishes his time with the City, we need to be prepared to elect new leadership again. Perhaps it should be Mayor Brown again as he has done well for the city. If we cannot coax enough good men and women to represent us, then we seal our fate by bringing in politicians. Now that we have the right people in place – the people we have in office today, we the public must take opportunity after opportunity to help shape its government and to help shape its city.

This is why I feel so good about our prospects as a city. From reading the local blogs and talking to people, the citizens of Wilkes-Barre would like things to be better. They would like a safe city, an affordable city, and a clean and beautiful city with jogging paths and bicycle path, and safe roads to travel. Surely, there have been great improvements and many have been substantial. Yet, the people you meet on the street are openly discussing making the changes necessary to put Wilkes-Barre back on the map again. The way I see it, Wilkes-Barre is a city ready to return to its glory days.

Who knows what the future of Wilkes-Barre may be in its return to glory. One thing we do know is that one of the only factors that may separate us from a wonderful future is if we choose not to pursue our dreams. If the Mayor were to make a decree that would have consequences, he or she would decree that "Dreams are back in style in Wilkes-Barre Pa." Pursuing dreams about our community and its people is a prerequisite for bringing back the glory days of Wilkes-Barre, PA.

Let the dreaming begin folks, and soon after, let our great ideas, plans, and actions help make our dreams come true. And if I might add, let none of us sit on the sidelines or somebody may deflate our goals. Get in the game Wilkes-Barre!

Now, how about going to a Wilkes-Barre bike shop and picking out a beauty!

Return to Glory: The Short Plan

In Chapter 1, I wasted no time to reveal my big life secret. I am a dreamer; a technocrat; and a solver of problems. Like many who are not in elected office, I too know that I have a solution to the ills that plague Wilkes-Barre today. It is part dream for sure, but there are enough ideas and plans in the mix that if we were to let loose and execute them all, Wilkes-Barre's days of glory would be well on their way.

Citizen action needed for City's return to glory

With the fine Wilkes-Barre leadership in place, we citizens cannot settle for the same old ideas from the past. After all, we elected our new leaders to get us out of our long-term funk. Our new leaders would be the first to tell us all that in order to get that done, we all must chip in and help. So, what are we waiting for?

Other LETS GO PUBLISH! Books by Brian Kelly:

America-First Immigration Innovative solutions which save $Trillions. Learn how!
Should We Cancel Student Debt ? What should the Biden Administration do about it?
What about Seniors??? Seniors have been "screwed" on SS Solution is a big Govt check
Hydroxchloroquine; Much Maligned Super Drug
Hydroxchloroquine; Worthless! Worthless! Worthless!
Lou Barletta Governor of California. Perfect candidate for Pennsylvania
Larry Elder Governor of California. Perfect candidate for California
WineDiets.Com Renews: The Wine Diet Includes three wine diets & an alcohol-free diet
Katie Kelly & Her Miracle Voice Singer, Songwriter, Musician and Producer
Beating Big Tech Monopolies! Just like when the Trustbusters beat the robber-barons in 1900s
The Great Story of Florida Gators Football Beginning of football to the Coach Dan Mullen's era
The Great Story of LSU Football The beginning of football to the Ed Orgeron era
The Great Story of Clemson Football Starts at the first football game to the Dabo Swinney era
The Great Story of Alabama Football From the first college football game to Alabama's last TD u
The Great Story of Notre Dame Football The beginning of football to coach Brian Kelly's last game
The Great Story of Penn State Football From the beginning of football to the last James Franklin game
Great Moments in College Football From the beginning of football to the 2020 post season.
Great Players in Tampa Bay Buccaneers Football From the beginning of football through the Bruce Ariens era
Super Bowl & NFL Championship Seasons: The Tampa Bay Buccaneers First championship to Super B
Great Coaches in Tampa Bay Buccaneers Football Begins continues through the Bruce Ariens era.
Great Moments in Tampa Bay Buccaneers Football Begins beginning of Football to Bruce Ariens era.
Donald Trump Governor of California After the Newsom recall, Trump is the perfect candidate
Ron DeSantis: The Best United States Governor To Governors what Trump is to Presidents—The Best!
Mike v Trump: Mike Grant takes on Donald Trump; Brian Kelly takes on Mike Grant;
SCOTUS Eliminatus No country needs a Supreme Court that refuses to hear critical cases!
The Corruption in the WB Area School District A Story about toxic corruption and other stinky things
Stolen Election ???   Democrats say: "fair and just;" Republicans surrender to Democrats
The Ten Commandments of Calipered Kinematically Aligned Total Knee Arthroplasty Color
The Ten Commandments of Calipered Kinematically Aligned Total Knee Arthroplasty B/W
About Alexa! Tell me how!
Chronicle of Inept Governance & Corrective Actions board from hell big question: better way?
Hey Alexa Create me my own personal musical paradise Unpublished with new book
FTC Case: LetsGoPublish.com v Amazon Fourth Edition big bully censored nine books
FTC Case: LetsGoPublish.com v Amazon Third Edition big bully censored nine books
FTC Case: LetsGoPublish.com v Amazon Second Edition big bully censored nine books
The President Donald J. Trump Book Catalog   Color Version by Brian Kelly & Lets Go Publish!
The President Donald J. Trump Book Catalog   B/W Version by Brian Kelly & Lets Go Publish!
FTC Case: LetsGoPublish.com v Amazon Original case bully censored nine books
What America Wins if Biden Wins Everything!!!!!! The answer is really nothing.
What America Loses if Trump Loses None of the 1000s of Trump wins for starters
What America Wins When Trump Wins Trump already gave the country more benefits and blessings
We Love Trump! Don't you? The President given to the people by God as the answer to our prayers
Amazon: The Biggest Bully in Town bully blocked eight books in 2020 by most published author
Trump Assured 2020 Victory President needs these two prongs for his platform for landslide
2020 Republican Convention—Speeches Blocked by Amazon Includes memento free Link
2020 RNC Convention Full Speech Transcripts Blocked by Amazon Memento of the 87 best
COVID-19 Mask, Yes? Or No? It's Everybody's Recommended Solution!!!
LSU Tigers Championship Seasons Starts at beginning of LSU Football to the National Championship
Great Coaches in LSU Football Book starts with the first LSU coach; goes to Orgeron Championship
Great Players in LSU Football Begins with 1893 QB Ruffin G Pleasant to 2019 QB Burrow
America for Millennials A growing # of disintegrationists want to tear US down
Great Moments in LSU Football Book starts at start of Football to the Ed Orgeron Championship.
The Constitution's Role in a Return to Normalcy Can the Constitution Survive?
The Constitution vs. The Virus Simultaneous attack coronavirus and US governors
One, Two, Three, Pooph!!! Reopen Country Now! Return to normalcy is just around the corner.

Reopen America Now Return to Normalcy

Enough is Enough Re: Covid, We are not children. We're adults. We'll make the right decisions.

How to Write Your 1st Book & Publish it Using Amazon KDP You can do it

REMDESIVIR A Ray of Hope

When Will America Reopen for Business? This author's opinion includes voices of experts

HydroxyChloroquine: The Game Changer

Super Bowl & NFL Championship Seasons The KC Chiefs From the 1st to Super Bowl LIV

Great Coaches in Kansas City Chiefs Football First Coach era to Andy Reid Era

Great Players in Kansas City Chiefs Football From the AFL to Andy Reid Era

Reopen America Now! How to Shut-Down Corona Virus & Return to Normalcy!

Why is Everybody Moving to the Villages? You can afford a home in the Villages

CORONAVIRUS The Cause & the Cure. Many solutions—but which ones will work?

Great Moments in Kansas City Chiefs Football. From the beginning to the Andy Reid Era

How the Philadelphia Eagles Lost Its Karma. This is the one place that tells the story

Cancel All Student Debt Now! Good for America, Good for the Economy.

Social Security Screw Job!!! Scandal: Seniors Intentionally Screwed by US Government

Trump Hate They hate Trump Supporters; Trump; & God—in that order

Christmas Wings for Brian A heartwarming story of a boy whose shoulders kept growing

Merry Christmas to Wilkes-Barre 50 Ways" for Mayor George Brown to Create a Better City.

Air Force Football Championship Seasons From AF Championship to Coach Calhoun's latest team

Syracuse Football Championship Seasons beginning of SU championships; goes to Dino Babers Era

Navy Football Championship Seasons 1st Navy Championships to the Ken Niumatalolo Era

Army Football Championship Seasons Beginning of Football championships to Jeff Monken Era

Florida Gators Championship Seasons Beginning of Football through championships to Dan Mullen era

Alabama's Championship Seasons Beginning of Football past the 2017/2018 National Championship

Clemson Tigers Championship Seasons Beginning of Football to the Clemson National Championships

Penn State's Championship Seasons PSU's first championship to the James Franklin era

Notre Dame's Championship Seasons Before Knute Rockne and past Lou Holtz's 1988 undisputed title

Super Bowls & Championship Seasons: The New York Giants Many championships of the Giants.

Super Bowls & Championship Seasons: New England Patriots Many championships of the Patriots.

Super Bowls & Championship Seasons: The Pittsburgh Steelers Many championship of the Steelers

Super Bowls & Championship Seasons: The Philadelphia Eagles Many championships of the Eagles.

The Big Toxic School Wilkes-Barre Area's Tale of Corruption, Deception, Taxation & Tyranny

Great Players in New York Giants Football Begins with great players of 1925 to the Saquon Barqley era.

Great Coaches in New York Giants Football Begins with Bob Folwell 1925 and to Pat Shurmur in 2019.

Great Moments in New York Giants Football Beginning of Football to the Pat Shurmur era.

Hasta La Vista California Give California its independence.

IT's ALL OVER! Mueller: NO COLLUSION!"—Top Dems going to jail for the hoax!

Democrat Secret for Power & Winning Elections Open borders adds millions of new Democrat Voters

Hope for Wilkes-Barre—John Q. Doe—Next Mayor of Wilkes-Barre

The John Doe Plan & WB Plan will help create a better city!

Great Moments in New England Patriots Football Second Edition

This book begins at the beginning of Football and goes to the Bill Belichick era.

The Cowardly Congress Corrupt US Congress is against America and Americans.

Great Players in Air Force Football From the beginning to the current season

Great Coaches in Air Force Football   From the beginning to Coach Troy Calhoun

Help for Mayor George and Next Mayor of Wilkes-Barre How to vote for the next Mayor Council

Ghost of Wilkes-Barre Future: Spirit's advice for residents how to pick the next Mayor and Council

Great Players in Air Force Football: Air Force's best players of all time

Great Coaches in Air Force Football: From Coach 1 to Coach Troy Calhoun

Great Moments in Air Force Football: From day 1 to today

Great Players in Navy Football: Navy's best including Bellino & Staubach

Great Coaches in Navy Football: From Coach 1 to Coach #39 Ken Niumatalolo

Great Moments in Navy Football: From day 1 to coach Ken Niumatalolo l

No Tree! No Toot! No Toot! Heartwarming story. Christmas gone while 19 month old napped

How to End DACA, Sanctuary Cities, & Resident Illegal Aliens . best solution remove shadows America.

Government Must Stop Ripping Off Seniors' Social Security!: Hey buddy, seniors can't spare a dime?

Special Report: Solving America's Student Debt Crisis!: The only real solution to the $1.52 Trillion debt

The Winning Political Platform for America Unique winning approach to solve big problems in America.

Lou Barletta v Bob Casey for US Senate Barletta's unique approach to solve big problems in America.

John Chrin v Matt Cartwright for Congress Chrin has a unique approach to solve big problems in America.

The Cure for Hate !!! Can the cure be any worse than this disease that is crippling America?

Andrew Cuomo's Time to Go? He Was Never that Great!": Cuomo says America never that great

White People Are Bad! Bad! Bad! Whoever thought a popular slogan in 2018 It's OK to be White!
The Fake News Media Is Also Corrupt !!!: Fake press / media today is not worthy to be 4th Estate.
God Gave US Donald Trump?   Trump was sent from God as the people's answer
Millennials Say America Was Never That Great": Too many pleased days of political chumps not over!
It's Time for The John Q. Doe Party... Don't you think? By Elephants.
Great Players in Florida Gators Football... Tim Tebow and a ton of other great players
Great Coaches in Florida Gators Football... The best coaches in Gator history.
The Constitution by Hamilton, Jefferson, Madison, et al. The Real Constitution
The Constitution Companion. Will help you learn and understand the Constitution
Great Coaches in Clemson Football The best Clemson Coaches right to Dabo Swinney
Great Players in Clemson Football The best Clemson players in history
Winning Back America. America's been stolen and can be won back completely
The Founding of America... Great book to pick up a lot of great facts
Defeating America's Career Politicians. The scoundrels need to go.
Midnight Mass by Jack Lammers... You remember what it was like Great story
The Bike by Jack Lammers... Great heartwarming Story by Jack
Wipe Out All Student Loan Debt--Now! Watch the economy go boom!
No Free Lunch Pay Back Welfare! Why not pay it back?
Deport All Millennials Now!!! Why they deserve to be deported and/or saved
DELETE the EPA, Please! The worst decisions to hurt America
Taxation Without Representation 4th Edition Should we throw the TEA overboard again?
Four Great Political Essays by Thomas Dawson
Top Ten Political Books for 2018... CliffsNotes Version of 10 Political Books
Top Six Patriotic Books for 2018... CliffsNotes version of 6 Patriotic Books
Why Trump Got Elected!.. It's great to hear about a great milestone in America!
The Day the Free Press Died. Corrupt Press Lives on!
Solved (Immigration) The best solutions for 2018
Solved II (Obamacare, Social Security, Student Debt) Check it out; They're solved.
Great Moments in Pittsburgh Steelers Football... Six Super Bowls and more.
Great Players in Pittsburgh Steelers Football ,,,Chuck Noll, Bill Cowher, Mike Tomin, etc.
Great Coaches in New England Patriots Football,,, Bill Belichick the one and only plus others
Great Players in New England Patriots Football... Tom Brady, Drew Bledsoe et al.
Great Coaches in Philadelphia Eagles Football. Andy Reid, Doug Pederson & Lots more
Great Players in Philadelphia Eagles Football Great players such as Sonny Jurgenson
Great Coaches in Syracuse Football All the greats including Ben Schwartzwalder
Great Players in Syracuse Football. Highlights best players such as Jim Brown & Donovan McNabb
Millennials are People Too !!! Give US millennials help to live American Dream
Brian Kelly for the United States Senate from PA: Fresh Face for US Senate
The Candidate's Bible. Don't pray for your campaign without this bible
Rush Limbaugh's Platform for Americans... Rush will love it
Sean Hannity's Platform for Americans... Sean will love it
Donald Trump's New Platform for Americans. Make Trump unbeatable in 2020
Tariffs Are Good for America! One of the best tools a president can have
Great Coaches in Pittsburgh Steelers Football Sixteen of the best coaches ever to coach in pro football.
Great Moments in New England Patriots Football Great football moments from Boston to New England
Great Moments in Philadelphia Eagles Football. The best from the Eagles from the beginning of football.
Great Moments in Syracuse Football The great moments, coaches & players in Syracuse Football
Boost Social Security Now! Hey Buddy, Can You Spare a Dime?
The Birth of American Football. From the first college game in 1869 to the last Super Bowl
Obamacare: A One-Line Repeal Congress must get this done.
A Wilkes-Barre Christmas Story A wonderful town makes Christmas all the better
A Boy, A Bike, A Train, and a Christmas Miracle A Christmas story that will melt your heart
Pay-to-Go America-First Immigration Fix
Legalizing Illegal Aliens Via Resident Visas Americans-first plan saves $Trillions. Learn how!
60 Million Illegal Aliens in America!!! A simple, America-first solution.
The Bill of Rights By Founder James Madison Refresh your knowledge of the specific rights for all
Great Players in Army Football Great Army Football played by great players..
Great Coaches in Army Football Army's coaches are all great.
Great Moments in Army Football Army Football at its best.
Great Moments in Florida Gators Football Gators Football from the start. This is the book.
Great Moments in Clemson Football CU Football at its best. This is the book.
Great Moments in Florida Gators Football Gators Football from the start. This is the book.
The Constitution Companion. A Guide to Reading and Comprehending the Constitution

The Constitution by Hamilton, Jefferson, & Madison – Big type and in English
PATERNO: The Dark Days After Win # 409. Sky began to fall within days of win # 409.
JoePa 409 Victories: Say No More! Winningest Division I-A football coach ever
American College Football: The Beginning From before day one football was played.
Great Coaches in Alabama Football Challenging the coaches of every other program!
Great Coaches in Penn State Football the Best Coaches in PSU's football program
Great Players in Penn State Football The best players in PSU's football program
Great Players in Notre Dame Football The best players in ND's football program
Great Coaches in Notre Dame Football The best coaches in any football program
Great Players in Alabama Football from Quarterbacks to offensive Linemen Greats!
Great Moments in Alabama Football AU Football from the start. This is the book.
Great Moments in Penn State Football PSU Football, start--games, coaches, players,
Great Moments in Notre Dame Football ND Football, start, games, coaches, players
Cross Country with the Parents A great trip from East Coast to West with the kids
Seniors, Social Security & the Minimum Wage. Things seniors need to know.
How to Write Your First Book and Publish It with CreateSpace. You too can be an author.
The US Immigration Fix--It's all in here. Finally, an answer.
I had a Dream IBM Could be #1 Again The title is self-explanatory
WineDiets.Com Presents The Wine Diet Learn how to lose weight while having fun.
Wilkes-Barre, PA; Return to Glory Wilkes-Barre City's return to glory
Geoffrey Parsons' Epoch... The Land of Fair Play Better than the original.
The Bill of Rights 4 Dummmies! This is the best book to learn about your rights.
Sol Bloom's Epoch ...Story of the Constitution The best book to learn the Constitution
America 4 Dummmies! All Americans should read to learn about this great country.
The Electoral College 4 Dummmies! How does it really work?
The All-Everything Machine Story about IBM's finest computer server.
Thank You IBM! This book explains how IBM was beaten in the computer marketplace by neophytes

Brian W. Kelly has written over 300 books including this book. Thanks again for buying this one.

www.ingramcontent.com/pod-product-compliance
Lightning Source LLC
Chambersburg PA
CBHW060236100426
42742CB00011B/1550